Uncle Sam's Prerogative

Perspectives on State and Economy

Zac Thompson

Contents

Introduction

"Government's view of the economy could be summed up in a few short phrases: If it moves, tax it. If it keeps moving, regulate it. And if it stops moving, subsidize it." - Ronald Reagan, 1986.[1]

Many of us have seen the blockbuster film *Cast Away* starring Tom Hanks. For those that have not, it is a film about a man who finds himself stranded on a small island in the middle of the Pacific Ocean. Presumed dead by society, he is forced by circumstances to fend for himself. If he is to avoid starvation, he must catch fish and break open coconuts. If he is to be sheltered from the elements, he must construct or find his own shelter. If he is to have a place to sleep, he must fashion a bed from whatever he can find on the island. Needless to say, the character portrayed in this film does not enjoy a very high standard of living while he is on the island. Eventually, he is found and returned to civilization. While at a reception welcoming him home, he takes a lighter and flicks it on and off several times while staring at the flame and the relative ease at which it makes itself available to the user. While on the island, he had no choice but to rub two sticks together for several minutes—often injuring himself in the process—before he could enjoy the wonders of fire.[2] What is the main difference between life on an island having only what you can create and life in a society where a quick phone call can result in food being personally delivered to one's doorstep? The answer, simply put, is other people.

When one person is alone, he is responsible for creating

everything he consumes. None of us would get very far under this arrangement. How many among us know how to hunt, forage, grow our own food, construct a house, craft tools, and make our own clothes? And these are just some of the more basic necessities. How many among us could single-handedly satisfy our more advanced needs? Who among us knows how to build a car, create pharmaceutical drugs for our illness, create a television set for entertainment, and more? None of us can do every single thing that allows us to enjoy the high standards of living that we experience today, and we're better off for it. Instead, we live in a world where labor is divided. Instead of supplying all our wants and needs directly, we focus on one trade or specialization—usually whatever we are good at or passionate about—and then trade with others for what we need and want.

Fortunately for us, we do not need to worry about whether the person we are trading with wants what we have. In a primitive economy where barter is utilized for trading, if the fisherman wants shoes but the cobbler does not want fish, either the exchange does not take place or the fisherman must find someone who does want fish and has whatever the cobbler wants in order to set up a more complicated transaction. Additionally, if the farmer wants one pair of shoes, but his cow is worth thirty pairs, he cannot trade a fraction of his live cow away in return for just the one pair of shoes that he needs. Money solves this problem. Instead of worrying about the other person needing what we have, we can simply exchange what we have for money, and then exchange that money for other things that we need. Money facilitates trading and cuts down transaction costs, but it is only useful so far as other people accept it. Again, people are the key. A person can have all the money in the world, but if no one is around to accept it, it makes no difference. In the 2008 hit film, *I Am Legend,* Will Smith plays the protagonist who is attempting to survive a zombie apocalypse-type event in New York City. All alone, he copes with his environment by "befriending" inanimate manikins and talking to them. He takes a movie from the video rental store and jokingly leaves wads of cash—presumably hundreds or thousands of dollars—on the counter as payment to the manikin he placed at the register to represent a store employee. In this movie, Will Smith's character has all the money in the city all to himself, but without other people, it has no meaning.[3]

People trade with one another for what they need and want, and money is the vehicle that facilitates trade. As people operate within markets, they come to understand that their actions and behaviors often affect others, as others' actions often affect them. People determined that it would be in their interest to establish authority to oversee events and transactions, as well as act as a referee to adjudicate disputes, thus modern government took shape. But how should this government take form? From what philosophical notion does its authority arrive...from a deity or from the people? How much control should it have over what takes place within its geographical zone of influence? Should people be allowed to alter their government themselves, or should it be unimpeachable? Such questions have grave importance on people's lives, and depending on how they are answered, people will live free and prosper, or they will live poor and under tyranny. In the United States, the answers to those questions are constantly changing.

When the United States was founded as an independent country free to forge its own path and govern itself, it established a framework—the Constitution—by which the government is to adhere. Although the Constitution is ink on paper, clear and dry, many people have different interpretations of what is implied. If all 535 members of the United States Congress were asked to define how government should be conducted on the basis of what is established in the Constitution, there would be exactly 535 different interpretations. Depending on who has power at a given time determines how the Constitution is applied to governance, and the implications can be severe. To what degree are property rights defined? How will law enforcement operate? What can we expect in terms of the burden of taxation? How extensive will the welfare system be? What does it mean for our health care and education systems? Once more, the answers are constantly changing.

Government involvement in the economic process is not absolute. It operates along a sliding scale that is fine-tuned by individual policies crafted by lawmakers. Sometimes we will experience a period of greater government involvement—usually resulting in economic decline, and other times we will experience a period of less government involvement—usually resulting in a burst of economic activity and rising incomes. If the government tends to harm people and lower their standards of living, why then does government involvement in the economy only seem to increase over longer time horizons? Sadly, not everyone believes that having less government leads to a stronger economy, especially those that have an already established reliance on government. They believe that more government is the answer, not less. It is not so easy as to simply wave a magic wand in order to have everyone believe that the free enterprise system is the best system for them and their families. People must be shown, convinced, and allowed to learn for themselves that the free market system is not just better than the alternatives, it is the only path to sustained prosperity. This is the greatest debate of all time, and the consequences of its outcome determine what kind of future will be had.

PART I

LEVIATHAN

1 Collective Action

"To act on behalf of a group seems to free people of many of the moral restraints which control their behavior as individuals within the group" - F.A. Hayek, 1944.[4]

Why Humans Cooperate

When two individuals voluntarily come together and make an exchange, be it goods for goods, service for service, money for either goods or services or some combination thereof, both parties are made better off by the transaction. If this were not the case, the transaction would have never occurred in the first place. Since the transaction was voluntary, it stands to reason that either party could have voluntarily abstained from making the exchange if he or she thought that the transaction was not in his or her best interest. Just as two individuals can trade with one another to increase their own welfare, likewise groups of people can trade with one another, both with other groups and within the group itself. There are many situations in which potentially profitable trades require more than two individuals to take part. When people come together and form cooperative groups in order to enhance their material well-being, the process is known as collective action.

Prior to grasping the concepts behind collective action, it is important to review the nature of cooperation. There is and cannot be an entity known as "the group." Any group is nothing more than a collection of individuals that have agreed to come together and cooperate for their mutual benefit. Likewise, groups cannot act, think, feel, or perform actions of any kind. Only the individual is capable of reason, understanding, emotions, actions, etc. A group always functions through the actions of a select individual or a smaller group of individuals who act on behalf of the group as a whole. Through these actions, a group derives its character, and its "will" is made known. A group itself has no existence beyond the individual members, and their actions give the group legitimacy and meaning.[5]

Humans are social beings; the story of human history is one of groups and their interactions with each other. The earliest humans often worked together for survival, as killing mammoths for food required the cooperation of dozens of spears acting in concert with one another to achieve a single goal. An individual's chance of surviving the harsh reality of the wild significantly increased when he banded together with others whose aim was also to survive, and this is precisely what separates humans from other animal species who mostly see others outside their tribe or heard as competitors. Humans understood very early on that they could increase their welfare by the division of labor, a process by which one person specializes in one trade, while another specializes in something else, and then they trade surpluses. Through the division of labor, a person can trade for things he lacks as opposed to being responsible for creating it himself. Imagine if you alone had to butcher your own meat, weave your own clothes, build your own house, etc. An individual's standard of living would be low indeed. Fortunately, a person can merely specialize in one trade, be it accounting, dentistry, auto maintenance, or any of the other countless professions, and then simply purchase what is needed and desired by trading the surplus. Having others to trade with is an obvious prerequisite for exchange, so why were humans able to understand this and not other animal species?

Humans and other animal species share some similarities as it pertains to the family unit. Food-sharing and mutual cooperation for survival has been observed in immediate families of other species, but only humans are capable of complex exchange that constitutes economic activity.[6]

The English philosopher Thomas Hobbes paints a picture of what he perceives to be human nature outside of society's bounds. In his most notable work, *Leviathan,* Hobbes explains how humans' primary objective is to avoid a violent death; therefore, a man's principal liberty is the right to preserve his life. He goes on to say that the condition of man is competition, with everyone competing against everyone else for the exclusive use of the world's scarce resources. His work can be best summarized with what is arguably his most well-known phrase, that the life of man without society is "nasty, brutish, and short."[7] To prevent the inevitable suffering of violent death, people may form groups in order to safeguard their own survival, establishing a government to oversee activities and enforce rules within the group, and secure the peace through which society is made possible.

When *Leviathan* was first published in 1651, England was engulfed in a civil war between Parliament and the King. Hobbes may have been influenced by events of the day which to his view may have shown a glimpse of what becomes of society when cooperation under a single government breaks down. Swiss-born Jean-Jacques Rousseau expands upon Hobbes' idea in his essay *On the Social Contract* a century later. According to Rousseau, people form groups for security, and thereby consent to living under the rules of the group so long as they enjoy its protection. Each member of a group is to give himself to the collective. Since all members have all given themselves fully, each member is equal to every other member and has no incentive to act against another individual's interests. By giving himself to no one individual, he gains everything he gave away, plus the collective force of a group to preserve what he has.[8]

Another well known English philosopher, John Locke, warns of the dangers of submitting oneself to a group authority. He expresses in his *Second Treatise of Government* that civil authority can easily turn to tyranny, denying a person of the rights and freedoms he seeks to protect. Locke expands upon Hobbes' view that humans have an inherent right to preserve their life by adding that human beings also have a right to liberty and the pursuit of happiness, and that a government's duty is to protect those rights. Should the government fail to do so, its citizens then have a right to change that government.[9] These are the fundamental ideas that led the Thirteen Colonies to revolt against Great Britain in pursuit of independence.

Since people are always seeking to substitute their current state of affairs for a more satisfactory one, they gravitate towards one another for mutual cooperation. If a man can find shelter and security in the formation of groups, finding others to trade and exchange with in order to increase his well-being, how should such groups be formed? Several other questions arise as to how large the groups should be, how they should act and make decisions, how they should consider the members' individual preferences, and which policies they should pursue in order to achieve objectives. Recall how groups can have no preferences themselves, only can the individuals within the groups. Since only individuals can act, rational action must be judged in accordance with the actions of those individuals. People make choices and commit to them because they believe that they can increase their welfare by committing to a specific action or by joining a specific group. Motivations are irrelevant and can vary wildly as to why people do certain things, but the bottom line is that they believe such actions will benefit them. When people make decisions, they analyze their current state, either consciously or subconsciously, and act on what they believe to be their optimal choice that will maximize their welfare. Oftentimes, that action is to become part of a group and cooperate with others to pursue a goal that would be more easily achieved with the help of others rather than on one's own. When people come together in groups, they form a body which is then incapable of acting on its own. Groups "act" only in the sense that the members of that group act, and then the group pursues a course of action that is reflective of the general will of those belonging to the group. Before a group can pursue a course of action, however, the members within that group must make up their minds and then somehow pool their preferences together in such a way that the single course of action for the group reflects their preferences overall. The whole purpose of collective action is to benefit the members of a given group, despite often relegating individuality.

Group and Individual Welfare

Prior to the 1960s, economists and sociologists widely believed that if individuals find common ground with one another and share common goals, they will naturally form a cooperative body and work together. In 1965, American economist Mancur Olson challenged this notion with his work: *The Logic of Collection Action,* in which he boldly claims that rational people will not cooperate within groups, but will instead attempt to free-ride off the efforts of others unless certain conditions are met. According to Olson, people will only cooperate if they are coerced into doing so, there exist heavy incentives for doing so, or if they believe that their free-riding would be noticed and rebuked.[10] Olson's view has largely been refuted through criticisms of his theory, though many will concede that there exist many situations in which his theory still applies. For the most part, however, his critics argue that he fails to take into account human emotions, such as passion, which also act as motivators towards driving people into cooperative groups. Furthermore, providing incentives within collective action settings is a collective action itself in that benefits are provided to all involved, not just those paying for the incentive to be applied. Therefore, it follows that Olson's free-rider stance corresponds equally to individuals providing incentives for other individuals to participate, just as it does to the original free-rider problem.[11] Simply put, if I am in a group and am attempting to free-ride off the efforts of others, and I nor any other individual will act unless provided an incentive, it stands to reason that I nor anyone else will ever provide that incentive, as an incentive for someone to act within the group benefits all if that incentive is acted upon.

Since groups themselves are not entities, it cannot be said that a group is made better or worse off after pursuing a certain course of action. Instead, it can be surmised that the individuals that form the group are made better or worse off, thus the "group" is made better or worse off only as its members are. In order to make the claim that a group or collective has been made better off by pursuing certain objectives, it must be determined whether or not that the members within the group have had their well-being increased. If on average, the individuals within the group have witnessed their circumstances improve after the group pursues an action, then it can be said that the group has been made better off. When an individual contemplates his choices and then pursues a course of action, he rationalizes which preferences he has and how he might increase his standard of living. From there does he follow through on his choice pertaining to his highest valued preference.

Humans tend to act in accordance with their highest-valued preferences because they live in a world of scarce resources that have mutually exclusive employment.[12] For example, if I find myself free on a Saturday evening and can choose between going to a rock concert or an art museum, I act in accordance to my highest valued preference and visit the museum, forever passing on the opportunity to attend the rock concert at that given time, as my body cannot be in two places simultaneously. However, if I am an active member of a social club that spends its Saturday nights together, some members may want to attend the concert, others the museum, while some others might have different ideas entirely. How then do we decide what the "group" should do? Naturally, conflicts of interest arise pertaining to decisions the group can make. What might benefit some members of the group could harm others. Since humans act in accordance with their preferences, and since groups are composed of sentient humans, groups must find a way to channel all individual preferences into one course of action, a difficult task indeed!

In the late 1800s, Italian Economist Vilfredo Pareto developed criteria by which we can measure a group's collective decisions known as Pareto optimal and Pareto superior. The main difficulty in passing judgment on a decision or policy that affects more than one person is that there is no real way to quantify one person's preferences over another. What a person likes, dislikes, enjoys, or detests is what makes him unique, and there is no rational basis by which we can say person A's tastes are better than person's B's tastes. These values that people hold are entirely subjective and not easily compared to the subjective values of others.[13] From this quagmire of uncertainty, Vilfredo Pareto developed his theory that since we cannot directly compare people's subjective values, we must analyze the decisions made from the standpoint of whether or not it increases people's welfare.

When dealing with a group of people, decisions will affect them in different ways. Some people are made better off while others are not. As the group grows larger, the chances of a given decision not making everyone better off increases, as more people are affected by the outcome. If a group policy is enacted that makes some members better off without harming others, it is known as a Pareto superior move. Once all Pareto superior moves have been made, the aggregate welfare of the group reaches the state of Pareto optimality. When a state of Pareto optimality exists, it is impossible to make a decision or reallocate resources in such a way that at least one person will not be made worse off.[14] Given the diversity of groups or the complexities of the situations they face, rarely is a choice a Pareto superior move. Someone will

17

almost always be made worse off, or at least find a reason to complain when a choice is made that affects them in a way they had not determined to be ideal. How then can a collective decide if it will make some members of the group worse off?

Popular vote is one method through which groups can enact decisions, going with whatever direction the majority decides upon, though popular voting has a multitude of drawbacks. With majority-rule voting, a policy will most likely fall among the preferences of the median voter, though this can lead to mob rule, or "tyranny of the majority." What is to stop the majority from simply voting away the rights of the minority? Under a system in which people can simply vote for what they want, and those that lose out have to live with the consequences, the costs born by the losers can outweigh the benefits to the winners.[15]

One way to ensure that everyone in a group or collective is made better off by a decision is to require all decisions to be unanimous. Since no one individual would vote against his own best interests, one can logically conclude that if a motion passes through unanimous agreement, it makes all parties involved in the decision better off. Perhaps achievable in smaller groups, unanimous decisions are almost certainly impossible in larger group settings, such as cities, states, or nations. To require each decision in a large group to be unanimous would be a tedious and costly process, having to seek approval from each member of the collective before proceeding, only to discard the motion at the first dissenting vote. As a result, unanimous voting is not a practical method by which groups can reach their decisions. If a group is to carry out a decision, there will usually be those that are either not content or made worse off by the ensuing result. Since there will be winners and losers with a group's decision, how then might that decision be deemed to be in the public interest or against it? Unanimity has been shown to be impractical, and simple majority rule could result in heavy costs for the losers and minor benefits to the winners.[16]

Costs of Decision-Making

Every choice carried out by a collective bears a cost. There is a cost in arriving at the decision in terms of time and resources spent—or internal cost—and there is an external cost levied against those that are not made better off by the decision's results. Both of these costs should be contemplated separately. The cost of obtaining unanimous consent would be high, especially if the group is large. Decision-making costs could even be unbearable if the group in question was a nation or some other large body of individuals. It stands to reason that for every one less person whose consent is required for a decision to be carried out, the net cost of arriving at that decision would decrease by the cost of obtaining the consent of that one individual. The fewer people needed to agree to a decision before it is carried out, the lower the cost will be. There is an inverse relationship between the number of people whose consent is required and the overall cost of decision-making. If a decision only required one person to enact a decision on behalf of an entire group, the cost would be zero. This is the case for absolute monarchies and despots. If one person, an emperor or king, for example, could carry out a decision for an entire group of people, the group would bear no decision-making costs, as the leader could just enact policies on a whim. However, if one person makes decisions for an entire group, there is a higher probability that the decision's outcome will not be satisfactory to some, if not a large number of the group's members. This is known as an external cost of decision-making.[17]

The external costs of decision-making are inversely related to internal costs. If a group requires 100% agreement before carrying out a decision, the internal costs of agreement would be extremely high, but external costs would be nonexistent; no one member would give his consent if the decision did not benefit him. If one person can make decisions for an entire group, the internal costs of the decision would be zero, while the external costs would be high, as there is a strong probability that many within the group would not be in agreement with the decision, and would suffer by its result. A group must decide on how it will arrive at its final choices. Should it allow one person to act on behalf of the entire group, minimizing internal costs but maximizing external costs, or should it take the opposite extreme and require unanimous consent, thereby minimizing external costs to its members but maximizing internal costs of reaching the decision? This issue could open a Pandora's Box of sorts, as a group could be inclined to first decide on which method it will use for deciding, thus spawning an infinite loop. Fortunately for any collective body of individuals, there exists a happy medium.

When a group embarks on a decision, both internal and external costs are realized. There exists a point, however, where the aggregated costs are at a minimum. This point will almost always be less than unanimous consent, as one who does not get his way in a given decision will accept being part of a group with low decision costs as a trade-off. He is still better off so long as the combined internal and external costs of decision-making are less than the overall benefits he receives as remaining part of the group, even if his group sometimes makes decisions that are against his interests. Majority rule is the usual go-to solution, as discovering which costs exist for each member could be difficult in large or even smaller group settings. Majority rule ensures that everyone has an equal say in the outcome of events, and it skews the group's choice towards the median individual preference.[18] Groups often impose certain restrictions on decision-making by majority rule depending on the nature of the decision itself. If a decision is largely irrelevant, such as deciding on whether or not a shared pizza should have pepperoni or sausage as its only topping, a group may decide that a 51% majority rule is sufficient to carry a motion forward. When potential external costs are high, a group may require a more unanimous agreement. For example, if a group charges a membership fee and is contemplating increasing benefits to members through the use of funds raised from increasing its subscription fee, it may consider requiring the consent of two-thirds or three-fourths of its members before the motion is carried. Each scenario that a group can face should be treated separately with regards to decision-making, as different scenarios will present different costs to the group's members.

Group Size

As humans began forming groups in the prehistoric era, they did so around familial ties. The first organized groups were primarily kin-based, as small groups of blood relatives roamed the terrain in search of food. There was no property and no state, and the primary objective of these primitive humans was merely survival and to subsist in an unforgiving landscape.[19] The earliest groups of people thus formed for the mutual benefit of protection and cooperation for sourcing food. Given the simple objectives of early humans, small groups sufficed to achieve them. As humanity evolved, agriculture, technology, and propensity for abstract thought pushed human cooperation to new heights. Early groups of organized humans were able to utilize river travel to begin trading their surplus goods with other groups. Survival and food were taken for granted while the division of labor allowed for ever more specialization. Over time, individuals could focus less on their needs and more on their wants, as their needs were taken care of by fewer people, evidenced by humanity's shift from an agrarian to an urban setting. As standards of living rose, people formed groups to achieve ends other than mere survival, though that has never ceased being one of the main reasons why people choose to cooperate.[20]

Regarding collective action, a problem then arises when ascertaining how to most effectively cooperate with others to achieve a specific end, and that is: how large should a group be, and what quantity should the good or service it provides to its members be distributed? There is no one-size-fits-all solution, as groups can range anywhere in size from two individuals to seven billion, and the type of goods or services provided has a potentially unlimited range, as people are always coming together to achieve new ends. One factor remains constant; however, and that is the reality that as more people join a group to take advantage of its benefits, those benefits need to be available in an ever-increasing supply.

Problems arise when the benefits of joining a group are only available in fixed amounts. For example, if a golf course is made available to members of a country club, they can enjoy the use of the facilities so long as their organization remains small enough to prevent crowding. However, if more people join the group, congestion takes hold, as the size of the golf course does not expand. Crowding may continue to the point where one person can not even use the course without someone else ceasing to use it. There comes a time when the group must impose a hard cap on enrollment to prevent congestion, but capping enrollment will impose costs to current users. When a number of people are consuming a shared good, and a new user is added, the marginal cost per user decreases, as there are now more individuals paying into a good or service with a fixed cost. On the other hand, as new users join, the marginal cost of congestion will increase, as now there is less of the good to go around. At some point, adding new users will no longer be worthwhile, as the marginal cost of an additional user in terms of congestion will outweigh the benefit received from lowering the marginal per-user cost, thereby signaling that the group is as large as it should be. When this point is reached for our members of the hypothetical country club, no new members should be admitted, and the most cost-effective way to grow the group further would be to open a second golf course in a new location or to find a way to expand the existing one.[21]

Democratic Methods

In the United States, we are all participants in collective action on multiple levels, as we all live under federal, state, and local governments that collect taxes and provide public goods and services in return. As previously shown, one individual making choices for all citizens would have low decision-making costs but high external costs, as a great number of people would be made worse off by that decision, while requiring unanimous consent to all decisions would have no external costs, but would be near impossible to achieve, let alone extraordinarily costly. How then do the people of the United States function regarding their collective decision-making process? The American spirit of liberty and freedom would never allow a monarch to make the decisions for us, while the nation is simply too diverse and populated to obtain unanimous consent to any given decision we could make. Even majority rule is flawed, as it would not be a cost-effective way to gather people's preferences to formulate a course of action. Instead, we rely on representatives to make our voices in the collective known.

Direct democracy would allow every person to have an equal say in all governmental decisions. The simple truth is that people have lives to lead and are far too busy in their day-to-day schedules to tune in to CSPAN every hour and maintain an informed stance on every current issue. The costs of collecting every citizen's "yay" or "nay" on every decision would prove extremely costly, not to mention that it would be a logistical nightmare. With representative democracy, people can simply select someone from their ranks to convey their preferences and represent their interests to the collective as a whole. This in turn

23

allows them to carry on about their daily lives while their elected representatives handle the decision-making process on their behalf. Theoretically speaking (assuming away bribes, lobbying, corporate pandering, and vote-buying with promises of increased social programs), and because the representative was elected locally, he or she can be said to reasonably represent the preferences of his or her constituents, for if that representative did not act in the interests of the people in question, he or she would simply lose the next election and be replaced with someone who does.

Legislators seeking reelection have an incentive to keep their constituents happy, or at least appear so by ramping up appeasement initiatives during election cycles. In the United States, this is evidenced by the fact that politicians no longer seeking reelection sponsor fewer bills, are less involved in committees, and are frequently absent from floor votes.[22] Despite the systematic flaws of politicians under the influence of lobbyists or serving their last term, allowing representatives to convey our individual preferences to the collective group alleviates most of the decision-making process costs. These intrinsic costs of gathering preferences to make decisions constitute a primary justification for why liberty-inclined nations use representative democracy, as it is more cost-effective to have a small number of people making decisions for the whole, while still generally reflecting the aggregated preferences of every member of the collective.

Scores of problems are then unleashed by government methodology in legislating and governance. When a representative democratic government embarks on a policy, it should theoretically be a policy that reflects the general will of the people, and also be said to be furthering their interests. From here arises the challenge of enacting policies in a cost-effective manner to minimize the costs born by those who will be made worse off by those policies. When the costs shouldered by "losers" in a policy decision outweigh the benefits of its "winners" the decision is not economically efficient. Another issue presents itself in the form of lobbying and special interests, whereby representatives are more than willing to inflict massive costs to people they do not represent if it allows them to score political points with those that voted them into office or contributed financially to their campaign. If a politician pursues a policy which would create a vast number of "losers" among other members of the collective but would make his constituents "winners," his efforts are in pursuit of an economically destructive policy, but it cannot be said that he is behaving in an irrational manner.[23] After all, it is his job to make his voters happy, and he is suspicious of a rising-star political upstart that seeks to dethrone him in the next election. Clearly the government needs strict constraints in order to ensure that its decision-making processes are efficient and that its policies minimize the costs of arriving at the decision as well as the costs born by any potential losers created by it.

Special Interest Groups

Representative democracies such as the United States tend to favor the special interests over the public interests, and there is a rationale behind this that goes beyond media headlines and the buzzwords they use to cast political agents as greedy, colluding, or even treacherous degenerates. Consider for a moment the position of the typical voter in a given election. Our voter can spend a great deal of his time and energy reading up on current geopolitical events, staying in tune with all the candidates' fluctuating stances on the issues, and can contemplate in-depth as to how each piece of legislation can affect circumstances. Having thus become perfectly informed on all the issues and candidates up for election, the voter can cast his vote among millions of other voters, and leave the polling site knowing that his vote influenced the election on such a minuscule level that his chances of winning the lottery or being struck by lighting outweigh the chances that his vote actually altered the outcome. Such is the reason why most voters are woefully ill-informed on political circumstances. Not having complete knowledge of candidates or the issues does not reflect apathy or lack of comprehension, but is instead a rational state of being. Given how little a person's vote affects change, being proportionality ignorant to current political circumstances is not unreasonable, as the personal cost of staying informed would be high, while the benefits of voting with a better understanding would be small.[24]

Special interests are another matter. They have a much larger incentive to stay informed on the issues that affect them over the average voter. Take for example a consumer who is in the market to buy printer paper for his copier versus the paper mill that supplies it. Assume now that there is a green initiative bill moving through the political pipelines alleging that deforestation levels are too high, and in response, it proposes a cap on the number of trees a logging company can cut down over a given length of time. With fewer trees being cut, the cost of producing paper would increase dramatically. A consumer may see the cost of his ream of paper go up by a few dollars, which would be a minor nuisance, but is likely not enough of a blow to encourage him to become informed on the logging issue and join the political fray to oppose the bill. On the other hand, the producers and suppliers of paper would see their profit margins suffer drastically as a result of the legislation due to increased production costs, so they have a strong incentive to lobby influential politicians and take extraordinary measures to oppose the bill and the interests of those supporting it.

In the United States, Washington D.C. is a hotbed for special interest initiatives, and this contributes to the issue of special interests prevailing over the public interest. Consider the power of special interests versus the public interest with regard to geographical concentration. The political influence of the public at large is dispersed among millions of citizens across 50 states.

26

Special interests on the other hand are able to employ their vast resources and bombard Washington D.C. with their lobbyists and lawyers, exerting control over the politicians that private citizens in their homes could not hope to match. A significant number of legal firms located outside of Washington D.C. have secondary offices in the capital, while several large corporations have administrative offices not far from governmental buildings. Surrounded by special interests and the resources at their disposal, politicians have little incentive to support the public interest when given a mutually exclusive set of options.[25]

Special interests often use their resources to fund political campaigns and support politicians, thereby providing incentives for government representatives to favor them over the average voter. The primary incentive politicians face is reelection, and special interest support carries more weight than support from the average voter, so naturally, politicians will favor those holding the purse strings. If benefits from certain policies are a zero-sum game, meaning that special interests can only win at your loss, and you can only win at the loss of special interests, the game is tilted in the special interests' favor. They have more to lose by not having political support, and they will thus put forth more effort to attain what they need than the average voter will. Returning to the paper supplier example, dispersing the costs of special interest-favored legislation to millions of consumers will not irritate too many people, as the consumers only see their tabs go up by a few dollars each...hardly enough to cause rallies and popular uprisings. Should the special interests fail in their quest to obtain favored legislation, the financial repercussions to them would be brutal.[26]

Keeping It Fair

Governments preside over and direct (to a more or less liberal degree) economic activities and market conditions for the collective society under their rule, and they enact policies that produce economic winners and economic losers depending on the legislation. When governments or mere group leaders dictate policies to people creating these winners and losers, by what standard can these policies be measured to ascertain whether or not they were generally fair and publicly desirable? It is important to judge policies by their actual outcomes and not by their intended results. Individual motivations behind decisions and policies can be as diverse as the individuals themselves, while intentions are often vastly different from the end result (for example, raising the minimum wage rate actually increases poverty levels by raising unemployment, while rent control laws raise housing costs by reducing the supply of affordable housing.)[27] A decision or policy enhances the public interest and general welfare if it is conforming to the preferences of the median voter without the costs imposed on the minority outweighing the benefits to the majority. The Rawls Veil of Ignorance provides a framework to determine whether or not a choice affecting the public is desirable or undesirable and would theoretically conform to the preferences of the median group member.

Son of a Baltimore attorney, John Rawls spent his early years pursuing theological studies before enlisting in the army during WWII. The rigors of war pushed Rawls from theology to behavioral philosophy, and he spent the remainder of his life expanding upon the theoretical principles of justice. In the 1970's he proposed the concept of the "veil of ignorance."[28] Under the veil, a person would judge a policy, group decision, rule, or regulation without ever knowing anything about him or herself first. A person would not know if he or she is male or female, old or young, rich or poor, attractive or unattractive, religious or atheist, intelligent or dull, etc. From there, not knowing anything about their own traits, race, gender, affluence, etc., people could predetermine how their group should be structured and what course of action it should take. For example, behind the veil of

28

ignorance people are proposed the following: every year the group is to take its richest member and sacrifice him to the gods, and then divide his wealth among the whole group. Would such a policy be agreed upon by the collective behind the veil of ignorance? From an individual's perspective, the chance that he or she would be cast as the richest member of the group would be slight, so everyone in the group except one unfortunate soul stands to benefit from this policy, but there is the small chance that any given person could be that one individual once the veil is lifted.

Hypothetically speaking, if a group of individuals lived together in a primitive society without a government, what type of government would they come up with, and what kind of policies would they then pursue? Everyone would live under the same government, so it could be expected that no one individual would argue in favor of a government that could make decisions going against the general public interest. If a body of individuals got together to form a government, and a majority argued against the government possessing certain traits or functions, it could be said that that idea of government would be against the general welfare, and it would not come into being without further brainstorming and negotiation. The great philosophers of previous centuries had much to say on this topic; they sought to answer the mystery of how an individual can maintain his liberty while still submitting to a collective body and the civil authority from which it is governed.

Rousseau is often considered by scholars to be one of the more prominent writers on social cooperation theory. He asserts that because all men are created equal no one man has a natural right to govern others. Instead, governing authority is derived from the consent of free peoples who come together in agreement with other free peoples to form a collective body. Once together, people's individual wills are replaced by a general public will, which when served is beneficial to all members of society, either directly or indirectly.[29]

If Rousseau's idea of an organized society is to be taken literally, members of the collective would need to come together frequently, or have elections, that periodically adjust the state of government and its course to ensure that it remains in concert with the public interest. Societies evolve, demographics change, migration patterns fluctuate, and some people's political stances change over time. During the formative years of the American Republic, Thomas Jefferson, author of the Declaration of Independence and the third President of the United States, understood this fact. In a letter to his friend and protégé, James Madison, he writes:

> The earth belongs always to the living generation. They may manage it then, and what proceeds from it, as they please, during their usufruct. They are masters too of their own persons, and consequently may govern them as they please. But persons and property comprise the sum of the objects of government. The constitution and the laws of their predecessors extinguished then in their natural course with those who gave them being. This could preserve that being till it ceased to be itself, and no longer. Every constitution then, and every law, naturally expires at the end of 19 years. If it be enforced longer, it is an act of force, and not of right.[30]

In other words, every rule or norm by which people live together collectively in a society must be reaffirmed with every new generation. Jefferson believed that individuals should not be forced to live under the rules and laws previously agreed upon by those that came before them. Instead, each generation is like a blank slate and should be allowed to form its own laws that can suit its interests better than the laws that were appropriate for the past but may not be so for the present.

Jefferson's vision of wiping the slate clean every 19 years and starting fresh with a new set of laws is too idealistic and impractical to be implemented on a grand scale, and Jefferson was probably aware of this fact himself. He might have been speaking to Madison simply in terms of what "should be" versus "what is." With a nation as populous and diverse as the United States, developing a system and political process that allows all laws to be voided after 19 years and then replaced with something new and agreed upon by everyone would be virtually impossible to design and employ. Instead, we rely on periodic elections to voice our opinions through representatives, as well as voting on amendments and new laws directly on a state level.

Given that members of a society have come together and agreed upon the laws and rules that will govern their lives, and also given that people will live their lives differently, inequalities will arise. In terms of morality, society should be such that everyone has an equal opportunity, but outcomes do not have to be equal. People are not all blessed with the same strengths and talents, and some will succeed when others fail. To forcefully deprive successful or wealthy people of their property or rights to boost the downtrodden is an abhorrent violation of individual rights and liberty, even if the cosmos seems to shine on one person and cast a never-ending gloomy cloud over another. When a system creates different outcomes for different people, there will be inequalities in wealth, land, status, prestige, love, happiness, you-name-it, that will become apparent. Even if someone is unhappy with a given outcome, as long as the process abides by previously-agreed upon rules, it must be considered fair and must also be allowed to stand without legal challenge (moral challenges may be considered separately, but behavior can be immoral and still legal).[31] If there is a disagreement on the rules by which people live in a society, the government can theoretically act as an arbitrator and ensure that the process stays true to the rule of law. However, if there is strong enough disagreement on the government process of interpreting the law and crafting legislation, the government itself must be re-examined and renegotiated to ensure a more proper and fair playing field through either peaceful means or violent revolution.

When the rule of law is just and equally applied, the resulting outcomes must be considered fair and equitable, even if they are unequal. As long as everyone is playing by the same rules, no one person may reasonably complain that another enjoys a higher standard of living. People do sometimes have valid reasons to complain, as some people are playing by a different set of rules. Society is full of double standards, corruption, nepotism, unjust discrimination, prejudice, and favor exchanges. One need not look very far to find ample evidence of this; it exists within our workplaces, communities, churches, etc. When faced with inequalities derived from unfair rules and double standards, the solution is not to violate one person's rights by realigning material wealth or property to ensure all have the same amount, but to instead adjust the rules to ensure that they are equally applied going forward.[32]

No Man an Island

Humans have a natural tendency to group up and form societies. Humans are social creatures, and even the more isolated ones understand that they are better off by cooperating with their fellow man than attempting a life of self-sufficiency. The image of a shipwrecked Robinson Crusoe comes to mind. Isolated and alone, he must fend for himself and build his own dwelling, grow his own food, and craft his own tools. He would be significantly better off if only he could specialize in one thing, making sandals for instance, and then trading sandals with others in exchange for food and clothing. Aside from the occasional isolated indigenous tribes found in the most remote parts of the world, everyone inhabiting the planet is connecting in some way to each other through the global economy that we as humans have created. In fact, most people do not even begin to understand just how interconnected are economic activities. Leonard Reed, the founder of the Foundation for Economic Freedom (FEE), wrote an essay published in 1958 titled "I, Pencil." In it he personifies a pencil telling its story of creation, how it is something so simple and ordinary, yet involves millions of people around the world, all acting in cooperation with one another. Consider the loggers who cut down the tree, the people who made their tools, the people who made the trains and railroads that transport the logs to mills, the people who built the mills and those that work within its walls, the individuals involved in making rubber for the eraser, the people that mine graphite, those that ship graphite to refineries, those that made the boats used in shipping, the crews of the ships, the assemblers of the pencil, and those that distribute and bring it to market. All of these people do not know one another, and they do not perform their individual tasks for the betterment of each other. Instead, they are motivated by the desire to increase their standard of living, and this is best achieved by working together to create something that is but a simple and pedestrian object through extraordinary means.[33]

Markets originate organically. In the case of the pencil, there is no single government body or ministry directing all the above-mentioned economic activities. There are of course different governments in the various regions of the world where these activities take place, but the process itself is largely untouched by governmental directives. Some might argue that the world's resources could be better allocated in the hands of the government, with ministers at the ready to direct economic activity, but nothing could be further from the truth. One merely needs to look through the lenses of history to see countless failed experiments of governments attempting to fully direct economies resulting in mass starvation and a squandering of labor and capital. Friedrich Hayek said it best in his notable work *The Fatal Conceit*, where he argues that government cannot possibly direct economic activity better than market participants can, because no small body of people can grasp the sheer amount of information that is diffused among millions (or billions) of individual actors. He writes:

> The curious task of economics is to demonstrate to men how little they really know about what they imagine they can design. To the naive mind that can conceive of order only as the product of deliberate arrangement, it may seem absurd that in complex conditions order, and adaptation to the unknown, can be achieved more effectively by decentralizing decisions and that a division of authority will actually extend the possibility of overall order. Yet it is that decentralization that actually leads to more information being taken into account.[34]

The message is clear: government must be used cautiously to craft and enforce new laws, establish new institutions, or replace existing ones. Likewise, people must be careful when choosing to come together and form governments to further the public interest. Government needs clearly defined functions with regards to the part it plays in the economy, checks and balances to ensure it does not breach its mandate, and a process by which it can be amended when needed.

2 Rights and Regulations

"It will not be denied that power is of an encroaching nature and that it ought to be effectually restrained from passing the limits assigned to it." - James Madison, 1788.[35]

Despite any protests or animosity, we may have over a given governmental economic activity, the fact remains that government plays an important part in our lives, and its ability to perform its role affects all of us. Government performs several key functions regarding economic activity, regardless of whether or not one agrees or disagrees that government should perform them to a greater or lesser extent, and they are: safeguarding an individual's right to life and private property, regulating economic activity, redistributing wealth and providing social welfare programs, providing macroeconomic guidance for the economy as a whole, as well as production and provision of certain public goods such as defense, education, and to an increasingly greater extent today than in previous generations, healthcare. Each of these functions has widespread effects on the economy. The specific handling of these functions by the United States government will be addressed later on, but for now the focus will be on the general functions of the state with regards to property rights and regulation.

Property Rights

In order for there to even be an economy, there must be clear property rights that are protected and ensured. Property rights are a necessary characteristic of any thriving market economy. Before understanding how property rights affect economic activity, it is worth discussing their characteristics and nature. Whenever there is a resource in question, what determines how that resource is utilized? There are always competing uses for any given resource, but a resource can often only satisfy one use at a time, with the cost of employing the resource for that purpose being what might have been achieved had it been employed for the other.[36] For example, a car cannot be used to take you to Chicago while it is also being used to take me to New York, and the cost of the car being used for my purposes is the loss of opportunity for you to use it for yours. Since the car can not go to both places at once, one of us will have to find another means of transportation, but who? The answer is whoever does not have property rights over the car. A property right is essentially the norm that dictates how a resource can be used and who owns it. If I own the car, I have the right to its use and can either drive it to New York or lend/rent it to you for your purposes, but the choice is ultimately mine.

When someone else owns a given resource, I have no right to requisition it for my own purposes without having first obtained consent from the owner. Aside from exclusive use, property rights allow for obtaining rental income from others using the property without loss of ownership. When a farmer uses his neighbor's tractor, the rightful owner cannot also use it during the time the farmer has it, so the farmer pays his neighbor for temporarily depriving him of his access to his property, though no transfer of ownership occurred. If the farmer sneaks into his neighbor's barn in the middle of the night and takes the tractor without consent, conversion of property has taken place, and this action is a strict violation of property rights. Even if the farmer left a cashier's check in his neighbor's front door for the fair value of the tractor, the neighbor's property rights were still violated, as he had the exclusive rights to determine how the tractor is to be used and did not consent to the arrangement. Property rights do allow for the selling, gifting, modifying, or destruction of one's property. The main limitation of property rights involves using one's property to interfere with the rights of someone else. If I own a baseball bat and enjoy swinging it around in the air, I am free to do so; I am not, however, free to swing my bat through your car's front windshield, as that action then violates your property rights. You have the right to destroy your windshield if you so choose, but I do not have the right to destroy it without your consent.

Before discussing how clearly defined (and protected) property rights are a necessary prerequisite of a thriving economy, it is important to briefly describe how property rights originate. There are essentially two ways to acquire property that do not involve forcefully violating the rights of others: homesteading or voluntary exchange.[37] Through homesteading, one takes an unclaimed resource found in nature and mixes his time, energy, labor, and capital with it in order to produce something new, thus making the new product his property. When I go to the ocean and collect unclaimed seashells, fasten them into a necklace with a piece of string, I have mixed my labor with nature and can now claim the necklace as my property. Through voluntary exchange one can acquire or dispense of property through buying, trading, selling, giving, etc. When I purchase a seashell necklace from a craftsman who made it himself, or if I purchase it from a merchant who purchased it from the craftsman, I have then made the property my own through voluntary exchange, and I now have exclusive rights to determine how it will be used in the future until I abandon, destroy, or trade it away.

Property rights are among the chief institutions necessary for a thriving economy. Without them, economic progress grinds to a halt, assuming there was any to begin with. Without respected private property rights, might equals right. People would never leave their houses for the fear that while they were gone, someone else would come behind them and take over their house, declaring it his, and then refusing to leave. With no private property rights, there is no recourse since no one could have ever owned the house in the first place. Any object would only "belong" to whoever is using it currently or whoever has the power to take it away from another. Fortunately, property rights are a fundamental institution of our society today, and we do not even need to be present for them to be recognized. When a person arrives at work but leaves her car in the parking deck, the car is still hers even though she has moved away from it. She can concentrate on her work and be productive knowing that when she returns to the car, it will still be there and will still be hers. Assuming the car is not there or vandalized, her property rights have been violated, and she will have legal recourse. Conversely, if she parked on someone's private property without permission, she still owns the car, but the property owner can have it towed away – that is his legal recourse. If we had no property rights, one would need to hire armed guards during periods of absence to protect what he has accumulated, and then hope the armed guards choose not to requisition his property while he is gone. Furthermore, no one would have the incentive to invest in anything, innovate, or even work, since one would not own the products resulting thereof, and this is key for explaining why property rights are a critical aspect of a market economy.[38]

The world's material resources are scarce, and property rights determine how they are employed. Those same property rights ensure that they are employed efficiently. If they are not, the person using them suffers financial losses, and after a while, that person will no longer be in command of a given set of resources. Since property rights apply, anyone in possession of anything has the incentive to look after it and ensure it is being used as productively as possible. After all, the owner of that resource will be the primary beneficiary when it is most productively employed. This incentive does not exist with resources or goods where property rights do not apply, or where the property is collectivized and "owned" by everyone.[39] I have the incentive to ensure my yard stays well maintained and attractive. It increases my home value, and I benefit from its routine maintenance. I have no incentive to exert energy maintaining the public park down the street. My efforts there only benefit me in the same proportion that they benefit all others that use it, which is less than the cost I incur to maintain it. A free-rider problem then emerges between the users of the park. Each will ask himself: "Why should I clean the park when others will get the benefit, and then dirty it up again?" This problem exists everywhere where resources are shared, and no one individual has property rights.

An anecdote to private property rights versus collectively owned goods can be found in Portland, Oregon circa 1994. Civic activists released hundreds of bikes into the community, all painted bright yellow to indicate that they are part of the program. The idea was simple: anyone could use a yellow bike at any time, all one had to do was leave it on a major street when finished so another could use it. The program fell apart almost immediately. Many of the bikes were promptly stolen. Some were vandalized, and the remainder fell into terrible disrepair.[40] Since no one owned the bikes, there was no incentive for a user to not attempt that sweet jump that he's too fearful to try on his own bike out of the fear that a rough landing could damage it. When a chain falls off a bike, it's much easier to just dump it and get a new bike rather than repair it. After all, everyone else will get the benefit of your efforts to fix it, so why bother? A much different story is told with private bicycles. Owners of their own bicycles have the incentive to lock them up so they aren't stolen, bring them inside out of the rain, repair them when they break...etc.

Lawful Protection

So where does the government factor in? Since private property rights provide people with the incentives to maintain their property and utilize it in the most effective way, protecting these rights and ensuring that property rights are honored becomes a significant factor affecting economic growth, and this is primarily left to the public sector. Protecting property rights is widely understood to be an important function of government, which is why protection eats up such a large portion of the public budget. In 2018 alone, the armed forces were budgeted over \$686 billion in expenses, comprising over half of all US discretionary spending at the federal level.[41] Each city, town, and municipality across the country will have its own police force that will consume a large portion of the local public funds as well, though data is sporadic and can fluctuate wildly regarding the proportions of the budget allocated to protection. Different municipalities will vary in terms of size, scope, and crime rates, etc. There are three primary instruments government uses to protect property rights, two of which were just mentioned: police to prevent individuals from violating each other's rights, armed forces to protect citizens' rights as a whole against foreign aggression, and a court system to settle disputes and mediate litigation between individuals, thus reducing the use of violence as a resolution.

When two private individuals engage in acts of violence, someone must violate the rights of another, with the rare exception that two individuals consented to fight each other under mutually agreed-upon terms. If one individual commits an act of violence against another in the form of physical assault, theft of property, trespassing, or any of the numerous alternative ways to violate a person's rights, the victim is permitted to engage in violence to the extent that is proportionate to the crime in order to defend his property and/or person. If someone uses deadly force against you, you are permitted the use of deadly force as well to defend your life. If you use deadly force against a juvenile spray-painting your mailbox, your response is out of proportion, and then you have violated that person's rights above any criteria of measurement

40

used to assess how violated your rights were when your mailbox was tagged in the first place. Bear in mind that a right to life and to your body constitutes property rights, as each person owns him or herself. In the United States, each state will have its own legal code that varies to some degree, but the general premise is that people are entitled to defend themselves and property with proportionate force as being used against them from aggressors.[42]

Regarding the use of force, the government and its agencies are unique in the sense that only they have a legal monopoly on violence. Government forces and police officers are charged with performing their duties and enforcing the law, and may thereby initiate violence where none otherwise would exist. This puts the government in a delicate situation: the people have granted it enormous power to use force to protect their rights, but given that the government enjoys the only legal monopoly on the use of force, it occupies an unimpeachable position easily susceptible to abuse and corruption. Government often uses its monopoly of force against people rather than for them, and it can easily become the single biggest violator of people's rights when its power was conceived in order to protect them. Evidence suggests we may have already reached that point. Government appropriation of private property under obscure asset forfeiture laws has increased significantly over the last few decades, with the total value of seized assets having gone from roughly $100 million in the late 1980s to more than $2.5 billion today. Many of these cases involve individuals innocent of any wrongdoing and not charged with any crime, leaving them to contend with the court system to reverse the damage done by the government.[43]

Government power must be heavily constrained to prevent the abuses that are increasing in frequency. Arbitrary asset seizure, confiscation of property without due process, penalties and fines for victimless crimes (such as the notorious seat belt laws and marijuana restrictions), and blatant excessive uses of force are all

41

problems that cause friction between people and the agents of government whose duty it is to protect and serve. Government must be heavily monitored to ensure that its agents are serving the people rather than abusing them. There must be strong guidelines in place that ensure police and military forces have strict mandates by which to abide, and punitive consequences when they are breached. Unfortunately for the citizenry, usually when police or other government agents push the boundaries too far and abuse the people, it is often the police or other government departments themselves that handle the investigation. In the United States even, there exists a "Law Enforcement Officer's Bill of Rights" that protects police when they carry out their duties. It shields police from public scrutiny by ensuring that any misconduct allegations will be reviewed by fellow officers, effectively choking off any potential civilian oversight of police and making it all the more difficult to hold police accountable.[44] Qualified immunity also protects police officers and allows them to violate a person's civil rights with little repercussion. Under qualified immunity, police officers can violate a person's civil rights without having to worry about being held personally responsible unless they blatantly commit a crime—usually, nothing less than murder will suffice. A person may sue the city or municipality that employs the officer, but the officer as an individual cannot be sued, and his assets are protected, effectively removing incentives for him to exercise his monopoly on violence more judiciously.[45] These doctrines warrant prompt and complete annulment. There needs to be established watchdog groups responsible for holding government police forces accountable, and a robust system of checks and balances on the power these forces wield.

For the sake of argument, let us assume that police and military do not exceed their mandates to protect our rights, and that they in no way violate our rights or the rights of others. All government agents tasked with protecting our rights and property

42

do so flawlessly, without falling into corruption or abuse of power. They carry out their duties as charged and only protect our rights, with no arbitrary penalties and convictions for victimless crimes or unjust laws. Only our rights are protected under this scenario, and they are protected to the extent we need them to be. Now the question arises: how much protection do we want? How much will we need? As you may have noticed the last time you checked your pay stub and realized how many of your dollars went into the government's coffers, protection is not free. Police need their cars and helicopters, the army its tanks, and the navy its aircraft carriers. These items come with a hefty price tag. In order to ascertain how much protection we should have, we must weigh the costs of protection versus the benefits at the marginal level.

Take for example a small-town police force. Perhaps the town grows in size, and new roads are paved, new businesses open up, and new homes are built. The small police department with its handful of officers may quickly find itself overstretched. Perhaps there are not enough police officers to patrol the roads while simultaneously protecting the businesses from theft and burglary. The police department would need to hire additional officers to accommodate the public's increased demand for safety and protection. The hiring of new officers will require the purchase of new cars for them to drive, new equipment for them to carry on the job, etc. Costs will be realized. At what point should the police department conclude that it has hired as many new officers as it needs? People's needs for protection vary from town to town, city to city, and nation to nation, as do the costs of provision, but everywhere the same fundamental truths apply: resources and manpower should be employed to protect people's rights until the cost of allocating additional resources exceed the additional benefits of protection. This can be achieved by calculating the economic damage suffered at the hands of crime weighed against the expenses of protection.[46]

Returning to our hypothetical town, let us now assume that our little police department has been able to grow its budget from the new tax revenue derived from the town's growth. It now has an adequate supply of officers and equipment to ensure protection. Would it benefit the townspeople to continue adding additional resources? There quickly comes a point where society is made worse off when there is too much emphasis on protection. Suppose the police department hired one extra officer that it did not need. Now the private sector has one less person to work in a factory or store providing the goods and services consumers demand. That surplus officer now derives a salary paid for by the public treasury, imposing costs on the people being protected. Suppose now that the police department quintupled in size when the town only experienced modest growth. Main street is now filled with police cruisers obstructing the flow of traffic, newly hired police officers stand idly by on the sidewalk waiting to be of use, and a welfare call to grandma's house prompts a literal army of first responders who have nothing else to do since the town is over-protected. Meanwhile, this excessive allocation of resources to public safety is draining the public treasury. In essence, the general idea is that the government should spend just enough to protect people's rights without bleeding them dry for protection above and beyond what they need.

Carried further, this same line of reasoning can be used to debate whether or not there exists an optimal number of terrorist attacks. Government is tasked with protecting our rights, which include our lives, against foreign aggressors and terrorist plots. Just like in our hypothetical town from before, there is a cost incurred with doing so. If the government successfully reduced the number of terrorist attacks the country experiences to zero through policies of protection, what would those costs look like? Any item that could be used as a weapon of terror would need to be confiscated. Immigration would need to be eliminated, depriving the country of access to labor and the innovators that would have engaged in our market economy. The size of the armed forces and local police would need to be increased a thousandfold to ensure that everyone who could commit an act of terror (essentially anyone capable of moving their arms) would be closely watched and monitored. The power and scope of duty that law enforcement agencies and military forces would have over our lives would explode to proportions that put totalitarian regimes to shame. The members of the armed forces and police would themselves also need to be monitored, for they have the means and capabilities to commit an act of terror if they so choose. Cameras would need to be installed in every house and building to ensure that no one is attempting to plot terror. All vehicles would need to be destroyed to ensure they cannot be used for terrorist purposes; likewise, all planes grounded. Food processing plants would need to be shut down to prevent anyone from ever being able to poison the food supply, and the same goes for water treatment. The costs of entirely eliminating even the most remote possibility of an act of terror would be so enormous, that economic activity would come to a screeching halt. One must, therefore, conclude that the optimal number of terrorist attacks we must endure is some number greater than zero. For the government to provide protection, the costs of provision should not exceed the benefits, and when "protection" is so absolute that it chokes off all economic activity, there are no benefits at all.

Government Control

The US economy is not a pure capitalist economic system, but rather a mixed economy. While primarily leaving the allocation of goods and services to the free market, there are sectors of the economy that rely heavily upon government intervention, if not outright direction. Supporters of the free market system hold that resources and capital are best utilized in private hands, as market incentives ensure that the world's scarce resources are most productively utilized in order to meet the demands of consumers.[47] Proponents of economic systems in which the government directs economic activity argue that the free market system allows for too much employer-employee exploitation while producing too many negative side effects. In their view, government involvement in economic activity will reduce what they perceive to be inequality in terms of wealth and income, thus creating a morally just society.[48] To what degree should governments be involved in markets? There is a wide spectrum on this issue encompassing many different scenarios and grades in which the government can play a part in the economy. Metaphorically speaking, one should not view government involvement in the economy as a light switch where government activity can be switched "on" and "off" in absolute terms, but instead as a dial where government intervention and direction can be turned to "increase" or "decrease" the amount of government involvement.

First, to understand how the government can involve itself in the economy, it is important to consider the end of the spectrum taken to its absolute extremity: the complete governmental control over all economic activity. Since Karl Marx argued that capitalism exploits the masses some 150 years ago, popular governments have risen up around the world to "seize the means of production" to ensure fair treatment for all workers and fair distribution of all goods. Marx and his followers believed workers are inherently disadvantaged by not owning any capital resources themselves, and by necessity must work for those that own means. Given the nature of this asymmetric relationship, Marx argued that the capitalist exploited the worker, and profits from production were attributed to the laborer's surplus-value, and should belong to the worker. Additionally, he argued that a good or service's value was related to the amount of labor that went into it, rather than the perceived subjective value determined by society.[49] In error, Marx either failed to account for demand or simply dismissed it as being an economic driver. I could spend a year designing and then sewing a sweater with five sleeves and two necklines, but if no one wants to buy it, then it has no value in the eyes of consumers. Regarding capital, Marx and his followers ignore the crucial service that the capitalists provide: investment and preservation of the capital structure.

Capital is created by delaying consumption. You could today spend your entire net worth on beanie babies and video games (consumption), or you could invest your savings in an original business idea or a business idea of someone else. You could also do neither by keeping your money in the bank, allowing it to be loaned to businessmen on your behalf. Regardless, delayed consumption provides capital which can then be used to increase production, thus enhancing our ability to consume in the future. Think of it this way: you could eat your corn seed today for a quick meal, or you could plant it and have meals galore in the future. When capitalists embark on business ventures, they take on risks by putting capital at stake in the production of future goods and services which will (hopefully) be in demand upon completion. Machines need operators and fields need harvesters, so workers are employed to help facilitate the process of transforming raw materials into consumer products which will be bought and consumed at the final stage of production. Throughout the whole process, the worker is rewarded with regular wages regardless of whether the venture pays off or not. If the venture does not pay off at the end, the business goes under and the worker is laid off – an unfortunate outcome for the worker, but utterly devastating to the capitalist who took on considerable risk. If the venture pays off, the capitalist is heavily rewarded for correctly predicting future consumer demand, and the worker is also rewarded with continued employment and the possibility of performance bonuses and raises.

Marxist governments fail to understand this relationship, and are quick to denounce capitalist entrepreneurs as exploitative and degenerate. By giving the capitalist the boot and collectivizing the means of production, there will no longer be any extraordinary individuals like Henry Ford or Bill Gates to revolutionize the way consumers have access to products. Instead, anything that can be presently consumed will be divided among the people, and there will be little to no production going forward. History provides ample horrific examples of what can happen when the government (always in the name of the people) seizes control of the economy and capital goods.

When the Japanese military was evicted from the Korean peninsula at the end of World War II, the Soviet Union occupied the northern half while the United States controlled the south. Seeking to stop the spread of Communism, the US supported anti-communist authoritarian leaders, while the Soviet Union backed Kim Il-Sung, a prominent figure in the communist anti-Japanese faction during the war. At the time, there was little difference in livelihood between a typical South Korean and North Korean. From the outset of both countries however, they would be placed on two different paths of economic progress that shaped their respective courses of history. The North Korean government took control of the economy and began directing economic activity. Markets and private property were and still are suppressed. Economic freedom is alien to North Koreans except for party insiders, but even those individuals have limited access to goods and services due to the limitations imposed on the markets by their current economic system. Agricultural activity has all but collapsed, there is no private investment anywhere to be found, and innovation and new technologies never emerge. South Korea on the other hand, after having embraced a more liberal market economy, has been dubbed an "economic miracle."[50] After just a few decades of these two government types, the outcome is apparent. South Koreans are more literate, healthy, and prosperous, while their northern counterparts are starving, uneducated, and oppressed. And yet, their northern cousins are the ones that live under a government that claims it does what it does in the name of "the people."[51] The Soviet Union, Cambodia, Mao's China, and other examples from across the globe highlight the catastrophe that awaits people whose governments seek to control the economy. In such a society, and assuming a person is lucky enough to even survive the resultant food shortages and purges of political dissidents, the future is bleak and grim with necessities becoming luxuries. Such is the way of economies under complete control of the government.

On the other hand, there are those that argue that the government can perform useful economic functions when properly restrained. I once attended an economics seminar in 2013 that featured a variety of speakers, all discussing the benefits and drawbacks of government intervention in the market economy. One speaker, whose name I sadly cannot recall, opened with the following line: "Everything you have, thank the government for," which was quickly met by a few snickers and chuckles in the back of the room. The speaker intended to evoke this reaction and allowed the moment to sink in before carrying on with his lecture, even briefly laughing with us. He then went on to explain how governments face different incentives than market participants do, which changes how they operate under different constraints.

Market participants are motivated by profit, and profit is the market signaling that scarce resources are being utilized effectively. Government has no such incentive. If a program is not profitable, the government can simply raise taxes to bridge the gap, something a private company cannot do. This phenomenon draws heavy criticism from the academic world of economics, but here is where the divergence between a government operation and private enterprise warrants further investigation. The government's ability to continue operating through long periods of loss allows it to perform certain functions in the economy that cannot be performed by the private sector alone. Namely, the government can make investments with such long time horizons that no private enterprise could afford to make them. Private companies need to earn profit to stay in business. Most companies operate through losses for the first few years of their existence—funding operations through short-term debt—and then they become profitable in the future. Since the government does not need to worry about going out of business, it can allocate resources to projects with time horizons that span decades, such as research and development for new medicine, subsidizing technological research firms, or funding extremely large infrastructure projects, etc. Private companies can rarely afford to wait multiple decades before turning a profit and are thus incapable of making the kind of long-term investments that the government can. The issue then becomes whether or not the benefit of government long-term investments such as the ones previously mentioned are worth the cost. In those cases, it will take a long time to actually find out. Regardless of whether or not it pays off, it is something that a private enterprise simply cannot attempt unless it has the cash to burn for many, many years.

The Theory of Regulatory Benefits

Tracing its origins to the Latin word "Regula," which translates to standard or rule, the word "regulation" alone is often enough to provoke passionate debates around the dinner table or conference room. A heated talking point for any contemporary political issue regarding the environment and finance, regulation is the knot in the rope in a game of political tug-of-war. The right declares that regulations are too many and too oppressive to business and general economic activity. The left cries that regulation is insufficient to curtail "bad behavior" of banks and other "greedy" financial institutions while also being too lax on environmental protection. Either side is rarely happy regarding regulation. But what is regulation, and why does it exist in the first place?

The theoretical framework for government regulation over economic activity goes something like this: government control over production or provision of a given good or service would be less efficient than private enterprise, but private enterprise itself provides the good or service in an inefficient manner as well, thereby necessitating a government action. The imposition of regulation can provide the incentives needed for private enterprises to more efficiently provide goods or services to the market without the government taking over the production process.[52] Government regulation in a market economy can have many faces. For starters, it can standardize a confusing set of measurements or procedures into one uniform set, reducing costs of translations and conversions for market participants resulting in greater access to information and a reduction in uncertainty. Imagine if every auto-maker had its own system for classifying the safety of its vehicles. A consumer would need to be familiar with all of them and be able to compare them with one another if he is to make an informed car purchase on the basis of safety. How would Ford's "A+" safety rating on its F150 compare to Chevrolet's "Gold Star" safety rating on the Silverado, and Dodge's "Two Thumbs Up" rating for its Ram trucks? Fortunately, we need not worry about such confusing translations, as we can simply default to the standardized criteria of the National Highway Traffic Safety Administration (NHTSA) to see universal standards applied to all vehicles.

Other cases can involve lopsided information whereby the consumer operates in a state of complete ignorance while the seller holds all the cards. Asymmetric information can be fatal in some extreme examples. In the 19th century, obscure drugs and tonics lined pharmacy shelves. Labels on the bottles boasted of their rejuvenating effects: longer life, better fortune, the gateway to happiness...and so on and so forth. Charlatans would drift from town to town selling elixirs and potions for the backs of wagons to easily-fooled townsfolk, and then they would disappear before the people realized they had been swindled. Not only were most of these "drugs" ineffective at achieving their stated purpose, many were also deadly. Mounting pressure from an increasingly outraged public eventually led to the Food and Drug Administration banning most of these hocus pocus medicines by the early 1900s. As a result of regulatory oversight, the dangerous elixirs with their exaggerated claims (and deadly side effects) vanished and were no longer able to be openly sold, thus protecting the consumer. Eventually, the Food and Drug Administration was granted the power to test all drugs for both effectiveness and safety prior to the drugs entering circulation. No doubt this has spared many patients from undue suffering or death by consuming dangerous drugs in cases where they would not have known what the side effects could be.[53] But like most government regulations however, the benefits usually come at a cost—a cost that often exceeds the benefits returned.

The Reality of Regulatory Consequences

The road to hell is paved with good intentions, as they say. Governments, like the market, do not always have access to the best information. When imposing regulation meant to protect consumers, governments can often hurt them in ways that outweigh whatever benefits the regulations were meant to achieve, thereby making regulation counterproductive at times. Returning to regulatory oversight over the pharmaceuticals market, oftentimes potentially life-saving drugs get caught up in the regulatory logjam which delay (if not outright terminate) their entry into the marketplace. Before reaching consumers, these drugs undergo test after test to be sure that no stone is left uncovered, and no side effects appear that were not already accounted for. All the while, individuals whose lives could be saved by the drug must wait months on end for a drug that may save them in a time when every day could make a significant difference in a person's deteriorating health condition.[54]

Regulation is a double-edged sword. One the one hand, the government can institute a regulation which at first glance protects consumers by ensuring that they have access to more information and protection from real dangers—making voters happy in the short term—but in most cases, regulation hinders progress and is counterproductive. More often than not, government regulations have unintended consequences, so most regulations operate like a controlled experiment. Market conditions X lead to problem Y, so regulation Z is strategically placed to correct the situation resulting in unintended consequences A, B, and C. The government, rather than repeal and replace the original regulation or modify it to mitigate the negative side effects, will usually just install additional regulations meant to deal with the consequences of the first regulation, which can have adverse consequences of their own. It is often a never-ending spiral of regulation for regulation's sake. And with each new regulation, companies must dedicate additional resources to interpretation. Compliance departments are expanded, lawyers are employed, and countless hours and manpower are now dedicated to ensuring that everything conforms to the rules. These are resources that could have otherwise been used for production. Government must tread lightly with its use of regulation, and must ensure that markets are not over-regulated or misregulated. The best course of action is for the government to allow markets to work naturally, abstaining from interference via regulation and allowing people to choose which businesses to patronize and which to avoid.

With zero regulations, businesses would need to rely on their established reputations in order to secure business. Critics of the free market hold this wild notion that if consumer safety regulations were all repealed, businesses would instantly put dangerous products on the shelves and take shortcuts with production that lead to unsafe products. They claim that food would be hazardous to eat and water dangerous to drink due to a lack of government oversight ensuring its quality. Safety and quality are not benefits bestowed upon consumers by a nurturing government, but rather are values created by profit-seeking businesses.[55] Businesses seeking to retain their customers will protect their reputation and withhold dangerous products from their shelves. In the event a business does not care to protect its customers or its reputation, it will not be in business for long, as angry consumers will abandon it for one of its competitors. Regarding information, the free market is capable of providing rating agencies, and these agencies would compete with one another the same way that other businesses compete. These agencies would stake their own reputation on the quality of their ratings, and any agencies that are known to rate loosely and over-generously will soon see their reputations diminished, thus incentivizing businesses to obtain their accreditations only from reputable rating agencies.[56]

The government discourages private certification firms by offering its own system of ratings through regulation "for free." Since the government goes around stamping seals of approval on things like food safety, drug safety, household product safety, etc., reputation is substituted with a reliance on government oversight. Strong reputations no longer distinguish companies' products from those of competitors, which negates the incentive to seek better reputations, and this comes at no benefit to consumers. Regulation forces consumers' hands by removing degrees of marketplace choice. In essence, regulation forces people to abide by what the government deems a person's risk level should be, not what the person chooses it to be. If a customer wanted to buy something that did not meet regulators' arbitrary standards—even if the consumer was willing to take the extra risk—he would not be able to. This is government interference in a person's rights to property.[57]

Regulation also breeds conflicts of interest between parties, and the government is not omniscient. Government bodies consist of human beings who are flawed and subject to human nature just like the rest of us. The imposition of a given piece of regulation is subject to the decision-making process of human beings, as are other government decisions and legislative acts. When potential regulation is put on the table for debate, the public interest is often pitted against special interests in a contest of determining who will benefit the most, and usually, it is the special interest. Average consumers are often rationally ignorant of what regulations are in place and how they are affected. Indeed, it would be an exhaustive task to understand how regulation affects each and every aspect of our lives. Corporations have a vested interest in seeing favorable regulations pass and regulations not favorable to them fail. They bring all their lobbying power to the politicians' doorsteps and take great efforts to ensure that their interests are protected, while consumers not only lack the lobbying resources to compete, they also lack the proper incentive. As a result of these circumstances, regulators face strong incentives to favor special interests over the public.[58]

Once regulation starts benefiting the special interests over the public, additional problems emerge that would otherwise be nonexistent in the free market. In a purely free-market economy, companies compete with one another to provide goods or services at the lowest cost to the consumer in order to capture business. It is very difficult for a single company to form a monopoly over a certain good or service in the free market, as newcomers will always be eager to enter the market and challenge the established company or innovate some new product that replaces the need for the monopoly company altogether. Multiple companies providing the same good or service can impose monopoly-like conditions on the consumers by agreeing to fix their prices or restrict output, otherwise known as a cartel. These arrangements work for a time, but each firm within the cartel has a powerful incentive to "cheat" and undercut other members on the price by just enough to steal business away from them. Once cartel firms begin eyeing each other with suspicion, the whole arrangement folds, and competition is restored.[59]

In most (but not all) cases, monopoly nor cartel control of resources is beneficial to consumers. Regulation, when used improperly or as an unintended side effect, has the power to create monopoly and cartel effects on markets at tremendous costs of quality, quantity, and value. Government regulation can impose strict barriers to entry through licensing practices requiring new entrants to navigate a labyrinth of red tape, costly fines, and bureaucratic hoop-jumping before being able to enter the market. These regulations are always enacted to "protect the consumer," but their effects tend to benefit the industries themselves. The next time you visit your local barber, look around the kiosk for a cosmetology license. In accordance with federal regulation, anyone cutting hair within the United States MUST have a license to do so, the requirements of such license being determined on a state level. Requirements vary from state to state, but beauticians and barbers must undergo significant training, complete cosmetology courses, fulfill hundreds of hours worth of on-the-job training, pass an examination, and have credentials accepted or rejected from an oversight committee. If anyone you know practices cosmetology without having undergone the appropriate steps, that person is a criminal. The reader might ask why all of this is necessary for the simple occupation of cosmetology? The response from regulatory supporters would echo something along the lines of public health and safety, but does a little piece of paper stating that a barber is "licensed" really make him that much more safe and qualified to cut my hair than my neighbor, who might be far more sanitary or talented? The suffocating regulatory requirements that beauticians endure in order to practice cosmetology may be in place for public safety reasons, but the resulting consequences are passed down to the consumers in the form of monopoly-like prices and lack of competitiveness in the cosmetology industry. Renowned economist Walter Williams elaborates further:

> The result of restricting entry to a business or occupation, and probably the intent of licensing, is to raise the incomes of incumbent practitioners. Evidence supports this self-interested behavior: (1) most licensure laws are the result of intense lobbying by (the) incumbents, not of consumers demanding more protection from incompetent or unscrupulous practitioners; (2) when incumbents in an unlicensed trade lobby for licensing (or when those in one already licensed lobby for higher entry requirements) they virtually always seek a "grandfather" clause that exempts them from meeting the new requirements, leaving the burden of the higher entry costs to be borne mainly by new entrants; (3) practitioner violations of licensing codes, such as price-cutting and extra hours, are nearly always reported to the licensing board by the incumbents rather than by customers.[60]

Since violating state or federal regulation is against the law and a punishable offense, monopoly effects are enforced leaving consumers to pick up the tab to the benefit of the special interests whom the regulation benefits. Regulation that blocks new entrants to industries suppresses the supply of that good, forcing the prices up, which is desirable in the eyes of those producers living under the protection of the regulatory umbrella. They may claim that regulation is necessary to secure public welfare, but oftentimes the public welfare suffers. The price effects of cartels and monopolies are allowed to persist due to the regulation when they would not be sustainable if the market was open to more competition.

Regulation can very easily destroy competition in the marketplace. One pitfall is that it often removes efficiency as a competitive factor between firms. If regulation prevents companies from reducing their prices below a certain point for example (no doubt to "protect jobs" in that industry), these firms are no longer allowed to undercut each other's prices to capture market share. Instead, they must find alternative ways to compete. They could distinguish their product by adding more features or customization options, or perhaps they could make a service available across a larger territory than they once served, even if it is inefficient to do so. Since they cannot compete on price, they must find alternative channels. The costs incurred from these new competitive measures will be passed on to consumers, absorbed by the companies, or some combination of both. If the costs of competing on a non-price basis are too high, it could eliminate the extra profits the companies once enjoyed at the onset of getting the favorable, price-fixing regulation. The result is a boondoggle affair whereby companies are made inefficient due to their non-price competition, but to repeal the legislation at this stage would impose massive losses on the companies who have by now tailored their operating models with the regulation already accounted for. This is the reason why regulation, once imposed on industry, is difficult to remove. The companies that once lobbied for its passage will now lobby for its staying in place.[61]

Political Incentives

Regulation tends to benefit some at the expense of others, usually in most cases the special interests over the public interests. Politicians must tread carefully, however, with over-appeasing the lobbyists. Politicians need those campaign contributions—and passing favorable regulation for companies is a good way to get them—but if their efforts to satisfy special interests at the expense of the public become too heavily scrutinized, it could prove detrimental to their odds of being re-elected. Appeasing special interests through regulation often bears political consequences, and when politicians favor legislation that appeals to certain special interest groups, politicians from the other party or political challengers in the upcoming elections will use those appeasements to discredit and slander. Politicians must find the balance between too little and too much regulation as it pertains to their reputations and political careers.

Regulation is enacted by legislatures who are human, and all humans must weigh the costs and benefits of their decisions before acting upon them. Politicians have the same constraints. Since regulation benefits some while harming others, politicians must determine whether or not the gains to their political campaigns/careers from enacting regulatory policies for the favored interests outweighs the costs they will bear from the disgruntled losers. Fortunately for the politicians, if regulation imposes costs on the public, most people are largely unaware of it. Did you really notice that your haircut cost $15 instead of $11 when you were unaware that it would cost less without licensure legislation in the first place? Indeed, most people are generally unaware of how legislation affects the cost. Still, there comes a point where people begin to realize the fact that goods and services provided by heavily-regulated industries tend to cost more, and the correlation is then easily inferred.[62]

Politicians debating regulatory legislation are bombarded with pleas, favors, campaign contributions, and sometimes outright bribes from the special interests who are meant to benefit from the regulation. From the view of the rational politician, it is difficult to piece together how political benefits from regulation will be offset by political costs from disgruntled parties, as well as to what degree the two will be related. Given how political benefits stack up against political costs, politicians acting in their own self-interest can be expected to pass regulatory legislation to the point where the political benefits from the special interests are exactly equal to the political costs imposed by angry constituents. Any additional regulation imposed beyond this point will incur political ramifications that do not pay off. This equilibrium of cost/benefits of regulation for the politician will vary across industries, but the concept remains the same.[63]

Special interest groups lobbying for regulation operate under different incentives. Those that benefit from regulation would prefer that regulatory stipulations extend to the point where benefits to them are maximized, whereby no new regulation can benefit them further. In most cases, this point will be beyond the politician's threshold of political costs equaling political benefits.

Because the amount of regulation desired by the special interests often exceeds the willingness of the politician to continue granting it, special interests lobby all the more. Usually, the special interest groups partially succeed. Not only do lobbying efforts elevate their interests above the public welfare, but the additional goodies and campaign funds they gift to politicians through lobbying efforts account for additional "political benefits" in the politician's cost-benefit calculation, thus allowing him to grant additional regulation until the new political benefits once again equal the political costs. As a result of lobbying, the public interest is underrepresented in regulatory legislation, thus giving regulation overall a special interest bias across the board.

In the 2015 film "The Big Short," based on the Michael Lewis book bearing the same title, one of the principal characters meets with his brother's ex-girlfriend at a resort hotel in Las Vegas during a mortgage-securitization conference. She had previously worked for the Securities and Exchange Commission (SEC), and he had hoped to pick her brain a bit on the current situation of the financial markets. Keep in mind that this film takes place in 2007-2008, just before the housing bubble meltdown that triggered the worst recession since the Great Depression. He floats the idea that he is interested in investing in mortgage bonds when in actuality he intends to bet against them, but he hopes to elicit a reaction from his brother's ex-girlfriend indicating that mortgage bonds are not sound investments despite their high credit ratings. Instead, she informs him that she does not regulate mortgage bonds, and due to budget cuts, the SEC in general pays little attention to them. Given this surprising fact, he asks her why she is there in the first place, to which she responds that her intention is to rub elbows with some big bank recruiters in the hopes of landing a new job at an investment bank. She then goes on to explain that there is no law on the books prohibiting a person who worked in financial regulation to pursue a career at the firms that person once regulated, much to the surprise of our protagonist.[64]

Politics, regulation, and lobbying work much the same way. When a given legislature retires from the public sphere, he or she often has a plethora of job offers from the firms that once lobbied for special favors. It is a classic case of "I'll scratch your back if you scratch mine." Otherwise known as the "revolving door" concept to illustrate the circular flow from politics to lobbying, and vice versa. Given that politicians can count on a lucrative career in the firms they grant special privileges to at the end of their political terms, politicians have an even greater incentive to favor lobbyists over the general interest.[65]

61

3 The Road and the Radio

"The government enforces a monopoly over the production and distribution of its alleged 'services' and brings violence to bear against would-be competitors. In so doing, it reveals the fraud at the heart of its impudent claims and gives sufficient proof that it is not a genuine protector, but a mere protection racket."
- Robert Higgs, 2007.[66]

The Public and The Public Interest

In a modern economy, there are two spheres of economic activity: the private sector and the public sector. The private sector consists of individuals and businesses that come together, and through mutually agreed-upon voluntary arrangements, exchange different goods and services with each other. This process satisfies consumer demand, creates wealth, and leads to economic growth. The public sector on the other hand does not rely on voluntary cooperation. Government activity comprises the public sector, and it can only be funded by siphoning off wealth from the private sector. Smaller governments require less private-sector fleecing, thus tend to yield stronger economic growth. Large, cumbersome governments, with their legions of bureaucrats and oppressive regulatory structures, require vast amounts of resources and wealth to maintain, and this funding comes from the private sector through taxation. When people pay taxes, the government is able to fund its operations, and public sector output is produced. Citizens are given a bundle of public sector goods in return for their taxes, some of which may not be needed or wanted, and some of which may conflict with people's moral sentiments, but regardless of whether or not a person agrees with or likes/dislikes the public sector output given to him in return for his taxes, he is compelled to "play along" and accept the status quo by virtue of living within the government's geographical territory. Government, through its monopoly on force, coerces people to obey its laws and pay for its production. Some people may be supportive of government activity—especially if their political party holds power at the time—but even if they are not in agreement, they are still coerced. The threat of punishment and further confiscation of wealth is reason enough for most people to pay taxes, therefore the public sector is defined by force and mandatory participation.

On her campaign trail to win the nomination for the Democratic Party's presidential candidate for the 2008 election cycle, Senator Hillary Clinton once remarked that "We're going to take things away from you on behalf of the common good."[67] Mrs. Clinton's remarks reflect a deeply concerning truth about how the government operates. Government takes the resources provided by its citizens and produces public sector output, giving back to the citizens according to what is perceived to be in the public interest. Defining the public interest opens up a big can of worms. There are as many competing definitions of what's in the public's best interest as there are people that comprise "the public." Everyone has an opinion on the matter—including the politicians—and they are the ones who get to make the decisions. Often their decisions are politically motivated, but through what methods are they to decide how to allocate public goods and services? One approach is to attempt to achieve the greatest benefit for the greatest number of people. This will benefit a large number of individuals but will be detrimental towards a few, and occasionally the benefits to the majority will not outweigh the cost to the losers. Although this type of policy might do the greatest good for the greatest number of people, it could have a net welfare loss greater than the benefits granted to the majority.[68] Take for example a proposed government undertaking, a new public power plant, which will provide lower electrical rates to those living closest to it. However, due to inefficiencies or bureaucracy, the cost of the hypothetical plant would be $100 million, while the benefits to society may only equal $75 million. A power plant backed by private capital would never be built under such circumstances, but the government does not face the same constraints, as it can finance its projects through taxes. Now assume that a majority of people in the area live near the power plant, while only a few live far away. Government raises the funds through taxation, forcing everyone far and near to pay for the project. Under the "greatest good for the greatest number" approach, those living close to the plant would enjoy subsidized electricity, whereby they receive benefits in excess of the loss incurred from increased taxes. Recall that the net social loss of this project is $25 million. This cost will be imposed on the few residents living farther away from the plant, as their raised taxes will result in a significant loss to them, while the benefits they receive from the new plant would be small. Thus, this project results in a net loss to the public welfare, but it does a lot of good for a lot of people in the process.

One redress for the above scenario would be for the residents living close to the power plant to compensate those living farther away. If an undertaking like the power plant scenario benefits enough people so that they may take some of their gains and distribute them to the losers, everyone could still wind up better off than they were before, in which case the proposal would be considered in the public's interest. For this to happen, however, the net societal benefit must be greater than the net cost. It is very unlikely however that the winners of any given policy would be willing to voluntarily give up a portion of their benefits to the losers, so government would once again be required to extract the required compensation through a special tax, but bear in mind that public policy funded by taxation is what caused the problem in the first place.

Public Goods

When the government has decided which objectives to pursue, it then distributes goods and services to the public. Most government-provided goods possess two defining traits: they are collectively consumable, implying that once produced, new users can be added without reducing the amount available to existing users, and they are nonexcludable, meaning that once produced, it is difficult to block other people from using it without paying.[69] Goods and services that have these traits are not limited to the public sector, but these are often referred to as "public goods."

Consider for a moment a typical 4th of July fireworks display. Someone must bear the cost of hosting the show, and that person may charge admission to see the fireworks. But once the fireworks explode in the air, how can the event host prevent non-paying persons from viewing outside the admission gate? Anyone with a decent vantage point within view can gaze upon the display free of charge. The most common public sector example of a nonexcludable good is national defense; the armed forces protect all citizens living within the country's borders regardless of whether or not they paid taxes contributing to the cost. Collective consumption goods will also not have their availability to other users diminished once consumed.[70] When was the last time you were listening to the radio when your neighbor knocked on your door to request that you turn your radio off so he can listen to his, as your radio is hogging all the sound waves? Once the signal is aired, anyone with a receiver can tune in without affecting the availability of the signal to other potential users. One of the most referred-to public sector goods exhibiting collective consumption is the roadway system. Once produced, another driver can use the road at little additional cost, that is until capacity is reached and congestion takes hold.

There can be a strong argument made for leaving collective consumption goods to the public sector. When certain collective consumption goods are produced and supplied in the private sector, considerable inefficiency results from abstaining nonusers who must subscribe at a cost if they want access to the good.[71] Take Netflix for example. As long as someone has access to the internet and a device capable of streaming, Netflix can extend service to that person at little to no cost, as the infrastructure is already in place. Given that Netflix charges flat rates for streaming packages, suppose that someone was willing to pay $5 per month for service, while the cheapest Netflix package may be offered for say, $12. Given that the would-be subscriber does not value Netflix at the minimum asking price, this individual will not subscribe, and no transaction will take place. But since he was willing to pay $5 per month for Netflix, while the marginal cost to Netflix extending service to him is nonexistent, society incurs a net social welfare loss. This individual has lost $5 per month worth of Netflix entertainment, while Netflix has lost a $5 per month subscription that it would incur no cost to obtain. How might this inefficiency be overcome?

Netflix, and other private companies like it, could offer a "pick-your-price" model whereby they allow their customers to freely choose whatever price they want to pay for the service, theoretically paying what the service is valued at on an individual basis, but Netflix would not be able to rely on the honesty of society at large. Far too many people would simply activate service at the lowest rate possible even if they valued streaming service at a higher price than what they choose to pay. Netflix would then need to rely on charitable donations or people willingly overpaying for the service in order to stay in business. The reality is that Netflix must maintain minimum rates which make it profitable, even if that means some would-be users who value service at a rate lower than the minimum will go without access.

Netflix could also attempt to instate a fluctuating price rate dependent upon individual demand, charging people who want it most at a higher rate, and people who want it least at a lower rate. This happens often in the marketplace in the form of bargain sales and discounts. Companies can offer variable prices on the same good in order to reach as many diverse customers as possible, but this poses another challenge: Netflix would have great difficulty determining who is willing to pay what price. The costs of this type of forecasting would be high as well. In response to the unknown, Netflix can simply offer several packages and different rates, and let consumers agree to or decline service at the given price points.

Another difficulty Netflix encounters as being a private provider of a collective consumption good is the widespread issue of free-riding. It is terribly common for an entire group of family and friends to all share a single account, freely texting the sign-on information back and forth. Netflix has addressed this by limiting the number of screens that are able to stream at one time, but the free-riding issue still remains, as is characteristic of collective consumption goods. As more people benefit from a collective consumption good without paying for it, the greater the likelihood that the good will be underproduced and over-consumed, which will lead to increased economic inefficiency.[72] However, it is worth mentioning the offset by highlighting certain (and ironic) economic efficiencies captured by free-rider cases like Netflix's. Say you have a friend that is willing to subscribe to Netflix for $5 per month, but the base rate is $12. Since Netflix could extend service to him at no additional cost, an inefficiency is born by having a person not getting a service he is willing to pay for, and a company not capturing business that it could acquire at no cost. When you agree to give your friend your sign-on information and password to allow him access to your subscription, he suddenly has the service he desires, and his standard of living has increased. Meanwhile, Netflix has incurred no cost since it would not have captured his business at the minimum rate regardless. Thus, the inefficiency is now removed. However, if too many people attempt to mooch—without enough actual Netflix customers paying for the subscriptions—the company could be forced out of business. A balance must exist to ensure that the volume of free-riders does not sink the ship.

With or without free-riders, there will plausibly be people who are always willing to buy a given service that satisfies their wants and needs, but they may not be willing to buy it at its current price level. The aggregate difference between what these people would pay for a service and what it would cost them represents an inefficiency in the market that could be remedied by the government. To ensure that everyone has access to a collective consumption good, the government can apply a tax to individuals and then supply the goods or services free of charge, allowing people to consume as much or as little as they demand. The issue here is that governments do not operate with the same incentive constraints that private enterprises do, and it will not have the incentive to serve their customers well or maintain any degree of internal efficiency.[73]

Before anyone concludes that I just suggested Netflix and similar services could potentially be nationalized, it should be emphasized that government provision of certain goods and services only remedies market efficiencies in certain cases, such as when a third and uninvolved party is harmed by a transaction between others, or when the provision of the good or service requires such a large collaboration of private individuals that it becomes virtually impossible to have it supplied, and only if it proves to be impossible for them to cooperate spontaneously. With regard to other goods and services, private sector provision is preferred. Government-provided goods and services tend to cost more to produce and are lower in quality (US Postal Service, pothole roads, failing schools...the list goes on and on).

Incentives, Costs, and Pricing

The reason why private sector goods are higher in quality and more efficient to produce rests in the fact that the owners of private sector resources have the incentive to make them so. The market pricing system conveys available information both upstream and downstream. It tells consumers how much the good costs while it tells producers what consumers will pay to acquire it. If a good or service costs more than consumers are willing to pay, this is an indication that the resources used to produce the good are more highly valued than the finished product, thus the company is wasting resources. Companies using resources efficiently to provide demanded goods and services are rewarded with profits, while those that are not suffer losses. The pricing system allows this information to flow freely between consumers, distributors, and producers to ensure that resources are being allocated to valued uses.[74]

Public sector goods and services are of a different nature. Rather than consumers choosing whether or not to consume, and in what quantities, the government applies sweeping taxes to fund production, and then distributes the goods or services to the consumer. Since consumers of public sector goods cannot operate on an individual basis but are instead grouped together as "the public," it becomes difficult to track which public sector goods and services are in high demand, and which are not. Furthermore, there is no way to calculate precisely just how much people value them since people cannot voluntarily withhold their money and decline consumption. Some people who place little value on a given good or service would likely decline consumption if asked to pay for it, but then choose to heavily consume the good when offered by the government "free of charge," leading to vast quantities of wasted resources. Government-provided goods and services do not make use of the pricing system the way private-sector production does, without which it is impossible to know if scarce resources are being used efficiently.[75]

To illustrate this point, imagine a large chunk of refined steel. This steel can be used in a variety of ways, but once used, it cannot be used towards something else. If the steel is owned privately, it could be used to build a hospital, office building, or something else. To determine whether or not any of these is a good use for the steel, simply observe the allocation of the material and witness the resulting profit or loss the company absorbs. Now suppose that the government purchases the steel with tax dollars, and then uses it to build a new battle tank. How are we to determine that this is a good use of steel? A tank is not a capital good, and it does not produce anything...on the contrary, it is designed with destruction in mind. One could say that the tank "produces" national defense, or is at least an instrument for that purpose. Very well, but how are we still to determine whether or not the amount of national defense "produced" by having an extra tank in our army is a good use of steel? Consumers cannot simply go to the supermarket and purchase quantities of national defense that suit their individual needs. National defense, once supplied by the military, is equally distributed among everyone living within the geographical region of protection, and no one living there can abstain. Consumer trends cannot be measured when it comes to goods such as national defense, nor can its value be adequately quantified. Jim, who is a multimillionaire and owner of vast properties, has much more to lose to foreign invaders than Bob might, so it can be expected that Jim would place a higher value on defense. The subjective values that people place on any given government-provided good have the potential to be as diverse and

70

numerous as the people themselves. Given all this incoherent information, lack of proper market pricing, and conflicting normative views, one cannot easily determine whether or not government-provided goods use resources more efficiently than their private-sector alternative uses.[76] In order to determine how much of a public good to supply, in this case, defense, the government should tally up the individual demands of all consumers, and then supply enough of the good to satisfy that aggregate demand. Obviously, such a feat is idealistic in nature and difficult to accomplish in reality.

Then there lies the matter of how to pay for it all. Taxes are the funding method for government-provided goods, but how should the government apply the tax? Because the pricing system cannot freely operate, there exists no market clearing price on government goods and services, making it rather difficult to calculate the accurate cost, a major issue for any government attempt at performing business functions.[77] Take for example, Lockheed Martin. A well-known brand in the defense industry, Lockheed Martin has been supplying the US government with weapons of war and new defense technologies for a couple of decades now, and the company is one of the largest recipients of government funds earmarked for military purposes.[78] Lockheed Martin contracts directly with the government to supply national defense instruments, and its products are not open to the general public. Imagine walking into the lobby of a Lockheed Martin location, having gone through the security checkpoints, and approaching the receptionist with: "Hi, I'd like to purchase one of your F-22 fighter jets please." Right off the bat, you might get a blank stare or a chuckle, but at the end of the day, fighter jets are not for sale to private individuals. Since they and other Lockheed products are not for sale to the general public but are instead supplied directly to the public sector market through government contracts, what is the actual market-clearing price for them?

We can calculate the actual cost of producing F-22 fighter jets with relative ease. First, calculate the cost of materials, wages of employees, cost of training and safety equipment, research and development, testing, etc. We can also know the price that the government pays for its F-22's, as that information is outlined in the Air Force budget.[79] Multi-billion dollar contracts between the government and Lockheed appear in the news frequently. Given that we know the cost of manufacturing an F-22 and for how much Lockheed sells each one to the government, we can deduce what the "price" of an F-22 is...or can we? Is the price at which Lockheed Martin sells its fighter jets wholesale to the government the same price that the market would set if private individuals could freely buy them in accordance with the subjective values they assign? Would Lockheed go out of business for failing to sell any of its equipment on account of its price being above the market-clearing price, or would there be a vast shortage of its products due to the price being too low? Since the private sector does not have a market on these products, it is impossible to say. We simply do not know how the private sector would value these types of goods if permitted; and since we cannot assess the values the individuals place on the defense products, we cannot determine if the resources going into their production are being used effectively, and also that the price the government pays for the contracts (which is the price we pay through taxes) is at the market-clearing price.

Taxation

Defense and other collective consumption goods are not paid for on an individual basis but instead paid for through widespread taxation. Everyone under the umbrella must pay for being dry. How are we then to determine how people should pay? People will be using the goods in different quantities. As earlier shown, people with more to lose in terms of assets and property will be "using" our national defense more so than one who has little. One method of allocating taxes is to apply different tax rates as people use a good more or less, charging them on a per-user basis. It could be said that this is a more fair approach, as those that enjoy the benefits pay more for their continuation than those that see little of them, while those that have little use for the good are not burdened with sustaining something they do not fully utilize.[80]

Many states have already moved into this type of system with the taxes levied on gasoline. Theoretically, the more you drive the more gas you will consume, thus the more you will pay for the maintenance of roads and highways. Though true in a sense, a gas tax also unfairly punishes those individuals who enjoy driving SUVs, sports cars, and other low fuel economy vehicles, as these individuals may not use the roads as frequently as others, but pay disproportionately for the roads' maintenance. Additional innocent victims of a tax levied specifically against gasoline designated for paying for the roads would be people who live on several acres of land and require additional gasoline consumption in Summer to mow their lawns. Since they own larger than average property lots, they must pay extra for highways? How does this make any sense? The plot thickens when politicians seek to impose taxes to pay for public goods in more creative ways that better appease their constituents. For example, raising gasoline taxes to pay for roads would greatly increase the cost of gas, and would thus be very unpopular among voters; however, raising sales taxes by a minuscule amount in order to pay for roads would raise even more revenue without even catching the eye of the average consumer.[81] Politicians would be much more likely to use this route in order to raise money for the public good, but now there is an even greater separation between the user and the good. He who spends more money at malls and stores must now indirectly be forced to pay more for the roads, even though he could potentially live within walking distance of his frequented shopping locations and seldom even use those roads. In conclusion, paying for public goods often results in unfair payment methods whereby people who seldom use the good could potentially pay more, while people who abusively use the good might be paying less. It all rests on the whims of the politicians' methods of taxation.

Like most forms of legislation, taxation policies have unintended consequences, and people are affected by them in different ways. Since most government-provided goods are funded through taxes and then distributed to the public, their actual cost must be shifted to other sectors of the economy. This can take the form of property taxes, sales taxes, inheritance taxes, capital gains tax, and many others. The individuals paying these taxes may not use the public good to the degree they pay taxes, or they may overuse it while paying too little. "Pay-per-use" is difficult to implement, subjective value is difficult to calculate and aggregate, and the true cost of provision is often unknown since market clearing pricing is absent. A mess like this will cause ripple effects in the economy that distort the prices in other sectors, interfere with individuals' budgetary practices, distort interest rates, and siphon resources away from their best alternative uses—or at least make it unknown or hard to determine whether or not they are being used productively.

Supply

We have explored and defined goods that exhibit collective consumption characteristics, now we will discuss goods that once produced, cannot be restricted in access to other users. Some public goods exhibit both features, such as national defense, which is among the more frequently cited examples of public goods that are non-excludable.[82] Once produced, prohibiting other consumers from partaking in its use without paying proves difficult, if not impossible. After the government supplies protection, everyone within its sphere enjoys its benefits, regardless of whether or not they contribute to its cost. If the army is protecting people in a certain area, there is no feasible way to prohibit others within that area from enjoying the same exact protection. As a result of this situation, once national defense is established there will be no incentive for people to contribute to its cost since it will be available to them either way. Likewise, nobody has the incentive to produce it, but everyone has the incentive to sit around and wait for someone else to supply it so they can free-ride off the producers' efforts. Free-riding benefits the individual, and every individual is faced with that incentive. If everyone acts on that incentive and tries to free ride, the good will not be produced, and everyone will find themselves worse off than they were before.[83] Given these incentive constraints, advocates for the government provision of certain public goods like national defense that are non-excludable argue that such goods will generally be in short supply if left to the private sector—if they are indeed supplied at all.

Next, suppose there are two ranchers, Jim and Bob, whose property lines meet in a pasture. Cattle freely roam between their properties, and though they can ascertain who owns which cow via the branding mark on its hide, Jim and Bob both believe that things would be a little easier if there was a fence separating their two pastures. Since both would benefit from a fence, who should be the one to supply it? There is no "no-man's-land" between the two property lines, so the fence must be located either at the edge of Jim's land or at the edge of Bob's, meaning one of them will need to pay to have the fence erected on his land, thus making it his fence. But whichever rancher builds the fence will be doing so at the other's benefit, while if the other rancher constructs the fence, he who refrained will be able to enjoy the benefits of a fence free of charge. Both ranchers have the incentive to wait for the other to pay for and build the fence, while neither have the incentive to actually build it himself.

In a situation such as this, cooperation is likely given the small number of parties involved. Perhaps Jim and Bob are good friends, and neither minds if the other enjoys the benefits of a fence at his expense. Perhaps they will mutually agree to split the cost with one of them volunteering to locate the fence on his land. Perhaps one will bear the full cost but will be given a few heads of cattle by the other as a gift. There are numerous possibilities for Jim and Bob to work out a solution and erect a fence. But what if instead of two ranchers, there were four ranchers and four pastures that all meet at a shared corner. Now the situation becomes much more complicated. Whenever groups are small, cooperation is easier and more cost-effective. The larger the group, the more difficult cooperation becomes. So how can a nation of several hundred million come together in cooperation to determine how they shall all contribute to costs and provision of certain public goods? Economists specializing in collective action and public choice have long theorized that larger groups cannot spontaneously produce public goods without the coercive force of government acting as a facilitator.[84] There are solutions to this problem.

Before contemplating solutions to the free-rider problem and other issues dealing with the provision of public goods, it is important to reiterate that there is no such thing as "society." Society is nothing more than a collection of individuals, and society cannot feel, think, or act. Only the individual acts. When approached from the perspective of the individual, public goods can be broken down, privatized, and subscribed to by people on an individual basis, eliminating the problem of free-riders and the difficulty of obtaining high degrees of cooperation among a larger group.

Privatization

Consider the public good of national defense. Under the current system of government-provided defense, no one has the option to opt-out. A person can not simply request to be left unprotected, and instead, have his taxes reduced accordingly. He is compelled by force to pay taxes and contribute to the funding of the public good, and therein lies the irony. For those claiming that the government's role is primarily the protection of people and property, it cannot provide defense without first violating the property rights of those it claims to protect.[85] The solution is to privatize public goods, including defense. Under such a system of privatization, anyone who does not want to enjoy the public good—in this case, protection of life and property—can simply abstain from paying and forgo the benefit. For those that do, they can subscribe to the private service.

Continuing the example of defense, the police and armies would be replaced by private insurance practices. Private insurance companies already operate effectively nationwide as it pertains to automobile, home, and life insurance, so it is not unrealistic to imagine scenarios in which it can be implemented effectively for defense insurance as well. These insurance companies providing defense for its clients will be subjected to the same market forces that current automobile insurance industries abide by. They will compete on reputation, services provided, and cost to clients. Superior companies that deal fairly and offer better protection will capture business away from companies that do not. Crime reducing behavior such as owning firearms for personal protection, living in safe neighborhoods, and conducting one's self peacefully will result in lower defense insurance premiums charged, while crime enhancing behavior will result in higher premiums...much the same as safe driving and maintaining a good driving record lower car insurance premiums and reckless driving raises it.[86]

Private defense insurance agents would patrol areas in which their clients live to maintain a visual presence—much like the police do today—only they would not interfere in peoples' day-to-day lives and initiate violent conflict where there otherwise would be none. If called upon by a client, a defense agent would provide protection to life and property, but what of those that do not have coverage with a particular agency or do not have time to call for help? If a defense insurance agent is patrolling a region and witnesses a violent crime in the making, he can intervene on behalf of the victim and render service. If the victim is not a client of the agent's company, the agent can submit an invoice to the client's actual insurance agency with the provision of proof of service. Should a client of one agency call for help, and one defense agent of another company is closer to the scene than an agent belonging to the client's company, the insurance companies may have a cooperative agreement whereby they dispatch each others' agents depending on urgency and then reimburse each other later. Such agencies utilizing network agreements will be able to offer lower premiums to their clients, encouraging the development of such networks. For those that can afford but simply do not want defense, that is their decision to make. For those that may be too poor to afford defense insurance, there would likely be private charitable groups and foundations that offer some measure of defense insurance for free to the needy, much the same as many of life's necessities can be found offered to the poor by religious organizations and other charitable individuals.

Critics would question the morality and motives of such companies. If they have arms and resources, what would stop them from simply taking over? For starters, one private defense agency would protect its clients from other private defense agencies in the event one goes rogue, thereby offering some degree of parity. Furthermore, no business has the incentive to extort its clients.

Raising private armies would cost the rogue insurance company significant financial resources, making it less profitable than its competitors. Clients would experience higher costs, and they would opt to change defense agencies for a cheaper and more efficient alternative, thereby pushing the offending agency out of business. Agencies would strive to maintain strong reputations and serve their clients well, as do other insurance agencies of today that are not protected from competition by the government.[87]

4 The Theoretical Framework of Government Intervention

"We are fast approaching the stage of the ultimate inversion: the stage where the government is free to do anything it pleases, while the citizens may act only by permission." - Ayn Rand, 1964.[88]

Imagine yourself sitting on your front porch by the river enjoying the summer weather. Perhaps you enjoy the occasional swim, perhaps you enjoy fishing, or perhaps you just prefer having waterside property. Whatever the case, your home sits alongside a water system, and you place great personal value on the river. As you sit in your rocking chair enjoying the day, you spot a small dead fish floating down the stream. *Not an uncommon sight,* you think to yourself, but then a group of dead fish floats up behind the first. Now paying closer attention, you see even more dead fish floating down the river. Dead bass, brim, and catfish now wash up on your property by the hundreds, filling the air with their stench. The summer sun amplifies the decaying process, and the cleanup requirements are so hefty that it will necessitate hiring contractors to remove the sheer volume of rotten fish. The river is now ruined until further notice.

This hypothetical scenario is all too real to those living on the Warrior River in central Alabama at the time of this writing. A poultry processing plant located upstream in the town of Hanceville owned by Tyson Foods dumped untold amounts of liquefied waste into the river, killing upwards of 175,000 fish and polluting the river up to 80 miles downstream.[89] By dumping its waste into a public river, Tyson has forced costs onto the residents, fishermen, and kayakers of central Alabama in the form of reducing their quality of life through pollution, otherwise known in economics as an externality.

Externalities occur whenever a person, company, or other organization commits some action that casts either costs or benefits onto another, uninvolved party, making that party better or worse off without those responsible bearing neither the costs nor receiving the benefit.[90] Externalities vary in terms of scale and significance. They can be small and limited to just one or two people, such as when you attempt to sleep in late but your roommate sings loudly in the shower; his action has a negative impact on you. Externalities can also occur on a global scale, such as governments and industries contributing to global warming that affects future children in Africa who are not yet even born. When externalities occur, it is often viewed as a proper function of government to step in and correct the situation, if it cannot be addressed privately.[91] The circumstances under which private solutions become feasible will be explored momentarily.

Externalities can originate either from the production or consumption of goods and services that have positive or adverse effects on people that were not involved in the original transaction, and they can be addressed in different ways depending on their nature. The ongoing Warrior River contamination is a classic case of a negative externality resulting from the production of goods. Tyson Foods processes millions of pounds of poultry from its Hanceville plant, which later finds its way into your freezer and ovens through the economic process. When you purchase Tyson chicken fingers from the grocery store, that transaction is between you as the consumer, and Tyson as the producer, with the grocery store acting as an intermediary to provide a marketplace for the transaction to take place. The poor fisherman on his canoe in the river had nothing to do with this transaction, yet he is forced to suffer by it, as he can no longer enjoy fishing due to Tyson's pollution-producing activities.

Negative externalities resulting from the production of goods or services need to be addressed for two primary reasons: the first being punitive in nature to prevent companies from imposing external costs on others with impunity, and the second being the elimination of economic inefficiency derived from their activities.[92] When firms engage in production, they incur costs, some that are fixed, and others variable. In the event of a negative externality occurring, there is a new cost imposed on bystanders. Without these negative externalities, the social and private benefits derived from voluntary transactions between consenting parties will outweigh the costs...otherwise, the transaction would not take place. When there is a negative externality involved, suddenly the summation of costs can outweigh the summation of benefits, and the difference represents a net loss to society.[93] From here we can splice the costs and benefits into two categories: private and public. The private cost of production is paid by the firm as their cost of doing business. The public cost is borne by innocent bystanders through the negative externalities they face. The private benefits of production are the profits allocated to the firm through the efficient use of scarce resources to provide products demanded by consumers. There can also be public benefits of production, and they are enjoyed by everyone who is made better off by a private transaction in which they were not involved.[94] For example, if a car mechanic eats Tyson's chicken, he is no longer hungry. If he is not hungry, he can focus on repairing my car to the best of his abilities without worrying about needing to forage for food. I indirectly benefit from his consumption of Tyson chicken, yet I pay nothing to him or Tyson for this.

Not only can the production of goods and services result in unanticipated costs foisted onto uninvolved third parties, but the consumption of goods and services can do the same. These negative consumption externalities occur when individuals or organizations consume goods or services that reduce the welfare of others who were not involved in consumption. When I was a teenager, I witnessed an individual making a serious error by consuming vast amounts of fried food prior to boarding a roller coaster in an amusement park. Though I'm sure the food was tasty and delicious at the time of consumption, I knew it would cause issues for him later in the day given the nature of our environment. For the other park-goers that day, his poor choices exaggerated his risk to them as a puke hazard, yet they had no say in whether or not he was allowed to consume that food. And yet, it was precisely a large crowd of those individuals that had to bear the costs of his decision when the contents of his stomach showered them from fifty feet above. Perhaps a more common example that one might relate to is a smoker standing too close to a building entrance as you walk in, or the local "cool guy" whose Honda civic makes excessive amounts of racket as he accelerates. You are not involved as a consenting party to either the smoker consuming cigarettes or the motorist tuning up his ride, yet you incur a cost for their choices.

Effects on third parties resulting from others' actions are not always negative; oftentimes, third parties can enjoy benefits that otherwise would not have been, as previously shown with the car mechanic. These benefits can result either from the production or consumption of goods and services, much the same as costs. When one drives through Birmingham, Alabama near the junction where Interstate 20 meets Interstate 65, the smell of freshly baked bread will often penetrate a car's air conditioning system, filling the vehicle with a pleasant fragrance. Of course, some may view this as a negative externality, as the sense of smell is subjective, but most would find the smell of fresh bread to be a pleasant aroma. The motorists driving down the interstate are not involved with the production of bread, and most may not be consumers of this company's bread either, yet they all get to enjoy the fragrances produced by the bakery. The bakery's daily operations increase the well-being of the motorists, yet the bakery is not compensated by them in turn for the benefits provided.

Consumption of goods and services can bestow positive benefits to others as well. Suppose a person visits a local health clinic and receives vaccinations for various diseases. This transaction is between the individual and his doctor, yet I benefit as well since the spread of infectious diseases is now less likely.[95] If my neighbor hires a landscaping company to take great care of his lawn through gardening and regular maintenance, the property value of my own house will increase as opposed to decreasing should he allow his property to decay. I also receive the free benefit of viewing his well-maintained lawn at my pleasure. When someone invests in his own education, I receive the benefit of living in a more highly-educated society. The list can go on and on regarding the benefits people can receive through transactions of which they did not take part.

Both positive and negative externalities are characterized by the fact that third parties are affected. In the event they are affected negatively, the offending party incurs no cost for reducing the livelihood of the injured individuals. Should the uninvolved parties receive an accidental benefit, the people and firms involved in the original transactions receive no compensation either.[96] These situations, especially in the case when costs borne by others are negative, are referred to as "market failures," and there are solutions available to address them.

Ideally, issues where costs are borne by others can be addressed privately, without needing to involve the compelling powers of government, but the range in which private solutions are feasible is limited. Before any private solution could be attempted, property rights must be well defined and respected. If I own a plot

84

of land and you cut trees on your adjacent property causing them to fall across my fence, this is a clear case of trespassing and damage to my property, in which case I have recourse against you. The less defined the property rights, the more sticky the situation. If I am enjoying a peaceful afternoon in my pool and you fly a noisy helicopter over my house disturbing the peace, I'm no longer able to enjoy my property as I once did. Flying your helicopter has imposed a cost on me, but can the case be made that I own the air above my house? If so, how high do my rights extend? Would I also be able to prevent major airlines from flying passenger jets over my house at altitudes exceeding thirty or forty thousand feet? Perhaps I do not enjoy the sight or sound of these jets flying over my house regardless of how high they are, therefore I stand to suffer any time something flies overhead. Milton Friedman proposed this scenario in his masterpiece, *Capitalism and Freedom,* when he presents the dilemma to the reader. Should the homeowner be compensated by the pilots for flying planes and helicopters over his house, or should he have to pay them not to?[97] As property rights are less defined and more ambiguous, the more difficult, philosophical, and subjective are the potential solutions.

Another drawback to private solutions depends on the size of the affected parties. If my roommate leaves his dirty dishes scattered about, this imposes a cost on me, as I now must live in less sanitary conditions while not being able to enjoy the shared living space. Given that I am the only injured party—and he is the only one committing the action that causes this injury—a private solution is easily configurable. I could convince him to be more courteous, pay him not to continue this behavior or request compensation of some kind. There would be no need to request state involvement in this dispute. Drawing once more on the example of Tyson Foods polluting the river, a private solution would be difficult in this case due to the volume of potential injured third parties. Negotiations, decision-making, and collective action become more costly as the size of the group increases, as does the cost for addressing externalities.[98] An assessment would need to be made to ascertain the extent of the damage on an individual basis, and each injured party would likely exaggerate the suffering. Synchronized cooperation among all the injured parties would be difficult to achieve, and suffering would continue as the process dragged on for years. As opposed to the inevitable boondoggle that naturally arises from trying to privately coordinate large bodies of people, the government can take some precautions to prevent externalities before they arise and discourage behavior that causes them in the first place.[99]

Theoretical Public Sector Solutions

When property rights are ill-defined and when the number of affected parties is too large to coordinate private solutions, the government must sometimes step in order to alleviate scenarios of market failure.[100] When industries engage in productive activities that cause harm to uninvolved parties, one tool in the government's arsenal is to impose a tax penalty on the offending industry that is equal to the cost of the harm done. This idea was made popular by the British economist Arthur Pigou, and has since been referred to as the "Pigouvian tax."[101] The idea is that by imposing a tax on producers equal to the extra costs their activities place on others, firms will lessen their harmful activities to compensate for the monetary loss of paying the tax. With the tax in place, costs of production increase, thereby providing firms sufficient incentive to reduce production and the harmful side effects thereof. At this point, one might assume that any revenue then generated by the government from this tax should be paid out to those that are harmed from the producers' activities, but this is a logical fallacy that warrants exposure. It becomes a classic case of a tree falling in a forest with no one around to hear it: does it make a sound? In order for an injury to occur, both parties must have contributed to it to some degree. If a company like Tyson Foods pollutes a river, homeowners living downstream would not suffer the negative externality if they did not live there in the first place. This is the same reason why insurance companies charge high premiums for insuring ocean-front houses, assuming they are willing to insure the houses to begin with. Some insurance companies will not insure certain houses that are subject to a higher risk of flooding without being subsidized by the government.[102] If homeowners lost their homes to hurricanes and could rebuild them every time with funds from (often subsidized) insurance claims, there would be many more beachfront homes built, thus creating a massive inefficiency within the home insurance industry.[103] It is likewise inefficient to live downstream from a polluter. "But I was here first!" Some homeowners might say. "This house was built a hundred years ago, and my family has been on this land ever since. That poultry plant should not have been built upstream." This is hardly realistic. Buying a plot of land does not give me the right to dictate who can or cannot engage in activities on adjacent lands. If this were the case, no one would be able to do anything, because everybody would be able to restrict everyone else.

Economic efficiency necessitates that both parties face the incentive to reduce harmful side effects. A Pigouvian tax gives the incentive to the polluters to stop their harmful ways, but the people living within the radius of harmful side effects should have the incentive to leave, not stay and continue suffering harm. If these individuals receive a payout from the government for suffering negative externalities, they not only have the incentive to continue suffering, but they have a new incentive to suffer more! People who originally did not live on the river will now want to build near it to suffer harm as well. Some dastardly individuals may even encourage pollution in order to receive additional payments, while others may attempt to block efforts to alleviate the polluting activities to ensure the payments continue.

But what of external benefits? When people and firms engage in productive activities, sometimes their actions provide other parties with benefits for which the producers do not receive compensation. Because these producers do not receive payment for the benefits they provide to others through their activities, that which they are producing may be undersupplied, or not supplied at all. In order to encourage production when positive externalities arise from these activities, the government may subsidize the firms and individuals in an amount that equals the value of the extra benefits enjoyed by third parties. If subsidized too heavily, firms would overproduce and exaggerate the benefits, while if subsidized too lightly, the good or service may still be undersupplied.[104]

Regulation

Governments can also theoretically regulate output in cases of external costs being forced on others. As either a supplement to or substitute for taxation and subsidies, regulation can often be the simple route for curbing the adverse effects on others caused by the production. The government can ascertain the optimal amount of production whereby the cost of producing, including external costs on other parties, just equals the overall benefit of that production. Whether or not the government and its army of bureaucrats are up to this task is another issue entirely. Regulation has the potential to completely alter the economic landscape. Regulation in favor of certain industries can make a company artificially prosperous while regulation against it can spell financial doom. Given how significant regulation is to most businesses, industry leaders form powerful special interest groups to petition lawmakers on behalf of their companies to pursue favorable regulation. Economist George Stigler gained traction in the early 1970s when he presented one of the earliest empirical theories of regulation. He discovered that regulation is primarily gained by the industry in question and designed for its benefit, and not for the protection and benefit of the public.[105] Since industries use the government to regulate in their favor, it can be surmised that the government does not have public interests in mind when passing regulatory laws, as the resources given to political hacks by the industries far outweighs anything the people could give to sway them the other way. When regulation is passed in favor of industry, there will likely be costs forced onto consumers.

Given how slim the odds are that the government would properly regulate the optimal amount of production to minimize external costs on others, a more efficient method would be to establish permits for production that can be swapped. Should production cause adverse effects on others by pollution, the government can issue a set amount of permits that allow for a certain amount of production-related pollution to be emitted by the producers. This ensures that producers can still operate without going overboard, but some activities are more productive than others, and not all productive activities would yield the same ratios of pollution into the environment. Allowing companies to trade these permits by purchase or sale would keep the overall pollution levels within the government-mandated amount, but it would ensure that consumers get the most value for having to suffer pollution. If one company's polluting activities are more profitable than another company's, the first company would bid away the permits and would be responsible for a larger share of the pollution quota, but its willingness to make that purchase would indicate that its productive activities are providing the most value to consumers. Companies that do not enjoy high-profit margins on their polluting activities can sell their rights to those that do, thus ensuring that pollution, since some amount of it must be suffered, goes to its highest-valued uses.[106]

One might suggest that the government outright ban any

activity that results in pollution in order to ensure a safe and clean environment whereby innocent bystanders do not suffer from the consequences of activities they had nothing to do with. Though it may seem romantic on the surface to save the environment and harmonize our existence with mother nature, there would be an enormous cost for doing so. Preventative measures have costs, and there quickly comes a point where these costs are not worth paying. Everything is calculated on margin, and some quantity of pollution is optimal; the trick is finding out how much. To reduce pollution to zero would not only be economically inefficient, but it would drastically lower our standards of living, as the costs to prevent pollution outweigh the benefits. Every step towards reducing pollution would be more costly than the last if the results are progressive.

Consider for a moment the air quality in Beijing, China. One of the most polluted places on Earth, Beijing's air is so polluted that it has a noticeable effect on life expectancy in the area. People have no choice but to walk around with surgical masks in an effort to breathe, while a glimpse of the sun is a rare occurrence. Entrepreneurs are actually successful in selling canned, breathable air, a product that would be doomed to fail in most cities. The smog is so thick that one could cut it with a knife, and this is not a metaphor. One individual even vacuumed enough pollution out of the air around him that he was able to transform the harvested smog into a brick. Indeed, Beijing has some of the lowest quality air on the planet.

Given how much pollution exists in Beijing, the Chinese government could commit very few resources to the problem and would see outstanding results. It could mandate that hazardous waste be disposed of in a more environmentally-friendly manner, or dictate how many miles one may drive in his automobile on a daily or annual basis, thereby reducing exhaust from cars. It could encourage pollution-alleviation efforts. The first baby steps would generate quick and fruitful strides in pollution-reduction initiatives, and Beijing would see its air quality increase dramatically. As the air improves and pollution is reduced, further reduction would become more costly. More and more resources would need to be dedicated to the effort, as each resource would have a diminishing effect on pollution levels. Eventually, the benefits of reducing pollution would not outweigh the costs of doing so. Therefore, it can be implied that there exists some optimum amount of pollution whereby the benefits of reducing it further are just equal to the costs of doing so. Efforts to reduce pollution past that point are simply not worth it, much the same as most common recycling is actually detrimental to the environment, as the amount of energy required to recycle an item is more costly than the final recycled product. However, it goes without saying that places like Beijing are not even close to the point where pollution-reducing efforts are not worth the cost.

All economic activity consists of transactions between people and firms, or simply limited to one person utilizing his own resources, but sometimes uninvolved parties to the transactions or activities will be positively or negatively affected. These effects can take the form of costs imposed or benefits distributed. If third parties incur undue costs, the government can hypothetically impose a tax to cause a reduction in the harmful activities that cause this cost on others. If third parties find themselves the recipients of benefits of which they do not have to pay for, the government can provide a subsidy to ensure the productive activity continues at its optimal level. When the government seeks to change an individual's or firm's behavior in order to address external costs or benefits, it can employ measures pertaining to the costs and price of the goods and services, such as taxes and subsidies, or it can impose measures pertaining to output, such as regulation. Effects vary, so the government must carefully consider its own goals before pursuing a certain policy. Measures that limit production ensure that a given behavior or economic activity does not breach some predefined amount, and in terms of pollution, would be the most environmentally-conscious option. Government can simply dictate that it will not allow pollution to exceed a certain level, and then impose strict regulations to ensure the threshold is met. Costs of such a policy would vary across firms, and firms that struggle to be profitable may be put out of business by such restrictive practices. Allowing pollution permits to be exchangeable would help with this problem. A Pigouvian tax would ensure that the cost of production will not exceed the cost firms pay in the form of the tax, but the desired amount of reduction may not be reached. In terms of pollution, governments must choose whether or not they want to ensure a given amount of environmental protection, or if they want to ensure a defined cost to the producers before embarking on policies that alleviate the external costs imposed on other people. Unfortunately, given the tendency for any of the above government actions to benefit special interests over the public interest, consumers should expect to draw the short stick in most cases of government involvement in market scenarios with third-party side effects.

PART II

TAXES TAXES TAXES

5 Income Tax

"When plunder becomes a way of life for a group of men in a society, over the course of time they create for themselves a legal system that authorizes it and a moral code that glorifies it."
- Frédéric Bastiat, 1848.[107]

Theory of Taxation

Government costs money. The cost of government depends on its size and scope, as well as on the commitments it makes to its people through the provision of public sector goods and services. Government finances itself primarily through taxation and the issuance of debt, the former of which will be the subject of this chapter. When people refer to government spending, gaining, or losing "its" money, make no mistake: the government has no money. Instead, it has either your money (taxes) or the money of future taxpayers (debt), which it then uses for its purposes and objectives. There is a strong argument to be made regarding the moral validity of taxation. Taxes are essentially a legalized form of theft. Before the taxes are paid, they are your property; the money you have earned through the sweat of your brow is yours, and no one else's. The government then comes along and demands a portion of it, the amount of which seems to only grow as time goes on. The requested amount is compulsory, meaning that you have no choice but to turn it over. Should you refuse, you are branded a criminal, and the fines and penalties associated with refusing to pay taxes are often more costly than the tax itself, thus making the surrender of part of your property the rational choice despite the fact that your private property rights have been atrociously violated.[108]

This relationship between people and government is what makes taxation work in the government's favor. The personal cost of resistance is too heavy, implying that taxes are paid out of fear, not a voluntary contribution or patriotic sentiment towards the government's initiatives. If ever you find yourself wondering whether or not this is true, ask yourself: "Would the government be able to sustain this level of spending if it relied on voluntary contributions from its people?" The answer is usually no, due in part to the free-rider dilemma discussed earlier, but mostly due to the fact that people simply would not voluntarily surrender that much of their property to the government if they were given a choice, therefore taxation can be appropriately defined as the "forced taking of money."[109] Government is aware of this and has devised newer and efficient ways to levy taxes that take the sting away. Today, American workers are permitted to have a portion of their pay withheld for tax purposes, and are then later refunded the difference or sent a bill. This is a significant improvement of the old methods of having tax collectors go door to door...the populace can tar and feather an automated withholding system. The Tax Foundation, a nonprofit tax policy think tank, has conducted a study annually for the past several years dubbed "Tax Freedom Day," in which they determine how long a typical American must work before he covers that year's tax liability. The studies vary from year to year depending on fluctuating tax rates, but generally "Tax Freedom Day" falls between early-mid April.[110] In other words, a typical working American spends roughly a third of the year just working to pay taxes. After Tax Freedom Day in April, his tax bill is covered and he can then begin working for himself. Visualizing how much of the year is spent just working to pay taxes adds perspective to the burden of taxation.

The effects of taxation are far-reaching, even beyond the obvious issue of people's deprivation of liberty and their rights to private property. In order to finance its activities through taxation, the government must first confiscate the wealth from the private sector, which then sends ripples throughout the marketplace taking the form of price and supply distortions. Taxation and its effects force a new set of constraints on suppliers and consumers within a market economy, causing them to face altered prices than that which would exist absent the taxes.[111] A result is a misallocation of resources that can bring about inefficiencies. If the government's use of the confiscated funds does not provide benefits equal to the inefficiencies created in the marketplace through the effects of taxation, society is made far worse off overall.

This type of theoretical resource misallocation is not ideal, but is simply a cost of government activity. There is no way for the government to raise funds through taxes without distorting market prices to some extent, so we as taxpayers must simply learn to live with the inescapable costs of resource misallocation through price distortion. Given that these price distortions are unavoidable, the government is faced with a new challenge: to implement a system of taxation that minimizes price distortions while maximizing the amount of revenue generated. Ideally, the government would only collect a given amount of tax revenue in such a way that it could not raise the same amount of revenue with another set of taxes that would make consumers worse off somewhere else, and this also applies to the overall rate of taxation.[112]

The economic cost of taxes is enormous. There is not only the dollar for dollar cost to consider but other, more serious, and implicit costs as well. For every dollar confiscated from the private sector in the form of tax, the government does not receive a dollar in turn, but some lesser amount. There are administrative costs of raising new taxes, punitive and judicial costs of pursuing and prosecuting tax evaders, functional costs of administering the government programs funded by taxes, etc.[113] Sadly, those are just some of the direct costs. People must pay money to file the taxes either through self-filing software or the hiring of a tax assessor, money which could have gone towards satisfying their other wants and needs and improving their welfare. They must sacrifice their personal time to file the taxes, time which could have been spent working, enjoying the company of friends or family, pursuing hobbies, or any other of the infinite uses one can imagine for time. The costs of financing government activity through taxation are also enormous, so in order to judge whether or not consumers are getting a good value for their tax dollars, one simply needs to casually notate the availability and quality of government-provided goods and services. The reality is that government-provided goods and services tend to be of significantly lower quality than their private-sector alternatives but come at a significantly higher cost. This is due to the government funding itself through taxes, not profits, and also due to the fact that the government often ends up spending money for political and not economic purposes.[114] If faced with financial loss, the government can simply raise tax rates to bridge the gap. Because consumers of government services are captive, especially in the case of government monopoly, the government does not need to worry about providing them with high-quality products at low costs.

Take Birmingham, Alabama for example. The metro area of Birmingham, encompassing roughly a fourth of the state's population, is serviced by a single, government-sponsored water provider that enjoys a monopoly over the provision of the utility. Private competitors are regulated out of existence, resulting in low-quality service at exorbitant prices mired in bureaucratic waste. It is not terribly uncommon for bills to reach consumers in erroneous amounts, often demanding excessive fees far out of proportion to the amount of water any one family could possibly consume in a month, and attempts to resolve the error condemn people to a week-long struggle of navigating a bureaucratic labyrinth of clerks and administrative assistants. Water leaks and burst main pipes along the road usually go unaddressed for weeks at a time, as the sole provider of water is not concerned with wasted resources or inefficiency. The Birmingham water utility company, like so many other public entities, fares terribly with maintaining respectable levels of customer satisfaction. As common with government-sponsored institutions, outside attempts at change and reform are met with hostile resistance by the established parties who seek not to improve their community relationships or find ways to better serve their clients, but instead only seek to protect their own interests.[115] In the words of one fiery review on Google: "In a free market, they'd be toast!"

Indeed, the government simply does not face the same constraints as do private companies and individuals, thus allowing them to operate in wasteful and inefficient ways that would sink anyone else; and yet, many still believe that the government should retain this position by virtue of being the government. Henry Hazlitt, author of *Economics in One Lesson*, said it best by highlighting the absurdity of believing that government can more judiciously spend money than its original owners who lost it through taxation:

> People who have earned money are too shortsighted, hysterical, rapacious, and idiotic to be trusted to invest it themselves. The money must be seized from them by the politicians, who will invest it with almost perfect foresight and complete disinterestedness. People who are risking their own money will of course risk it foolishly and recklessly, whereas politicians and bureaucrats who are risking other people's money will do so only with the greatest care and after long and profound study. Naturally the businessmen who have earned money have shown that they have no foresight; but the

politicians who haven't earned the money will exhibit almost perfect foresight. The businessmen who are seeking to make cheaper and better than their competitors the goods that consumers wish, and whose success depends upon the degree to which they satisfy consumers, will of course have no concern for "the general social advantage"; but the politicians who keep themselves in power by conciliating pressure groups will of course have only concern for "the general social advantage." They will not dissipate the money....There will never be even a hint of bribery or corruption.[116]

Regardless of how inefficient the process of taxation is or the moral ambiguity created by its coercive and compulsory nature, taxes exist, and the consequences of not paying them outweigh the potential reward for successful resistance. Consequently, private money fills the government's coffers and allows it to provide public goods and services to citizens.

Government employs many different forms of taxation to transfer wealth from the private sector to the public, and it finds new and creative ways to raise taxes as time goes on. The growing length and complexities of the tax code in the United States have even become a campaign platform for some grassroots candidates who argue that it needs to be cut down and simplified despite the fact that as public sector bureaucrats, their offices and colleagues are often the ones benefiting most from the current tax policy. For evidence, one should simply observe the happenings in and around the nucleus of this bureaucratic apparatus: Washington D.C. The nation's capital and the surrounding residential areas encompass some of the highest per capita incomes in the United States, but unlike other high-income areas like Silicon Valley, the Washington D.C. metropolitan area produces nothing outside of laws. There are no major industrial activities, no great financial centers, and yet it is one of the richest geographic regions. This is possible because the powerful bureaucrats and lawmakers that live there keep voting themselves more pay increases and greater benefits, all funded by taxing the American people.[117]

From an additional tax on playing cards in Alabama to a tax on sliced bagels in New York, some taxes are so bizarre that one must step back and wonder if they are actually just a joke.[118] Despite the extraordinary length of the current tax code and all the different taxes contained therein, most can be categorized in three compartments: taxes on income, taxes on wealth, and taxes on production and consumption. Wealth taxes and consumption or production taxes will be addressed in subsequent chapters, but for now, the focus will be on income tax.

Taxes on Income

The taxes levied against income by the government fall primarily into three broad categories: taxes on earnings, personal income tax, and corporate income tax. Taxes on earnings are the primary contributor to financing social programs such as Medicare, Medicaid, Social Security, unemployment insurance, and others. When people engage in productive employment, part of their earnings are confiscated in the form of the payroll tax which comprises the bulk of these funds.[119]

Individuals experience a wider, more broad tax levy on their income than just the tax on their earnings. During the year, income is accrued by individuals from a variety of sources, and then a tax is levied against all of it with rates depending on the type of income earned. The amount of tax paid depends largely on what tax bracket a person resides in, with higher-income earners paying more in tax on each accrued dollar, with lower earners paying less. Unlike the payroll tax, income tax applies to all forms of income, such as interest on savings and rental income, as well as on the income generated from selling assets.[120]

Taxes are also applied to the income of corporations. One of the primary goals of taxing corporate income is to tax the owners of capital that might otherwise escape taxation by the individual based income tax system.[121] A key distinction to make here is that corporate taxes are still taxes paid by individuals. Large corporations have become a popular boogie-man in the political arena with regards to their earnings. People often look at the extraordinary wealth of corporate leaders and believe that these individuals were able to enrich themselves at the expense of the public by not paying their "fair share," and by exploiting workers and the environment. Encouraged by popular resentment towards corporations, radical politicians usually attempt to appeal to potential voters by publicly condemning these corporations and demanding that they pay more in taxes. Usually, the larger and more visible the corporation the better. Politicians are able to convince people that a tax on business is a tax on a thing and not a tax on people, but this is a delusion.[122]

When corporations face high tax rates, society bears many detrimental consequences. Capital which would fund American investment projects is moved overseas to tax shelters, depriving potentially beneficial domestic investments of necessary capital. Corporations that are unable to move capital overseas are forced to bear higher costs and lower profit margins which will inevitably reduce the value of the company to shareholders, force higher prices on consumers, reduce the wages and number of jobs available to employees, or some combination thereof. Businesses are composed of individuals, and a tax on business affects their ability to provide goods and services at lower costs to consumers. A tax on business is a tax on individuals, only it has been pushed through a corporate balance sheet beforehand; though it remains a tax on individuals nonetheless.[123]

No permanent income tax existed in the United States prior to 1913. At the conclusion of the Civil War and throughout the late 1800s, the size and scale of government grew dramatically. Previously, the United States government relied on other forms of taxation as well as tariffs to fund its activities, but President Woodrow Wilson, after having easily seen the bill glide through the House of Representatives but become entrenched in the Senate, eventually convinced opposing senators to approve of the new legislation, paving the way for a federal income tax.[124] With a new revenue source, the Wilson Administration was able to cut tariffs, another one of its desired policies. Government officials realized that the costs of increasing government's role in the economy and American way of life would require new sources of cash, and also that an income tax would generate more revenue than the current tariff policy, thus came into being the Revenue Act of 1913. The first permanent income tax began small and only affected a minority of income earners, but its modest nature was quickly swept aside by the initiation of hostilities in Europe and the subsequent American involvement in the First World War. In 1917, the United States entered a war like none before it, and logistical demands of maintaining a large fighting force half a world away strained the economy. Warfare had grown to be an evermore expensive endeavor in the 21st century, and American taxpayers were called on to foot the bill through significant increases in tax rates.[125] It is worth noting that eventually tariffs were raised again to levels even higher than those before the implementation of the income tax, and yet the tax persists to the present day as a painful reminder to workers that Uncle Sam always gets his due.

The allied victory shortly after the American entry to the war witnessed a brief period of peace in Europe that allowed the United States government to lower its tax rates, though the rates did not fall back to prewar levels. The Great Depression of the 1930s and the Second World War in the 1940s also had similar effects on tax rates. Whenever a crisis emerges, the government dramatically raises tax rates to help pay for its programs and solutions. Once the crisis has abated, the government lowers tax rates again, as the intense financial demands of the crisis have passed, but never to pre-crisis levels. Economist Robert Higgs has characterized this as a "ratchet effect," whereby each passing crisis widens the scale of government and increases the financial burden of those who must pay for its activities.[126] Top tax rates during World War II reached a staggering 94%, while the Great Depression-era saw the top rates reach a high of 79%. The highest marginal rate for 2019 was 37% for individuals earning half a million dollars per year or more, but that rate only applied to any dollar earned above $200,000.[127] Income up to that amount was taxed at lower rates, and that is the nature of the progressive tax system.

Taxes on income discourage work. If marginal tax rates are too high, as they have been during times of crisis and even during some calm periods, many people determine that the effort they must put forth to earn that extra dollar is no longer worth it since they keep a smaller and smaller portion of that extra dollar earned. Actually, *any* tax rate discourages work to some degree, and even the smallest tax rate will prevent some productive work from being done. In the absence of taxation, people will continue to work so long as it increases their welfare and standard of living. Once taxation is applied, additional work may actually decrease their standard of living, as the cost of paying the tax must now be added to the cost of doing the work.[128]

In the mid-1970s, future Vice President Dick Cheney and economist Arthur Laffer were having dinner in a D.C. hotel one evening discussing the implications of tax policy. To illustrate the relationship between tax rates and government revenue, Arthur Laffer scribbled a graph on a napkin which would become known as the "Laffer Curve."[129] The Laffer Curve shows how government revenue changes as tax rates are raised or lowered. Take the two extreme rates of 0% and 100% taxation for example. Without a set tax rate, government tax revenues would be equal to zero, as no one is paying taxes. At a 100% tax rate, whereby every dollar earned is taken by the government in its entirety, government revenue will still be equal to zero, as the incentive to work has been completely abolished. The Laffer Curve points out that there exists a tax rate whereby government revenue can be maximized, and once this point is reached, raising taxes actually decreases revenue, as the incentive to work and be productive has been reduced. As tax rates increase, that incentive is chipped away piece by piece until none remains, and no one will see it worthwhile to earn anything if it will be taxed away from them. Alternatively, if taxes are too high, the government can actually increase its revenue by decreasing the tax rate, as more people will have the incentive to earn income.[130] It is difficult to determine where the government can set its tax rates in order to maximize its revenue, but if it raises tax rates too much, people will no longer have the incentive to earn income. This occurs often in areas with despotic regimes that fleece their people in order to maintain power, and also in places with large government interference in an economic activity whereby the governments do not intend to be tyrannical per se, but simply lack an understanding of basic economic principles, human nature, or simply believe that all of their nations' social or fiscal dilemmas will be solved with increased taxes.[131]

When the French Socialist Party took the reins of power from the more moderate UMP Party in 2012, newly elected President François Hollande announced his intent to raise tax rates for France's top income earners in order to generate more public revenue. His policies did not have the desired effects. Tens of thousands of France's millionaires packed their bags and bid "bon voyage" to their homeland, seeking citizenship in nations more friendly to productive individuals. Among these individuals was arguably France's most famous actor, Gérard Depardieu, who left the country as a tax exile and announced his intent to liquidate all his assets there. Depardieu was then granted Russian citizenship resulting in an international humiliation for France.[132] If any government raises taxes to the point where individuals believe it to be in their best interest to leave, and if they have the freedom to do so, many simply will depart and take their income-potential with them. When the government believes it can increase revenue by raising taxes, it may be in for a surprise when all the would-be payers of those new taxes end up paying nothing because they are no longer around.

Progressive, Flat, & Negative Income Tax

Progressive taxation is designed to shift the tax liabilities to ease the burden of low-income earners; the idea being that since higher-income earners can more easily afford necessities, they will be less hurt by the surrendering of their money to the government. Another justification revolves around the well-being of the higher earners afforded them by society at large. Higher-income earners theoretically benefit more from a well-educated populace and an adequate national defense than do low-income earners, thus they are expected to contribute more to the public cost of providing them. Finally, there is the argument of diminishing marginal utility of income which implies that one who earns a larger income will see diminishing returns on each dollar earned, and therefore the last dollars earned should be taxed at a higher rate.[133]

Many argue that the United States should abandon its current tax system and adopt a universal flat tax, whereby every dollar earned is taxed at the same rate. Without question, a flat tax would be easier to implement and manage. Abolishing the current lengthy and confusing tax code and replacing it with a streamlined flat tax would free up resources previously spent on interpreting and administering the current tax system for new and more productive purposes.[134] When Gérard Depardieu fled France due to its high taxes, he sought a safe haven in the Russian Federation, which had been operating under a 13% flat tax since 2001. After the breakup of the Soviet Union in the early 1990s, collecting taxes in the newly organized Russian Federation was a messy business. A complicated, decentralized, and overall weakened collection process led to rampant tax evasion and accounting fraud. Plagued by broken institutions and an inability to collect taxes, the Russian government defaulted on its debt in 1998, leading the world to wonder if the post-Soviet revival was doomed to fail, but everything changed when Russia adopted a financial reform package with a flat tax rate. When Russia became the first large economy to adopt a flat tax, it saw income tax revenues increase by 25% over the course of just one year, while the economy grew at a pace of 5%. Russia witnessed a significant decrease in tax evasion, an increase in tax compliance, and extraordinary economic growth, only to be curtailed by the 2008 financial crisis.[135] Russia's economic success after adopting a flat tax serves as a strong argument that the United States (if it MUST tax its citizens) should follow suit, as many other nations already have. The tricky part of adopting a flat tax would involve how to treat deductions.

Charitable contributions to hospitals and universities also account for a large proportion of the wealthy class' tax write-offs, and if those deductions were to be removed, charitable giving by the rich could be expected to decline significantly. Additionally, the wealthy could expect to further benefit from a flat tax with deductions, as they do not consume as large of a proportion of their income as the middle and lower class, implying that in order to retain the same amount of revenue as a progressive system, a flat tax would have to increase the net burden on the lower-income strata.[136] But under a flat tax rate with deductions, any allowed deductible amount actually transforms the flat tax back into a progressive tax, as higher earners would see effective rates go up compared to their lower-earning peers. Consider the two following individuals, Jack and Jill, who have different incomes under a flat tax system. Jack earns $45,000 per year while Jill earns $90,000, and the government has allowed for a one-time deduction of $10,000 on an overall flat tax rate of 25%. Jack reports a taxable income of $35,000 while Jill reports her taxable income of $80,000. At a 25% flat tax, Jack pays $8,750 in tax compared to Jill's $20,000 after the deduction has been made. Due to the deduction, Jack and Jill experience different rates. Jack's effective tax rate is 19.4% (8,750/45,000), while Jill's is 22.2% (20,000/90,000). Even though there is a single flat tax rate, deductions cause the rate to become progressive, thus nullifying the arguments of a flat tax rate being a more fair and equitable alternative to progressive marginal tax rates.

If we truly wanted a completely fair and flat tax rate that affected everyone equally, deductions would need to be entirely eliminated. Paid mortgage interest, business expenses, charity contributions, and others would no longer be deducted from a person's taxes, and this could cause some upheaval if implemented all at once. A recession in the housing sector would likely ensue by taking away the mortgage interest provision in the tax system while removing deductions on energy-efficient vehicles and other green initiatives would cause a decrease in those sectors as well. Removing deductions for education expenses would increase the effective cost of attending university, and philanthropy would become a more costly endeavor as there are higher opportunity costs for the donated funds without being able to write them off. On the other hand, without deductions, people would be less able to creatively misrepresent their taxable income in order to reduce their tax burden. Should a person really be able to consider toothpaste a medical expense and list it as an itemized deduction on his taxes? A flat tax cuts through the bog of deductions and streamlines the process.[137]

Nobel laureate and American economist Milton Friedman suggested a different approach: the negative income tax. Serving as both a replacement to the tax system as well as an alternative to the welfare state, a negative income tax kills two birds with one stone. It works like this: there is a predetermined level of income at which any income earned above that level is taxed, while any income earned below that level is subsidized. This ensures that people living in poverty can still have the advantage of a social safety net without having the incentive to work removed. Under the current system of welfare, there are many people receiving government benefits that increase their standard of living above and beyond what they could achieve by working. And should these individuals obtain employment, many of these government benefits would be stripped away, thereby lowering their standard of living below what it would be if they remained unemployed. A negative income tax does not remove this incentive to work, because any dollar earned under a negative income tax system represents real income to the earner. Friedman did warn us, however, that the subsidy must be capped so as not to interfere with this incentive. Under a negative income tax, income earned underneath the rate would not be reimbursed dollar for dollar, thereby enhancing the incentive to increase one's income through work, while still providing them with a guaranteed basic income should they fail to be productive enough to meet the minimum income requirement to be taxed.[138]

Corporate Income

A corporation is legally defined as being detached from its owners (shareholders) but operates from a legal perspective as if it was an individual. Corporations are recognized by law as one entity, and they can perform most of the same roles and functions that individuals can in terms of business proceedings. When the owner(s) of a company decide to incorporate, they do so to capture several strategic advantages. Large corporations are drawn to Delaware as a corporate home due to the lenient business laws there, while smaller businesses tend to incorporate in their principal state of business operations.[139] The primary reason for incorporation, and perhaps offering the most significant advantage, is the construct of limiting liability. Under a corporation, the owners of a firm cannot be held personally liable for any business debts or obligations, allowing the owners to keep their personal assets safe. If a corporation fails, the shareholders are not required by law to use their personal assets to pay the company's debt. All they can lose in the event of bankruptcy is their investment in the firm.

Large, profit-seeking corporations fall into two main categories: S-type and C-type, with the difference being the tax status applied to the firm. Under an S-corporation, income earned is treated as personal income, with the corporation itself being the entity, and is subject to the individual income tax. Income earned as a C-corporation is subject to the individual income tax once again as the income is distributed to shareholders. Most production occurs under C-corporations. Incorporated companies tend to segregate ownership of the company from managerial control, especially among public corporations. Partial ownership of these companies are traded on stock exchanges, so any investor big or small can buy or sell ownership. Other corporations are privately held so that only a select few investors are able to have an ownership stake. Shareholders are usually permitted to vote annually on who will run the company, and they are also permitted to vote on certain proposals that affect company direction and management compensation, but shareholders do not make the daily decisions on how to run the corporation. The segregation between ownership and administrative control is especially necessary for larger corporations. The thousands of shareholders cannot possibly congregate and vote every single time a small decision needs to be made, although separation of ownership from control creates certain problems dealing with incentives; namely the misalignment of interests between the company's owners and its managers. A more potent misalignment of interests within a corporation, however, involves the groups of financiers responsible for providing the capital for the company to function: debtholders and shareholders. Both of these individuals provide required capital investments for a company's operations, although both face different risks and can have different opinions on how a company should operate. This difference is magnified and skewed by the antagonizing presence of the corporate income tax, which can create management-level problems for a company.

Governments tax corporate income just as they tax personal income, only different laws apply and the rates vary. From the corporate perspective, taxes will be equal to the firm's earnings less its expenses, multiplied by the corporate tax rate, less any applicable deductions and investment credits. Earnings are the revenues a firm generates by selling goods or providing services to consumers, while expenses are the costs of conducting business (salaries, advertisement costs, rent, supply costs, etc.). Certain deductions are allowed for, just as personal income taxation allows for deductions. Interest payments on debt are deductible, as are certain qualified investment expenditures. Corporations may also deduct depreciation, or the declining value of their capital assets, though the tax code does not permit the full costs to be deducted all at once. The tax code instead permits firms to deduct small allowances that are designed to approximate the rate at which its assets lose their value over time.

The current corporate tax rate is 21%, down from 35% as of 2017, allowing for companies to retain a larger share of their profits, invest in additional productive assets, or hire additional personnel.[140] Many argue that corporations need to be heavily taxed in order to fund the government and punish "corporate greed," such as the excess and lavish lifestyle associated with private jets, yachts, and golden parachutes for ousted executives,[141] ultimately stemming from the viewpoint that corporations are exploitative organizations that trap desperate workers and coerce them into low wages while enriching its owners and directors. With this fallacious view in mind, it is easy to see how some might want to extract wealth from corporate productivity and distribute it back to the people in the form of public goods; however, this view not only falsely characterizes the corporation in general, but it inadvertently overlooks several macroeconomic dangers of income taxation when applied to business.

Consequences of Corporate Income Tax

When politicians demand that corporations surrender a higher percentage of their income to the government in the form of taxes, they greatly underestimate the economic-altering effects these taxes will have. Recall how taxes levied against businesses are still paid by individuals at the end of the day. When taxes are levied against income generated by corporations, either the business owners (shareholders) pay by seeing the value of their equity decrease, the customers pay in the form of higher prices, the workers pay in the form of lower wages, or some combination of two or more of these circumstances occur. The group that will be hit hardest depends on the nature of the product, good, or service offered by the business. When taxes are levied against corporations that produce things that are in high demand, customers will end up paying most of the cost, as they will continue buying the product regardless of a price increase. If the corporations produce goods in low demand, they will bear most of the cost, as they cannot pass the costs of taxes onto customers without losing substantial amounts of business.[142] Corporations are not "things" in the same sense as the buildings they occupy are things. Corporations are groups of people working together to provide goods and services to the market, acting as one legal entity under the direction of a committee of directors. When taxes are levied against corporations, people foot the bill. So how does that affect the economy at large?

For starters, a higher corporate income tax rate reduces corporate net revenue; this is a no-brainer. When corporations are faced with decisions on how to most effectively deploy their capital, they put their financial analysts and project managers to work forecasting which capital-demanding projects will yield the highest rates of returns. Generally speaking, capital investments with higher returns will be undertaken before investments with lower returns, and those with negative return rates will not be undertaken at all unless there are some other factors at play, such as a corporation needing to embark on a capital-loss project that improves their public image. In any case, taxes distort the picture on what projects will be profitable and which will not be. In the presence of a corporate income tax, some projects that would have yielded a profit without a tax may yield a loss; and as a result, the project will not be undertaken. Already, the corporate income tax has deprived consumers of valuable goods and services which they could have purchased to enhance their lives, thereby reducing our aggregate standard of living. Empirical data further suggests that the corporate income tax reduces corporate innovation, which also leads to a lowered standard of living.[143]

Aside from reducing the availability of goods and services to consumers, taxes on corporate income also rearrange the entire structure of the corporation itself, which present new hazards to the economy and have consequences of their own. Corporations are financed primarily through two capital-raising instruments: debt and equity. Debt is money raised through the issuance of corporate bonds that investors purchase. The investors then receive regular interest payments until the note reaches maturity, or is converted or rolled over. Investors that purchase debt enjoy a fixed-income return on their investment, and in the event of bankruptcy, creditors have a claim on that company's assets to make their investments whole. Furthermore, corporate debt investors will still receive their anticipated returns even if the overall market capitalization of the company is reduced through a declining share price, provided the company can still make the payments. The drawback to investing in corporate debt is that holders of debt do not share in the profits of the company as they pertain to an increasing share price. Debt investors are limited on the return of their investment.

Corporations also raise capital through equity. They divide their company into pieces of ownership, or shares, and sell them to investors. The money raised from this practice can then be used to fund corporate investments or operations, just as the capital raised from debt issuance. Investors that purchase equity investments then become owners of the company, not creditors. In the event of company bankruptcy, equity holders may lose the entirety of their investment, and they do not receive preferential payoff treatment as creditors do. On the other hand, should a company thrive, equity investors may see the value of their investments rise ten or a hundredfold. They are not limited on gains in the way corporate debt holders are.[144]

Given that there are two primary ways for a corporation to raise capital, how is the company to decide which method will be used? What percentage of the company's capital should be debt, and what percentage should be equity? How a company structures itself financially will no doubt affect its operations in the future, as well as its abilities to grow its business and adapt to changing market conditions. Both present and projected market conditions, interest rates, investor demand, and of course the corporate tax rate are just a few pieces of information that go into the corporate capital structure equation, but as we shall see, the corporate income tax plays a larger role than one might otherwise suspect at first glance.

Due to the nature of the tax code, corporations are taxed on profit, and people are taxed on their income. When a corporation turns a profit, it must pay taxes on that profit to the government, the amount of which depends on the current corporate tax rate. After those taxes are paid, the corporation can then reinvest the remaining profit in the company, hold it as retained earnings, or return it to those that financed the company's operations through investment in the form of debt or equity. For holders of equity, the returned value takes the form of dividend payments; however, those are also taxed for the recipients. This concept implies that corporate profits are taxed twice, once when earned by the corporation, and then again when returned to equity holders.[145] The tax code is significantly more friendly towards debt financing. If the corporation returns value to investors in the form of interest payments, it can deduct the interest from its tax liability, thus shielding its profits. Debt investors still pay taxes on the interest payments they receive, but at least corporate profits are shielded, thus allowing more capital to flow down through the company.[146]

Imagine a pipeline of water flowing through it, with the water representing corporate profit. At the top of the pipe is a valve which represents corporate operations. As the company turns the valve, water flows down to the end of the pipe where investors may fill their cups with returns on investment made possible by the flowing corporate profit. Now picture the government coming up to the pipe and drilling holes into the middle of it, allowing water to flow into their cups as well and leaving less to flow down towards investors. This is the effect of the corporate tax rate. When a company finances through debt rather than equity, it is able to plug more of those government-drilled holes. An incentive exists for companies to finance through debt rather than equity due to the corporate income tax structure.

The incentive to finance through debt rather than equity can vary in intensity depending on where the interest rates are set. As interest rates decrease, debt becomes the cheaper financing option, furthering the incentive for its use.[147] Debt allows current company operations to be financed with future cash flows, and the cost of doing it is extremely low. As a bonus, those costs can be deducted from corporate tax expenses...what a deal! During the 2008 financial crisis, the Federal Reserve lowered interest rates in an attempt to stimulate economic activity. Interest rates have since remained at historic lows, and corporations have responded by adding significant amounts of debt to their books, which could impact their ability to conduct business in the future.[148]

Corporate debt can prove hazardous and repressive to corporations. Once a corporation releases debt to investors, it must pay that amount back plus interest. A particularly bad fiscal year does not release a given corporation from paying back its financial obligations, so the amount of debt a company carries on its books can correspond to risk. As a company becomes more indebted, the larger the risk that it could experience financial strain at some point in the future, especially when business operations are stifled. Additionally, the more debt a company carries, the more it is seen as a credit risk. Banks and investors will want to offset this risk by receiving additional compensation, and they will usually demand more collateral or higher interest payments on additional debt that the company attempts to raise as a result. When companies are heavily indebted, a larger portion of their profits is used to service the debt by making regular interest payments and paying off principal. These are funds that could have gone towards useful and profitable projects within the company that could have increased the company's value or provided goods and services to the market, but instead will have been allocated to debt service. One possible solution is to even the playing field between debt and equity by allowing equity financing to be deductible the same way debt financing is, and also to further reduce or remove altogether the taxes on capital gains, thus eliminating the double taxation problem. These circumstances are currently not met, thus creating a strong incentive for companies to finance through debt, and not equity, especially as interest rates remain at historic lows.

Holders of debt and holders of equity for a given company often face a conflict of interest. So long as a given corporation does not experience bankruptcy, holders of debt receive a fixed return on their investment. The returns that equity holders receive is not fixed but instead linked to the company's performance. As a company grows in value, so too does the value of equity holders' investment, but they will see their investments decline in value if the company performs poorly. Equity holders are limited as to how much they can lose in the event of bankruptcy, namely their entire investment. If the company does well, there is no limit on how well the holders of equity can do, as the value of their holdings can increase by multiples. It stands to reason that if an equity investor only holds a small share of a given company, he or she will want the company to court excessive risk. The equity holder, in this case, has a potential for a much higher return should the risk pay off, but losses are limited to the relatively small size of the initial investment.[149]

Debt holders get nothing extra if a risk pays off, other than additional peace of mind knowing that there will potentially be a reduced likelihood of interest payment interruption. If a company takes excessive risks and fails, debt investors not only lose their principal investment, but also the future interest payments they would have received. The conflict of interest arises as both debt and equity holders face different incentives on corporate strategy, but it is the equity holders that elect board members and make decisions on what personalities will be hired and which capital projects will be pursued.[150]

117

Given that a corporate income tax places an incentive on financing through debt, the conflict of interest shifts in favor of shareholders. As the proportion of debt that comprises a company's capital structure increases, the holders of that debt increasingly shoulder the costs of failed projects that are not profitable, while shareholders see a decreasing scale of risk. As the percentage of a company's financing that is equity declines, equity holders have even more incentive to pursue potentially higher-risk gambles, as the excess risk is picked up by the debtholders who receive no additional compensation. Since shareholders elect the company's leadership, the corporate income tax ensures that a smaller amount of capital at risk can dictate strategy to a larger amount of capital, provided that the company acts on the incentive to finance more through debt rather than through equity. Acting on the incentive to finance through debt increases the incentive to pursue risky behavior among corporations, and the burdensome presence of the debt makes any attempts to adapt to changing market dynamics or consumer preferences that much more difficult, especially when the risky behavior backfires. As more companies turn towards debt financing to shield themselves from the corporate income tax, risky behavior will increase, bankruptcies will become more common, and corporate diligence will decline. The solution then is to address the perverse incentive created for companies by the corporate income tax by either reducing it to such a level that the incentive to finance through debt rather than through equity is no longer such a dominating factor, or to eliminate it entirely allowing companies to retain additional earnings, return more value to shareholders, and invest in themselves by improving their processes and hiring new personnel

6 Consumption Tax

"There is no art which one government sooner learns of another than that of draining money from the pockets of the people."
- Adam Smith, 1776.[151]

In a given economy, goods and services are bought and sold depending on price and availability. Consumers will purchase goods and services they want, and producers will supply them. For every product or service, there exists a price where the amount of goods and services produced is equal to the amount demanded by consumers, and this is often referred to as the market-clearing price. The laws of economics dictate that as the price of a good or service increases, more producers will be willing to supply it at that price, but fewer consumers will demand it, thus resulting in a surplus. The opposite is true if the price goes down. As prices decrease, consumers are willing to buy more of the goods or services, but producers are less willing to supply them, thus resulting in a shortage.

The goods and services purchased by individuals and the quantity consumed by them vary wildly. People are different from one another ethnically, culturally, religiously, etc; their tastes and preferences will vary. What some find appealing, others may find revolting. I have a strong demand for cheese, but my lactose intolerant neighbor has no demand for it. Needless to say, our consumption habits will differ. I am willing to go to the store and exchange dollars that I earned for cheese whereas he would be unwilling to consume it even if it were available to him at no charge. Even though our demand for cheese differs to such an

119

extent that we could be considered consumer opposites, we are both still aggregated in the cheese market, and the average of our two levels of demand is the market demand for cheese between us as individuals.

Given that every product has a market, and that each product has a market-clearing price where consumers will purchase the exact quantity of product supplied, how might a tax levied against the consumption of the good affect the way consumers behave? Just as people's demands differ across markets, people's code of ethics and morals differ. What some consider harmless, others may consider to be an egregious vice. As you read this, somewhere there is a government official or bureaucrat—either elected or not—that is conjuring up new ways to control how you spend your money. He or she can be working on new legislation right now that could affect your consumption habits; after all, no one "needs" a second refrigerator dedicated exclusively to cheese, right? Perhaps a person's consumption habits violate another individual's religious creed, or perhaps it is simply offensive.

Everywhere, people will be trying to impose limitations on the things you do and the products you consume. Evidently, these people have more insight into how you can live your best life, whereas you—the individual who is most affected by your own choices—clearly need their guidance and wisdom to determine which products you buy and how much you can purchase. When these people achieve positions of power in government and are able to pass into law and influence legislation, a person may find access to his or her desired products limited by a consumption tax.

Effects of the Consumption Tax

A tax levied specifically against the consumption of a good increases the cost of consumption, and when faced with increasing costs, consumers will consume less. Although this is not always the intention of consumption taxes, it is the inevitable result. Sometimes legislators apply consumption taxes on goods simply to raise revenue, feeling no need or desire to limit how much of a good is consumed. By raising the costs of consumption, however, people are simply less willing to consume at the same levels that they otherwise would without the tax in place, provided that their demand for that good is elastic, meaning that the amount they consume is more responsive to changes in price. There are certain goods in which consumers have inelastic demand, implying that they will continue consumption regardless of price. Depending on how strong consumers' demands are for goods and how reactive they are to changes in price will determine how effective the consumption tax is at either raising revenue or on cutting down consumption, depending on the politicians' motives for applying the tax. Regardless of motive, consumption taxes raise costs, and those costs must be borne by someone.[152]

As the government levies taxes against the consumption of goods, consumers are forced to pay more for what they buy, while sellers receive less for what they sell. What would otherwise be a private transaction has had a new cost inserted, and this cost must be shouldered by the participating parties, but the weight of the burden may not be evenly distributed. It all depends on the type of good that has had a consumption tax applied. When consumption taxes are levied, costs increase, and the act of selling that good becomes less profitable. From the seller's perspective, he would seek to raise his prices so that the total compensation he receives is at least equal to the compensation he would receive without the tax in place, only now he is faced with fewer consumers willing to buy his product at that price. To avoid losing business, sellers will usually decline to raise prices to fully accommodate the tax. Instead, most sellers only partially raise their prices, effectively splitting the cost of the tax between themselves and their consumers. Sellers of these types of goods may be less willing to take on some of the new tax-related costs if the goods they sell are in high demand. If the goods are in low demand, or if drastically raising prices would result in catastrophic loss of sales, the seller may be forced to shoulder the entire cost of the consumption tax by not raising prices at all, but instead by simply selling less and taking less profit. In either situation, consumption taxes impose costs to consumers and sellers that limit economic growth and reduce the welfare of all parties involved in the transactions.[153] Consenting adults should have the right to consume what they please and in whatever quantity they please, provided that their consumption does not directly interfere with the rights of other individuals. When the government imposes consumption taxes to alter people's spending habits, it is effectively interfering with their freedom to choose how they will lead their lives. Without the tax, and if consumers acknowledged that consumption of a particular good was not in their own interest, they would abstain from its consumption. Forcing them to abstain, or at least financially punishing them for continuing the behavior, does not benefit them.

Aside from the moral objections of consumption taxes regarding interference with people's freedom to make their own choices, there is a more practical objection that emphasizes how consumption taxes are economically destructive. A consumption tax reduces the overall consumption of a given good by raising its costs, thereby lowering the amount of that good demanded by consumers. Given that taxes impose costs to market participants, and also that wealth lost from the marginal transactions no longer taking place as well as from the reduced wealth of the market participants still engaged, one need not strain himself to realize that the amount of wealth directly transferred to the government is less than the aggregate amount of wealth prior to the tax. The tax revenue flows through bureaucratic legions and is doled out special interest favors before ending its sad journey into the government's coffers where it will be frivolously spent on public goods of inferior quality at double or triple the cost of its superior private sector equivalent.[154]

Private transactions that would be beneficial to both buyer and seller may no longer benefit one or both parties after a consumption tax is imposed, resulting in that transaction being canceled or cost-prohibitive. If consenting individuals who have signaled that they are willing to engage in voluntary cooperation by their own market behavior are no longer willing to engage in a given market activity, it proves that the tax will make them worse off after the transaction has taken place than before...if they still follow through with it; assuming that these market participants are acting in their own self-interest, they won't. Consumers abstaining from conducting economic transactions indicate that the benefit they would receive from consumption does not outweigh the loss of wealth used to make the purchase. If the consumption tax is lifted and they engage in the behavior once more, they show that the benefit received from consumption does outweigh the financial cost of the purchase. In such a case where the consumption tax is high enough to prevent a transaction from taking place—even if the tax is relatively small—the total amount of the tax equals a net loss to society, as that amount would have been equal to the created wealth through the transaction taking place.

When Philadelphia introduced its controversial soda tax designed to punish drinkers of soft drinks while promoting citizens' health, consumers responded. Soft drink purchases within city limits declined significantly, while soft drink purchases just outside of city limits increased, resulting in a general decrease in economic activity for Philadelphia, and a loss of wealth for its people. The city itself raised less revenue through the tax than originally forecasted, while the most adversely affected individuals were among the city's poorest residents who do not have the means to leave the city in order to make their soda purchases. Rather than encouraging healthier diets, the consumption tax merely added a new and oppressive cost to people's lifestyle choices, resulting in a loss of wealth for everyone.[155]

Regrettably, very few individuals will notice the lost wealth, as it can be difficult to imagine how lifting consumption taxes will benefit us all. Indeed, the taxes levied against goods or behaviors that society deems "bad" or "unhealthy" tend to be perceived as a moral obligation to limit the amount consumed in order to protect each other from the negative attributes associated with these goods.[156] Sadly, this results in mass confusion among the people as to the true effects of consumption taxes. When politicians denounce the consumption of certain goods in order to curry favor with potential voters, they are often met with applause and commendation. People celebrate their bravery for suggesting the tax and standing up to the corporations behind the production of these evil products, while also agreeing with all of the new studies that suddenly appear out of the woodwork to support the energetic politicians' claims. People lick their chops at the idea of taxing bad behavior into oblivion and making the world a better place. What little consumption does remain will be so heavily taxed that schools and roads will be better funded at the expense of greedy corporations who are seeking to get rich off our own deteriorating health, while the few holdout consumers become ostracized as evil-doers for continuing to engage in consumption. Ironically, when businesses are forced to raise prices to negate the loss of sales due to the costs of taxation, they are again denounced for trying to squeeze every last cent from the people—even though people wanted the policy and cheered its governmental approval.

Businesses operating under heavy consumption taxes are faced with a set of difficult choices: raising prices will lead to loss of sales and public outcry, but inaction could cut too deeply into their margins, making their ventures unprofitable at the expense of the shareholder. A common practice then is for businesses to play the political game themselves. Firms can launch their own public outreach program and employ lobbyists to represent them in D.C. They can both attempt to win the public favor back by disproving the allegations against their products and also convince the politicians that they have been led astray in passing the consumption tax. The companies will attempt to justify the need to consume their products by appealing to the loss of jobs should consumption be rolled back as a consequence of a tax, or they will attempt to obtain a federal subsidy so they can continue operating profitably despite the new losses from taxes.[157]

Subsidies are quite common among firms under heavy consumption taxes. On the one hand, government policy has made their line of business less profitable, thus harming the company by lowering the amount consumers buy. The government will collect tax revenue from whatever consumption remains. From there, the government will turn around and make direct payments to the company in the form of subsidies to keep it operating. Usually, these two functions are carried out by two very distinct government bureaucratic agencies who are relatively unaware of the actions of the other, even though their government-mandated objectives are in direct conflict with one another. The result of these consumption taxes, and all taxation for that matter, is a back-and-forth economic fiasco of private wealth being forcefully confiscated from the marketplace and subsequently flushed down many governmental toilets. When a handful of pennies finally trickles down through the pipes and is returned to the public via government-provided goods and services, or used for one of the government's many other unnecessary functions, one cannot help but be amazed at how wasteful the entire system is.

As a final, sad anecdote to the consumption tax, it should be mentioned that the poor are those disproportionately affected. Lower-income individuals spend higher proportions of their income on consumer goods, while higher-income individuals invest more of their income. Even though a higher-earning person

125

may spend more on consumption overall than a lower-income individual, it is the lower-income person that has spent more on consumption as a percentage of his income. When consumption taxes are in place, the poor are disproportionately affected since the tax will be more of a burden on them than it will on their higher-income earning peers.[158] Finally, consumption taxes that are levied against certain products are often products that are consumed more at the lower end of the income strata, such as soda and cigarettes. These products are among the most likely to have their cost raised by consumption taxes, and poor people are going to be hurt as they continue consuming these products in greater quantities than the wealthy do, as the wealthy have for the most part moved on from such products into healthy alternatives.[159]

7 Taxes on Wealth

"An unlimited power to tax involves, necessarily, a power to destroy." - John Marshall, 1819.[160]

Taxes on wealth and taxes on income are often confused with one another, but the difference is quite simple. A tax on wealth is a tax on the value of what a person owns, while a tax on income is a tax on what a person earns. Wealth taxes are used to fund government activity, just as other types of taxes, but a key difference is that taxes on wealth are levers the government uses to address wealth inequality.[161] For some, taking wealth from those with plenty and giving to those with little is a necessary function of the state, based upon the common misconception that wealthy individuals did not earn their wealth or that they see themselves as superior to their fellow man and should be cut down to size.[162] While some come into wealth through fortunate birthright or lottery-style luck, the vast majority of wealthy individuals in the United States are first-generation, meaning that they started with little and earned what they have.[163] The government employs several tools for extracting wealth from these individuals, and those tools along with the implications of wealth taxation will be discussed momentarily, but it is first worth detailing the origins of wealth to gain a better perspective.

Wealth is derived from two primary sources: productive labor and natural resources. The earth is a planet with bountiful resources, and though being so endowed with them, humans can not achieve a wealthy state of being relying on nature alone. If a man is left alone and isolated in nature, he will have plenty of natural resources, but little wealth. Should he find another person with resources of his own, the two may engage in voluntary exchange to begin creating wealth for themselves. Even toddlers are aware of the effects of this phenomenon. If two toddlers voluntarily trade a juice box and a cookie with each other, they have created wealth even though no new additional resources were added or produced. A good classroom demonstration of this concept involves selecting ten or so student volunteers to come forward. Distribute at random ten items to them, giving one item to each student, ranging from soft drinks to candy bars. Ask each student to quantify his or her satisfaction with the random item received on a scale of 1-10, and then record the responses. Then allow the students a moment to trade with one another, whereby each student can exchange his or her item with that of another. After the period of trade, record the students' satisfaction levels once more. In every instance, each student will record a higher level of satisfaction than the one he or she gave prior to trading, or at the very least, the satisfaction level will remain unchanged. No student would make himself worse off by trading something he values for something he does not. The aggregated satisfaction levels between the students will always be higher after the period of free trade than before it commenced. The students took a pool of resources, traded them, and created wealth. Imagine now a "government" that appeared at the end of the trading period and siphoned off a part of each item as a wealth tax. Would the student with the chocolate bar have traded it for the can of soda if he had to give a third of the drink to quench the government's thirst? Perhaps he values two-thirds of a soda greater than one full candy bar, or perhaps he does not. In either case, where once wealth was created through trade, a tax on that wealth ensures that the wealth-producing trade does not raise standards of living as high as it otherwise could have, assuming the trade still takes place. Many voluntary and wealth-producing trades between consenting parties would not take place in the presence of a wealth tax.

Throughout most of human history, people remained poor. Even the kings and queens of a few centuries ago were poor by today's standards. Electricity, supermarkets, cars, refrigerators...all of these contribute to our wealth in ways that no king could even comprehend just a few hundred years ago. For the peasant living under his rule, things were much worse. Working hours were long, conditions brutal, and life short. For most of history, wealth was not created but instead plundered. Indeed, many warrior societies were culturally ingrained in this thought process. The constant pillaging of wealth reduced the incentive to produce wealth in the first place, and the high costs of preserving and protecting what little wealth that was created often prevented additional productive activities from taking place. Even as recently as the Enlightenment era when nation-states emerged, so-called civilized peoples could not understand this concept. If the Dutch are becoming wealthy due to their overseas trading, it must be at France and England's expense, or so the faulty thought process went. Entire schools of economic thought were developed around this line of thinking, and they impoverished nations for centuries while the advocates of these economic systems believed them to be the pathway to national wealth.[164] "Your wealth-producing activities are making me poor!" This is known as the "Fixed-Pie Fallacy," where the total amount of wealth in existence is believed to be fixed, and if one person's share of the pie grows, others' shares must be shrinking.[165] This fallacy is a driving force for the current demands to increase taxes on wealth, even though the fallacy was blown to smithereens long ago. It has been proven and shown time and again that wealth is not fixed but can be created and destroyed depending on policy and people's activities.[166] Unfortunately, so long as people believe the amount of wealth to be fixed, where one person's gain is another's loss, they will always believe that plunder, theft, fraud, and other dishonest means are the only ways to become wealthy. Their beliefs will be no different from those of the people that came before us who also believed such fallacies, and who also failed to realize that wealth is created from scratch through production and services. Economist Walter Williams said it best:

> Prior to Capitalism, the way people amassed great wealth was by looting, plundering, and enslaving their fellow man. Capitalism made it possible to become wealthy by serving your fellow man.[167]

Just as trading resources valued less for resources valued more can create new wealth, using those resources for productive purposes can create wealth as well. Man can mix his labor with resources to create wealth if the resultant product can be used to satisfy his wants and needs, or if it can be used to satisfy the wants and needs of others. Trees mixed with labor become timber, which can be used to build houses. Ore mixed with labor becomes steel, which can be used to make cars. Coal can be mixed with labor to create energy, which powers our lives...etc.

A major fallacy found within Marxist doctrine and some Keynesian circles is the idea that labor alone can create wealth. Karl Marx explained in his Theory of Labor Value that the price of an item should be based on the labor employed to create it, and not based on the level of demand by the consumer.[168] By this logic, one could spend a lifetime painting and repainting a rock many different colors, and then be able to sell it for an astronomical fortune. At the end of the person's life when he is finally ready to sell his rock that has been painted a hundred thousand times, he should be able to fetch a very high price for it given that an entire lifetime of labor went into the completion of this piece of art.

Instead, our poor laborer will find that no one will buy his rock simply because no one values it. Such is the fallacy of the labor theory of value. In the 1930s, the US government fell into this trap during the Great Depression. As unemployment increased, the government created multiple work programs for people to get paid to complete random tasks and projects, many of which did not create wealth. Digging a hole only to have another laborer fill it back up and tumbleweed chasing are just a couple of examples.[169] The Roosevelt administration, inspired by the labor theory of value, believed that formerly unemployed individuals can now have the ability to spend money and stimulate the economy due to their newfound jobs. What the administration did not comprehend is that doing mindless tasks is both a waste of time and energy, both of which are scarce resources for an individual.

Only productive labor can create wealth, not labor for labor's sake. Therefore, industrial nations with extensive capital stock have become rich while labor-intensive economies remain poor.[170] Labor economies can evolve by discovering ways to make labor more efficient, increasing output on the same or a lesser amount of labor input. Prior to the industrial revolution, clothing items and textiles were produced in small quantities by skilled craftsmen for a limited customer base, resulting in high prices and few textile products. During and after the industrial revolution, the textile industry was made more efficient and productive by new machines like the Spinning Jenny and Flying Shuttle, enabling vast quantities of textiles to be produced at a fraction of the cost.[171] Skilled craftsmen became relatively obsolete, as these machines could be operated with limited training. As a result, the availability of textile products went up, prices went down, and society became wealthier. It is the same story with every market sector that is made more efficient by capital goods replacing labor pools.

Certainly, not everyone immediately becomes wealthy from the widespread adaptation of new inventions and technologies.

Some, like skilled weavers prior to the industrial revolution, lose their livelihoods to automation. If threatened, labor that is soon to be rendered obsolete can form powerful lobbying movements to convince politicians that efficiency and increased productivity acts contrary to the public good. They describe horrific scenes of people losing their jobs and homes, of quality-made domestic products being replaced by cheaply produced and imported foreign goods, and of a great loss in employment with the introduction of new technologies. "We must protect our jobs!" cries labor advocates as a loyal echo reverberates back to them from the duped public. This is the fallacy that labor equates to wealth, and this concept is illustrated by Frédéric Bastiat in his work *Economic Sophisms:*

> The immediate effect of the invention and use of an ingenious machine is to render superfluous, for the attainment of a given result, a certain amount of manual labour. But its action does not stop there. For the very reason that the desired result is obtained with fewer efforts, the product is handed over to the public at a lower price; and the aggregate of savings thus realized by all purchasers, enables them to procure other satisfactions; that is to say, to encourage manual labour in general to exactly the extent of the manual labour which has been saved in the special branch of industry which has been recently improved. So that the level of labour has not fallen, while that of enjoyments has risen.[172]

For those that believe wealth is derived from raw labor, and not from increased levels of productivity, I put forth the question as to why bother with certain household items. Why mow the lawn with a lawnmower when a person can give himself countless hours of labor by cutting it with scissors? If one's basement is prone to flooding, why install a pump when he can provide labor for himself by using mops and buckets? People understand that efficiency makes them better off in their personal lives, but regarding public policy, they often take the opposite stance.

As processes become more efficient and more productive, wealth expands. What then are the effects of government taxation on the processes that make us wealthy, or on the created wealth itself? The immediate and easily observable effect is that it makes society less wealthy than it otherwise would be. This is apparent, as taxation takes wealth which could be used for additional productive purposes or to satisfy wants and needs, and then redistributes them to bureaucrats, foreign wars, bridges to nowhere, or any other number of government pet projects. Even if government is able to redirect the confiscated wealth towards something useful, the satisfaction and utility derived from it will still be less than the satisfaction and utility derived from the wealth had it been left in the private sector, as no one dispenses with wealth as carefully as he dispenses with his own, and this is especially true in the case of private versus public spending.[173]

On a deeper level, taxes on wealth discourage incentives to become wealthy. Given that wealth is primarily derived from providing in-demand goods and services to the market at better prices—not from plunder and pillage—confiscating part of the net benefits from the economic process acts as a dissuasion from engaging in the productive activity in the first place. For example, when taxes are imposed against wealth generated by productive economic activity, entrepreneurs and innovators that engage in that activity must now factor in these tax expenses as part of their costs, thereby creating an upward inclination in the costs of creating wealth resulting in less wealth being created.[174] Investments, lending, capital preservation, property upkeep, and other methods of employing wealth for the benefit of society are punished via wealth taxation. People and organizations with wealth face new incentives considering wealth taxes, mainly the incentive to dispose of more wealth than they otherwise would, especially with regards to the tax on inherited wealth. With high taxes on wealth, there will be fewer investments and less wealth preservation. The incentive applies pressure to individuals to shift their behavior from saving to consumption, which satisfies wants and needs today at the expense of being able to better satisfy the wants and needs of the future. Consumption of wealth can take on many forms, as there are many different types of wealth in question. Just as there are many different types of wealth categories, there are individual taxes to confiscate a given amount from each one, the degree of which will vary from person to person depending on his or her life circumstances.

Capital Gains Tax

One of the more obvious forms of wealth taxation is that which is levied against capital gains, or the difference between the cost to purchase an asset and the price at which it is later sold. Most financial assets typically held by individuals and institutions generate wealth for them in the form of regular interest and dividend payments, even if they are not sold at a price higher than that at which they were bought. Interest-earning assets are taxed on accrual, with taxes being paid each time interest is earned. Capital gains are taxed on realization, meaning that taxes only come due when the asset is sold, not throughout the period on which it was held.[175] The primary justification for taxing capital gains upon realization and not on accrual relates to the potentially tricky situation of being able to actually afford the tax while holding the asset. If capital gains taxes were to be applied to accrued value, many investors would need to sell their assets to make the payments. Furthermore, an asset may increase in value and trigger a tax payment, and then subsequently decrease in value, leaving the investor further in the hole. Fortunately for the investor, accrual taxes on increased value are not reality, which generally leads to an overall lower tax burden than would otherwise be his obligation if he held an interest-paying asset with regular periods of taxation. By paying taxes at the sale of an asset only rather than on accrued value, investors are able to earn further returns on capital which otherwise would have been their tax obligation. This favorable outcome tends to pull capital away from interest-earning assets and towards value accrual assets, as overall tax burdens on this style of investing are generally lower. Unfortunately, however, this tax structure creates incentives that influence investor decisions which lead to unintended consequences. Capital gains taxes provide limited revenue to the government in comparison to the damage they can cause. Capital gains tax has the potential to distort capital markets and increase volatility levels within those markets as investors allocate a disproportionate amount of capital to equities rather than fixed-income.[176]

Many outspoken individuals in favor of forced government wealth distribution advocate for a higher capital gains tax. They segregate people into those with plenty and those with little, pitting the two against one another. Denouncing the fat cats as becoming wealthy at the general public's expense, they further go on to imply that becoming rich off capital returns is not an honest path to wealth since those returns are only made possible by the productive activities of laborers down the line. There are several concepts to understand here, the first being that labor by itself is not productive. Only through plentiful access to capital can labor become as productive as possible, and that capital is provided by investors who reap a return proportionate to their contribution to the productive enterprise.

Another fallacy is the notion that capital gains embody wealth at the public's expense: if Wall Street gets rich, Main Street must be getting poor. This is simply not true. Capital is constantly in motion as it seeks out its most productive uses. When it finds productive employment, everyone is made better off by the finished goods and services. A final fallacy is the straw man argument pushed by those that want to devour the rich. Clearly we need to cut the greedy cats down to size, and raising capital gains taxes and redistributing that wealth to the people is the way to go about it, right? Well, increasing capital gains taxes would affect Main Street worse than one might assume at first. Almost every American is participating in the capital markets either directly or indirectly. Raising taxes on capital gains affects pensioners, 401(k) accounts, retirement accounts, and more. Ordinary people who have been saving for retirement throughout their entire working lives would have significantly less of their own wealth waiting for them when they reach old age due to higher levels of government confiscation. Lastly, higher capital gains taxes play havoc on market prices as well as wealth creation and preservation—a concept that warrants deeper investigation.

One could argue that the creation of modern capital markets by Dutch financiers in the 17th century marked a turning point for civilization. With the creation of the stock market, companies needing capital can readily find investors needing opportunities. The consumer products we see on the shelves are there due to the simple fact that the companies behind them secured the funding to make them. There is no shortage of entrepreneurial ideas...anyone can have one. There is however a limitation on how much capital can circulate. Some projects and companies will find investment, others will not. The investment process determines which goods and services will be produced and consumed. If a producer secures capital for his project and the final good is worth less than the capital deployed to make it, both he and his investors will suffer losses. This is an efficient process that ensures scarce capital finds its way to higher-valued uses. Just as the economic markets require efficiency to ensure capital is being employed productively, the capital markets themselves require efficiency to ensure capital can be efficiently moved from one productive project to the next, and financial markets that are less entwined with state involvement in the economy will be more able to efficiently allocate capital than those that have higher degrees of state involvement.[177]

Human beings are not perfect, and since the capital markets operate with human participants, the markets cannot be expected to be entirely perfect either. Humans operate under constraints and act upon the incentives they face, and taxation creates huge incentives within the marketplace that alters people's behavior...capital markets being no exception. When a capital asset is sold for more than its purchase price, that difference is a financial gain to the investor and is subject to taxation. The presence of capital gains tax in the case of selling an asset creates an incentive not to sell that asset in order to avoid the tax. Money today is worth more than money tomorrow, so the longer an investor can delay selling his asset, the lower will be the discounted value of his tax payment.[178] By holding his asset longer than he might otherwise ideally like to, he can at least lower his tax burden. Problems then arise which conflict with the nature of efficient capital markets. A robust capital market requires efficiency and fluidity, allowing capital to move from one productive project to the next, funding business ventures and ideas that raise standards of living. When taxation provides the incentive not to sell assets, capital tends to remain parked in one place longer than it would otherwise be if there were no capital gains tax. With higher capital gains tax, productive projects are delayed or foregone due to lack of capital, while a lower capital gains tax would allow capital to more readily flow between its highest-valued uses.

Alternatively, investors that sell their assets for a loss are permitted to write off the loss on their taxes. Every December, retail investors everywhere participate in capital-loss selling of their underwater equities in order to secure a tax write-off for that given year. Many of these assets are sound investment decisions and portray temporary paper losses to investors that will become gains with time, but due to the perverse incentive created by the tax write-off, investors are pressured to deprive productive projects of capital in order to secure a tax benefit. This creates the "January Effect" in capital markets whereby some investment sectors explode in value as all the newly freed capital from December selling is reallocated.[179] This amount of capital transitioning over such a short period of time creates microbubbles in capital markets which distort asset prices relative to their true values and can be directly attributed to government capital gains/loss tax policy.

Further incentives are created due to higher capital gains taxes as they pertain to preserving one's wealth. It is common knowledge that money hidden under the mattress as savings will lose its purchasing power over time due to the inflationary monetary policies of the Federal Reserve, so people must find productive ways to invest their money in order to generate a return. With higher capital gains taxes, investors require larger returns before they can sell their assets for profit and redeploy the capital to more productive use. If one purchases an asset and sees its value increase over time only modestly, selling the asset for a profit may actually result in a loss of purchasing power for him if the asset's value increase is equal to or less than the rate of inflation. Paired with punitive capital gains taxes, an investor may find himself worse off after the sale of an asset than he would be if he just held it, creating the incentive not to sell the asset and move capital to a higher-valued use.

Entrepreneurial activity is also stunted under a system with high capital gains taxes. Every time a businessman embarks on a new venture, a craftsman sets up his trade, or a merchant purchases his inventory, he takes a risk. If his venture fails, he suffers losses which indicate that he is not using scarce resources effectively. If his risk pays off, he is rewarded by the market with profits for creating wealth. Without risk, there is no growth. Risk has always driven business and innovation throughout history, and the adventurous personalities of our most famous entrepreneurs and inventors spurred them to court the necessary risk needed to develop their products which have revolutionized the world.

Higher capital gains taxes is effectively a tax on this type of behavior. Investors will be more reluctant to fund projects, as they now require higher returns on their investments in order to justify suffering the tax payment.[180] If the capital gains tax is too high, entrepreneurial activity will cease altogether, as capital will cease its flow from one productive use to the next. Businesses and innovative ideas will go without capital, and many potentially world-changing goods and services will never get off the ground, being condemned to exist only as hypothetical ideas. Those advocating for capital gains to be taxed at the same rate as income—or even at higher rates—overlook this reality. What many also fail to grasp is that capital gains taxes actually act as a double whammy. When a person earns income, he is taxed. When he invests that after-tax income into some form of asset, later to sell that asset, he is once again taxed on capital gains. Such a deluge of tax penalties may convince the would-be investor to abstain from injecting his capital in the markets, given that his money has already been taxed once.

Transfer Taxes

In the United States, assets can not only be taxed by having a portion of their gain in value upon sale confiscated, but also by having their values taxed at a set rate (depending on jurisdiction) when transferred from one person to another, usually in the form of a gift or inheritance. Whenever a person makes a gift to another over a certain amount, he must surrender a portion of its value to the government.[181] Currently, the gift tax rate does not apply for items worth less than $15,000, so most instances of gifting will be permitted without being subjected to the tax; but there are still many circumstances where one cannot give a gift to another without paying the government. The law is currently arranged so that the recipient pays no tax.[182] The entirety of the gift tax is shouldered by the giver unless the recipient agrees to cover some or all of it. Regardless of who is legally liable, the gift tax carries severe implications. Essentially, a gift tax settles the question once and for all over who has sovereignty over property: the individual or the state in which the property is located. Given that a portion of a gift's value that is subjected to the tax must be surrendered to the government, it can be asserted that an individual does not completely possess the item in question since he cannot fully dispense it at will without paying homage to the state. This is a blatant infringement upon the natural rights of people to own property and use it for whatever means that they deem most appropriate.

Similar to the gift tax is the estate tax, or the fee that must be paid to the government upon the death of a person. Described at the onset of the Great Depression by a disillusioned President Herbert Hoover as "one of the most economically and socially desirable—or even necessary of all taxes,"[183] this fee will have rates that vary across jurisdictions, with some jurisdictions having higher minimum thresholds than others, but generally the fee is calculated upon the market value of a person's assets at the time of death once the minimum threshold value is met.[184] Once more, double taxation is at play with the estate tax. An individual earns income and pays taxes, and then his beneficiaries are taxed on that same earned income upon inheritance, even though by now the earned income may likely take the form of many different assets

140

apart from a pile of cash.

Benjamin Franklin once said in correspondence that the only two certainties of our world are death and taxes.[185] Perhaps even he would be surprised that the government has recently decided that the two should be permanently joined, with death itself being a taxable event. During Franklin's day, a very modest estate tax was levied against bequeathed assets in the form of a stamp tax, but it was shortly thereafter repealed during the first decade of the 19th century.[186] Today the highest tax rate for estates hovers at 40%, but it is worth noting that the estate's value must be substantial before the tax applies. Indeed, almost all estates are exempt from the tax due to the minimum value thresholds required to trigger it. It is estimated that less than 10% of all estates will be subject to the estate tax upon a person's death.[187]

If so few estates are subject to the estate tax, why dedicate time and energy to understand its implications? Growing in popularity is the notion that the top income earners should be forced to pay more in taxes to cover the costs of public goods enjoyed by the population at large, so is it not better if wealthy estates are heavily taxed, especially since the individual is deceased and is no longer around to complain about it? Even though most estates get by without paying estate tax, with only the wealthiest of them being subjected to it, a dissection of the policy is warranted on two grounds: the first being the practical reason for abolishing it, and the second being attributed to the perverse incentives it creates.

For the small minority of individuals whose estate is large enough to trigger the estate tax, their death becomes a taxable event. For most of us, our deaths are not taxed. The moral implications of this policy are such that heirs of taxable estates should be punished for their predecessors' success, and should be forced to give part of the inheritance to the state in the name of economic equality. Many argue that being endowed with massive

141

fortunes creates an injustice, as so very few of us are fortunate enough to ever receive such inheritance. This arbitrary advantage will give the select few a leg up against us in life; and as such, they should be cut down to size to equal the playing field. What these advocates of the estate tax fail to grasp is the fact that the playing field has a way of leveling itself out on its own.

Most of the wealthy individuals in the United States are first-generation, meaning they made their wealth for themselves and did not receive it as an inheritance.[188] Even for those that do receive their wealth as an inheritance, at some point that fortune had to be earned through innovation or the provision of goods and services that people demand. Advocates of the inheritance tax often assert that people should not benefit from wealth they did not earn, and the inheritance tax creates a more equal distribution of wealth. Inheritance taxes do not account for a large portion of government revenue—less than one percent—and therefore cannot benefit many people through distribution in the form of direct payments (welfare) or through provisions of public works.[189] For those whose inheritances are taxed, they become noticeably worse off. The taxation of inheritable wealth can thus be said to be a Pareto inferior policy, as some are heavily punished while the benefits to others are so insignificant that they do not raise their standard of living by any measurable amount.

The free market has its own way of distributing wealth that does not require government force and a violation of individuals' rights. In order for wealth to grow, the activities which caused it to form must continue. When someone who does not possess entrepreneurial talent inherits wealth, that person will likely spend more than he earns, and the wealth will dissipate over time. The money will flow from his hands into the hands of people that are providing him with the goods and services he wants, and the producers will then become wealthy, without the need for an inheritance tax. Advocates for higher inheritance taxes, such as

Thomas Piketty in his best-seller *Capital in the Twenty-First Century,* paint a scary picture of wealthy aristocrats who inherited rather than earned their wealth, and of how the world's wealth will continue gravitating into their hands unjustly unless we step in and seize it.[190] The reality of the situation is less fictitious.

If a person who does possess an entrepreneurial spirit inherits wealth, he will use the newfound wealth to either continue in the economically beneficial activities that allowed its original formation, or he will embark on new economic activities now that he is in possession of capital. If the state were to step in and deprive him of a portion of the inheritance, he now has less to work with towards providing consumers with goods and services.

In either of these two cases in which the inheritor is entrepreneurial or a big spender, wealth will find its way from those who do not understand how to create and preserve it to those that do, without the need of a tax. Ironically, an estate tax often preserves wealth in the hands of those that would otherwise lose it due to a lack of good stewardship. In the presence of an estate tax designed to confiscate wealth from those unworthy heirs that did not earn it in order to redistribute it in the name of equality, wealthy estates often employ lawyers that will help them navigate the legal channels necessary to avoid paying the estate tax or at least reduce its impact. These channels often involve tying the wealth up in alternative vehicles less penalized by the tax, or by setting up restrictive trusts that ensure its preservation. As a result, inheritors not capable of preserving wealth that did not earn the wealth they receive end up keeping it longer than they would without the presence of an estate tax.[191]

An inheritance tax is unnecessary for the purposes for which it was designed, and it often achieves the opposite of what it intends. The United States is not a land of wealthy aristocrats that inherited their wealth, and we live in a society of great upward mobility. A majority of America's millionaires are self-made and first-generation rich, and studies have shown that a majority of families that did inherit their wealth lost it all by the second generation.[192] Wealth flows like a river from those that understand its properties and are good stewards from those that are not.

Government involvement in this natural process distorts capital flows and destroys wealth. When wealth is confiscated through taxation, it must pass through bureaucrats, special interest groups, and layers of red tape before making its way to some public works project or welfare distribution. The amount of resources wasted in this process amount to a deadweight loss that ensures there is less wealth at the end of the process than at the start, and whatever project the wealth is funneled towards will be more costly and less desirable than its private sector equivalent, making the inheritance tax both economically destructive and wasteful.[193] Third-party observers may feel good about seeing wealth being taken by the state away from those that did not earn it directly, but they fail to realize that the destructive power of government makes them worse off by destroying wealth which could have been invested in new entrepreneurial projects. More dangerous still to the proper handling of wealth is the incentive the tax creates for people to frivolously consume their wealth before the state has a chance to take it. Such over-consumption ensures that less capital is used for more productive outlets, which lowers standards of living across the long term.

When the government, or any entity for that matter, states that it intends to seize a portion of a person's wealth upon his death, that person has just been given the incentive to ensure he has as little wealth as possible at the time of death, or at least to reduce his wealth to a point that is below the tax threshold.[194] Although the current estate tax only applies to a minority of estates, the wealth of these estates is considerable. Due to the size of these estates subject to the tax, it follows that the amount of wealth that will need to be disposed of before death to avoid the tax will also be considerable. People who might have been willing to leave more wealth to their heirs will now be inclined to take more ski trips, buy more sports cars, go on another cruise, or do any number of things that consume wealth. Although there is nothing inherently wrong with consumption per se, frivolous consumption is economically destructive. Even though we produce so that we may later consume, our present consumption choices indicate that we value the consumption more than any future consumption we might enjoy if we delayed consumption in the present. If forced to spend and consume due to an imminent tax penalty, this might not hold true. People may engage in present consumption that they do not value more than future consumption while shrugging their shoulders saying "better spend it up now before the government gets it." This is wasteful for the same reason that Christmas is wasteful.

Assume at Christmas time little Johnny receives a toy he did not want, and the toy has a retail value of $10. If little Johnny only values the toy at $6, the amount of wealth destroyed in the process of him receiving the gift equals $4.[195] Taxing estates and providing incentives to spend has the same effect. If a hypothetical estate is worth ten million dollars, and five million must be spent to reduce the estate size to avoid a tax, wealth will potentially be dissipated on consumption that otherwise would not happen. The five million might be spent on consumption that is only valued to the consumer at two or three million, but it is spent regardless in order to avoid having the state seize it. Wealth is inevitably destroyed.

While the inheritance tax provides the incentive to reduce the size of an estate prior to death, there are more rational ways to avoid the tax that can preserve wealth. Briefly mentioned earlier were trusts. Family trusts can be established to pass estate wealth from one generation to the next without being subject to heavy taxation.[196] The beneficiaries of the trust will be taxed on income earned by the trust, and also on special distributions, but the return of principal itself will be allotted certain tax deductions. Managed trusts can be invested in interest-earning securities which will grow wealth while the beneficiaries slowly receive payments from the trust amounting to a proportion of the estate's value, often a much-preferred option among wealthy families as opposed to lump-sum inheritances reduced by the burden of taxation.[197]

Financial securities themselves are another way to spare beneficiaries a painful tax burden. Stocks passed down through death to a beneficiary are not taxed upon receipt, though the cost basis changes for the new owner.[198] If Grandma bought her Ford shares for two dollars a piece in the 1980s, and then she dies today leaving them to you as the beneficiary, you will inherit the shares with a cost basis of whatever the current market price is, not what Grandma paid for them. Selling the shares after inheritance will however trigger capital gains taxes if they are sold for a price higher than whatever the new cost basis is. Fortunately for beneficiaries, this is a superb way to avoid both inheritance tax and capital gains tax. Suppose Grandma bought X amount of stock in the 1980s for $10 per share, and at the time of her death, those same shares are worth $100 each for a net gain of $90 per share. Suppose also that Grandma meets the minimum requirement for the federal estate tax, and she has no exemptions. Finally, suppose that Grandma sold off her stock shortly before her death, leaving her estate flush with cash. Poor Granny would be subject to a capital gains tax on the increased value of her stock, leaving her with significantly less cash from the proceeds of the sale. Then, after her death, that cash would be heavily taxed as part of the estate, a double whammy. After her passing, you may only receive a fraction of Grandma's estate when it's all said and done.

Now assume that Granny had a little more sense than to sell her stock prior to her death. Instead of inheriting cash, you inherit her shares. Her cost basis of $10 per share is now disregarded, and you receive the shares with a new cost basis of $100, the current market price. If you sold the shares immediately at $100, there would be no capital gains to you, since you sold them at the cost basis. But do not forget that the shares were originally purchased at $10 per share, not $100. You have just been spared capital gains tax on the entirety of the position and accumulated wealth; the wealth that rightly belongs in your family remains in your family. Granny took the risk when she bought the stock...why should the government get part of her reward through taxes? Passing stock down in an estate that has accumulated in value is a great way to avoid taxation.

Property Taxes

One of the primary sources of funding for city and other municipal governments in the United States is the property tax, essentially a recurring tax assessed against the value of real estate or vacant land.[199] Every few years, government-employed property assessors appraise the value of private land or real estate using prevalent market conditions multiplied through a formula that includes their paymasters' tax rate, usually set by a board or commission. The resulting assessed value of property can be quite different from the actual market value, so the government-assigned value can be said to operate on a "best guess" basis for tax purposes.[200] Property taxes are generally used to fund localized government spending that is valued and utilized by most property owners, such as fire and police forces, public education, and public works development. If however, the property owners do not value the public goods funded by their tax payments, society incurs a net economic loss.

In a little town called Gardendale, located in North-Central Alabama (where much of this book was written), a festival is held every year whereby local merchants set up booths and tents to peddle their wares and crafts. Hometown fiddle bands take the stage to provide light entertainment, and food trucks set up along the roadside to offer munchies to hungry festival-goers. Without question, a good time is had by all in attendance. This annual festival requires that each vendor register himself with the city, and he in turn is offered a designated spot where he can erect his merchant tent. This process ensures that no unknown merchants show up to sell unverified crafts in zones that are designated to others that have registered and paid their dues. Furthermore, this registration process ensures that each merchant knows exactly where to set up his equipment, and that chaos does not reign over the festival with merchants all vying for the prime locations. With this in mind, how long might an average person expect the festival registration and planning process to last? Perhaps the city designates one of its council members to devote a month or two leading up to the festival to make preparations. Perhaps someone from the chamber of commerce might also step in, right? I'm afraid not. The city of Gardendale has full-time staff "working" year-round to plan the festival that occurs over a single weekend, the logistics of which are limited to assigning certain plots to certain merchants, and approving which people can and cannot attend as vendors. Although nearly all of the work is done in the week(s) leading up to the day of the festival, salaries are collected year-round, and as with most public sector jobs, responsibilities are few, while the pay is generous and benefits superb, much more so than could be found in the private sector job equivalent of secretary or private event manager. Are the residents of Gardendale truly receiving value from the property taxes they pay? Perhaps some resident taxpayers enjoy the festival so much that they can answer in the affirmative, but this will not be the case for everyone. With the 2020 Coronavirus pandemic, the event was canceled altogether, thereby offering no value whatsoever to the payers of property taxes. Gardendale residents will of course not see a rebate on their property taxes for the canceled event, and those dollars have still been spent on public sector salaries for duties unable to be performed.

Unfortunately, all across America stories like this provide testimony to the fact that tax dollars are so easily squandered, and people would be much better off if they were allowed to keep their money and spend it on the goods and services they demand, rather than see it frittered away on nonsense. It is not terribly uncommon for a given town to have a mayor, police chief, or some other high ranking city official whose nephew/niece earns a tax-funded six-figure salary working for the city as a special projects coordinator or executive consultant, with questionable if not nonexistent duties. To be fair, the private sector has some of those abuses as well, but they are far more scarce, and there are real consequences for the firms that engage in that behavior such as a decline in profitability unless the state is involved, in which case the offender is often protected at the expense of competition. City governments will often grant large contracts to favored private companies through which they have personal connections to perform certain services for the city, often at a much higher cost to the taxpayer than if several different private companies were allowed competitive bidding.[201] Corrupt city officials will look after their own, and this corruption is enabled and exacerbated by the payment of property taxes.

Agency problems arise with property taxes, as those that utilize public goods without owning property are not subject to the tax. When I pay property taxes on my house and land, and then later enjoy the use of the public sidewalk to stroll to my favorite burger joint, I am using the goods that I paid for directly through taxes. If Jim from the next town over or Bob who lives in a local apartment also uses the sidewalk—potentially crowding me out—they are enjoying public works that I paid for while they incurred no costs of funding. Consider also the varying size of tax

149

payments made and the disproportionate funding of public services compared to the value received in return. When I pay X amount of dollars to the local government in the form of property tax on my modest home, I receive police "protection" in return. John Doe may have a much larger, much nicer home than I, and his property tax bill may be four times higher. Can it be said that he receives four times as much police protection as I do, with the police arriving at his house four times faster than they would to mine if we both dialed 911, or can it be more reasonably said that he receives the same amount of protection? Property taxes, like most all taxes, hit certain individuals harder than others, usually, the hardest hit are the ones demonized for needing to "pay their fair share," when it is actually they who pay most of the total tax amount collected.[202]

As property taxes are higher in some areas and lower in others, the effects on certain individuals can vary greatly depending on that individual's circumstances. Having highly valued property in a region with high property taxes can be extremely detrimental to a person who may not necessarily be wealthy. Retirees on fixed-income or those with low incomes will be disproportionately injured by higher property taxes if they own their own homes, but the same can be said of other taxes as well. Additionally, higher property taxes increase the cost of owning a home, penalizing those less well off and those looking to transition from renting to buying.[203]

Property taxes are highly political in nature, and they have significant effects on capital flows. Higher or lower property taxes will determine how land is used and how much of it is bought, sold, and owned. Like all taxes, property taxes provide incentives for people to behave in certain ways. In the United States, agricultural land is typically taxed less than residential or commercially zoned land.[204] As a result, people who own cows and horses will often build their enclosures from the edge of their

150

property to as close to their houses as possible in an effort to maximize the amount of agricultural land they own and minimize the acreage of residential land. Though cows may be happier with this arrangement, cow patties baking in the sun just outside the bedroom window will not be pleasant to the homeowner, and the fact remains that government has once again created an incentive for people to use their property in ways they might not otherwise have, making them worse off in their efforts to reduce their tax burden.

In my home state of Alabama, the property taxes still resemble their Victorian-era design. Being a core state of the old Confederacy, Alabama's political atmosphere at the time was greatly influenced by the wealthy, landed class. The gentry, looking out for their own interests and seeking to minimize the tax paid on their cotton-producing plantations and estates, were able to keep property taxes low through favorable legislation. Alabama still boasts low property taxes, while the local governments bridge the gap with higher than average sales taxes.[205] High sales taxes and low property taxes create incentives for capital to flow from consumption to real estate. Wealth and income that might have been spent on goods and services desired by consumers, hence making both consumer and producer better off and stimulating the economy by creating wealth, is instead channeled into property, as the tax rates are more favorable there. Although land and houses are cheaper in Alabama than in most states, they could be cheaper still if their prices were not being bid higher by capital flowing from higher-taxed consumption into lower-taxed property. Such a policy also greatly affects those without a house or land, mainly young people and impoverished people.[206] These individuals find themselves paying additional taxes on their weekly groceries, while they are unable to enjoy the break allocated to real estate owners, as they do not own property. Even though many of them will one day own property and enjoy the same reduced tax rate, their eventual owning of land will be delayed, as a larger proportion of their current incomes are consumed by the higher sales taxes.

Businesses also face property tax incentives. Since property taxes apply to commercial real estate as well as residential, businesses must include potential property taxes in their decisions on where to open new locations or expand existing ones. Local governments often provide strong tax incentives to businesses in the form of exemptions to convince the businesses to locate in their communities, bringing jobs and sales with them, thus creating two new revenue streams for the government in the form of occupational taxes and sales taxes.[207] These tax breaks offered to businesses in order to get them to locate in a specific region, or at least not to move out of that region, can cause companies to operate in an area where doing business is not economically efficient, but instead where they can get the most tax breaks. All of these taxes against wealth are economically destructive and should be reconsidered from the ground up.

PART III

QUID PRO QUO

8 Redistribution

"But let me offer you my definition of social justice: I keep what I earn and you keep what you earn. Do you disagree? Well then tell me how much of what I earn belongs to you - and why?"
- Walter Williams, 1987.[208]

Redistribution is a very polarizing issue. While many on both ends of the political spectrum argue in favor of or against the general redistribution of wealth and income, the vast majority of governmental activity already engages in redistribution, and its efforts are ever-increasing. From general redistribution of wealth from rich to poor, the concealed redistribution of wealth from poor to rich, or from specifically targeted redistribution from certain interest groups to others, the government employs legions of bureaucrats and administrators to entertain the efforts of lobbyists and work to achieve various redistribution ends.

When the government collects tax revenue, it uses that revenue on certain public goods which people have access to, but it also uses those tax dollars to directly bestow benefits to others or to certain interest groups for the purposes of increasing their welfare in the form of direct transfer payments. Transfer payments have been growing substantially as a proportion of government expenditures, and their growth has also been increasingly outpacing revenue to back them, forcing the government to increase its borrowing to finance the deficit.[209] Given the nature of the current progressive tax system, the wealthy as an interest group pay the vast majority of total taxes collected by government while redistribution programs are often directed at benefiting those worse off, and while this is mostly the case, it will be later shown how some programs actually work in reverse. The power of government is often used to benefit special interests at the expense of other groups and the public at large, and often government policies have consequences that far exceed their stated intent.

Intent

An often-cited justification for government is its ability to take from some and give to others, to act as a force that can level the playing field between rich and poor, enacting policies that strive to achieve equality between people, especially as it pertains to wealth and income. Although this power to redistribute wealth and income amounts to theft by definition, it has grown to become one of the principal functions of government.[210] There are some arguments in favor of such redistributive power worth mentioning, and these form the cornerstone of the scholarly debate advancing the notion that society needs more government force taking from some to give to others.

Societies that have too great a disparity in welfare between the few rich and the many poor can succumb to social upheaval and revolution. Advocates of government redistribution argue that it stands to reason that some measure of redistribution is desirable in order to foster more social harmony.[211] Another argument leans more on our morality. There will always be those that are too poor or too helpless, and we should be compelled by charitable nature to see that they are taken care of, or at least be compelled by shame to prevent their living situations from deteriorating further. Some egalitarians go so far as to assert that all economic inequalities should be erased, with all the wealth and resources equally divided among all.[212] Such a philosophical outcome is not only impossible but would cause irreversible damage to human progress going

156

forward.

Seizing all of the wealth and engaging in a single, grand redistribution scheme would be a one-trick pony. Resources intended for long-term productive use would be consumed in the name of economic equality, and the incentives to produce wealth going forward would be erased.[213] Advocates of this insanity and perhaps even the general public might be in favor of this policy, as short-termism convinces them that they are being helped now while blinding them to the future troubles, but governments would know that they cannot continue such a scheme in perpetuity. Instead, governments pursuing redistributive policies must be tactical in their execution, and they must only take enough to ensure that the promises they have made to their voters can be met without causing too much harm to the entrepreneurs who created the wealth. How much taken will be determined by the intent of the government takers.

While pursuing redistribution theoretically involves transferring resources from the well-to-do to those that are less fortunate, a difference of intent can have a different set of consequences. If the intent of redistribution is to achieve more income equality, a policy could be enacted that lowers everyone's income, with the rich having their income reduced by a greater proportion than the poor, but the policy will adversely affect the poor as their incomes are reduced as well. They will have more income equality compared with their rich peers, but will have less income, and will thus be made worse off. Likewise, a policy that raises everyone's income overall but perhaps raises the income of the rich by a greater percentage than the poor would result in the poor being made better off in terms of income, but income inequality would be increased. Too often people assume that policies aimed at achieving income equality simultaneously work to benefit the poor, but often such policies have trickle effects. By reducing the income of the wealthy, their incentives to engage in the activities that made them wealthy are taken away, and those activities are more often than not the efficient provision of goods and services to the marketplace at a lower cost or better quality than the competition. By going after these industrious individuals, the economy becomes less efficient due to their receding activity, and this will hurt the poor in the long run.[214]

On the other side of that coin is the law of diminishing marginal utility, stating that each additional unit of something brings less benefit to an individual than did the unit before it, and this includes money and income.[215] Suppose a homeless individual chances upon a $100 bill drifting in the wind. It lands at his feet and he picks it up, and he can now spend that money to fulfill his basic needs like food or shelter for the night. Suppose now that he finds a second $100 bill. Once again his welfare is increased, but the second $100 will bring less marginal wealth than his first. For people like Bill Gates of Microsoft, the marginal return of an additional $100 is so low that he may not even bother to pick one up if he found it. In a society such as this, the argument for redistribution states that it is practical to take some money from the wealthy and give it to the poor.[216] The poor will have immediate increases in their welfare while the rich will barely notice the loss of what was taken.

Through some redistribution, aggregate social welfare can be maximized, but only in the short-term, and an increase in aggregate social welfare will be more than offset by the long-term detrimental effects of societal institutions that endorse such a blatant violation of property rights, and such policies also tend to ignore individual preference.[217] Furthermore, the arbitrary quantity of redistribution necessary for maximizing aggregate social welfare on paper may be impossible to discover altogether because it involves so many variables and undefined concepts that are always in a state of continuous change. Crudely speaking, if for example the benefits to the recipients of redistribution are X, and

158

the loss of welfare to the wealthy individual who had wealth taken from him is -0.01X, utility is maximized when 100X is taken and redistributed.[218] Only after this goal is met will further confiscation of wealth harm the wealthy more than it does good to the poor, and this crude model assumes away the law of diminishing marginal returns. Furthermore, it remains undefined as to what "X" is exactly and how to discover it, and who is to say what it should be. Lastly, the costs of government administration are not included, and government activity will destroy wealth in the process of redistributing. With undefined variables and incongruousness, redistributing wealth to maximize social welfare may never be a possibility, and even if it were, it would likely take a different form than a redistribution of material wealth and income.

Although most people agree on policies that support the poor and are willing to pay taxes to fund social safety nets—with the disputes being to what extent the social safety net should be applied—they are reluctant to provide cash directly to the poor and downtrodden. Taxpayers tend to agree that society's worst-off cannot be trusted with direct cash payments, as these recipients will not wisely spend the money on essentials like food and housing, but instead on vice. Instead, taxpayers are more willing to engage in redistribution if the recipients receive goods and services in lieu of cash, as these will directly meet their needs without giving them the chance to repurpose the redistributed resources on drugs, prostitutes, and other iniquitous outlets.[219]

Even if maximizing social welfare through redistribution was both possible and practical, moral arguments must be made against the idea. If high-income earners are forced by the government to surrender a portion of their earnings to low-income earners, they must, therefore, work without receiving the fruits of their labor. Essentially they become the slaves of low-income earners up until the redistribution threshold is met, after which they are then permitted to work for themselves.[220] This policy punishes industrious individuals and by extension also punishes higher productivity work, while it simultaneously rewards lower productivity. When higher productivity is forced to allocate resources to lower productivity, scarce capital is not used as efficiently as it could otherwise be. Income left in the hands of he who earned it will be used in one of several ways: it will either be 1) invested, allowing capital to find its way to productive outlets, 2) saved, allowing entrepreneurs access to it in the form of loans through banking intermediaries which will then be used to fund small business activities in the local community or lent out to a potential home-buyer, etc., or 3) it will be spent on consumption. Many take issue with this final possibility.

How can we as a society allow low-income people to struggle while high-income earners purchase their third beach house? The answer is complex: first and foremost, it is immoral to take by force what rightfully belongs to someone, regardless of one's personal opinion on the disparity of those that have and the have-nots, provided that what was earned was earned through voluntary cooperation through free and consenting transactions.[221] Second, by taking income that the high-income earner would have spent, the individuals who would have received that income as earnings on the other side of his transactions are now deprived of their livelihoods. Since the large-scale implementation of the welfare state under President Lyndon Johnson's war on poverty in the 1960s, trillions of dollars have been transferred, yet low-income groups have been made worse off by these policies of redistribution, especially those that work in sectors that serve high-income earners as consumers.[222] If a high-income earner enjoys collecting sports cars, but his income is seized through taxation to satisfy redistribution requirements, he will no longer be buying as many cars as he otherwise would have. The auto manufacturers will produce less and be less profitable, and they will be unable to offer as many job opportunities to potential job seekers. Less productive companies imply workers with lower wages, and these workers will have less income to spend in order to satisfy their own wants and needs. Businesses they patronize will feel the effects as well, and the cycle continues down through the economy resulting in a situation where each dollar of private economic output lost does not grant a dollar in public economic benefit.[223]

A counter-argument will here be made by dissenters, such as former Vice-Chair of the Federal Reserve Alan Blinder, who will argue the following: if income is taken from a top earner who was going to spend it, and instead given to someone on the lower end of the spectrum to spend, aggregate consumption stays the same or is only ever so slightly diminished.[224] This is a fallacy that warrants exposure. For starters, wealth is consumed by the government during the process of redistribution, so while $100 may be taken from the top earner, perhaps only $50 or $60, or maybe even less, will reach the recipient, as a large portion of the wealth is sunk into administration costs and supporting a large government bureaucracy that oversees the transfer programs.[225]

A majority of empirical models suggesting otherwise largely ignore or understate the significant impact government will have on the net amount of wealth when acting as a facilitator of the transfers. The bottom line is that wealth is destroyed, and the recipient of the redistributed wealth cannot stimulate economic transactions to the degree the original owner of that income could prior to government involvement. This argument compares apples to apples, however, and one should also consider the apples to oranges scenario whereby wealth taken from a higher-income earner who would have *saved or invested* it is then redistributed to someone on the lower end who will *spend* it. When this happens, aggregate consumption is actually increased, providing a limited short-term boost to economic output as suppliers work to satisfy this increase in consumer demand. This short-term stimulus comes

161

at the expense of future generations, as resources are pulled away from investing and pushed into consumption, ensuring lower standards of living in the future than would exist if those resources had been allowed to find uses as capital.[226]

Proponents of redistribution will continue pleading and imploring the government to take more from high-income earners and redistribute to low-income earners. They will say that without having a government being able to take by force, there will not be enough charity to prevent the lowest income earners from living in squalor. While people would probably agree that it is undesirable for others to struggle financially in the land of plenty, few may be willing to actually do something about it that involves personal sacrifice. In order for a voluntary charity to work, the supply of charity must be able to meet the demand, and the demand will always be growing.[227] Those who believe that their lives would be improved with more material wealth will be quite willing to accept money as long as it flows to them. Meanwhile, those who are giving are only going to be willing to give so long as they believe that their charity is appropriately used, and also so long as they retain the "feel good" aspect of giving, or at least so long as they believe they are doing the right thing.[228] In short, the giving would die out long before the willingness to receive provided that the initial willingness to give was able to meet the demand in the first place. Even worse still, some potential givers who enjoy feeling good about giving may try to piggyback off the charity of others in order to capture that feeling without suffering the financial loss,[229] and making charity a public good provided by the government through the redistribution of wealth ensures that piggybacking becomes easier for those seeking to engage in such lewd behavior while crowding out more efficient private charity efforts.

Advocates for redistribution may take one final stab at selling the policy to skeptics. If income redistribution exists to shift income from higher to lower earners, higher earners become protected in the event they are met with an unfortunate change of circumstances. Should they lose their source of income and join the ranks of lower-tier earners, they will begin receiving subsidies that can help them recover.[230] Whether or not current high-income earners would agree that redistribution is desirable on these grounds is hard to assess without polling a large sample of them and projecting those findings on the entire class at large. Redistribution as a desirable policy could still be rejected on these grounds by the fact that those receiving benefits may grow comfortable in those benefits and choose not to strive to become more productive in order to break out of the welfare trap, especially if those benefits offer higher payouts than can be achieved by working and earning a wage.[231] The damage here is two-fold, as policies to redistribute wealth are more rigorously pursued, those that create the wealth have the incentive to create less, while those that receive the distributions have less of an incentive to join in the processes of its creation. Productive activity should always be encouraged by our institutions.

Redistribution has been in effect in the US for a long time. While some redistribution shifts resources from poor to rich or from special interest groups to other special interest groups, as will be seen later, the majority of income redistribution is intended to benefit the poor at the expense of the rich. As the government seizes the property of the well-off and gives it to those at the bottom of the spectrum, those that have their income taken from them are made worse off—even if only marginally so—yet those recipients may not always be better off.

In the 1980s video series adaptation of Milton Friedman's book *Free to Choose*, Economics professor Thomas Sowell appeared as a guest debater in the episode dealing with the rise of the welfare state and its fiscal shortcomings, and he made the argument that wealth redistribution and welfare are subsidies of individuals' failure. He stated that as people fail they are given benefits, and insofar as they succeed, those benefits are taken away.[232] So long as the recipient of distribution remains poor, his subsidies will continue. Should he gain a better job opportunity and see his income rise, he may actually make himself worse off by raising his income, as the loss of cash transfer benefits may not outweigh the gain in income, leaving him with less money than he had when unemployed or underemployed. With a higher income being reported, he could breach the minimum threshold by which he qualifies for benefits—and his payments would cease—while his new income may not provide him with the material welfare he once enjoyed as the beneficiary of redistribution.

Under these circumstances, this individual has the incentive to remain unemployed or underemployed, as well as to remain unproductive in order to keep his income suppressed enough to continue receiving benefit payments. People that choose to leave their position as beneficiaries of redistribution in order to become low-skilled workers will not only see their wealth level decrease, they will have to work for the money as well. While true that one could temporarily take the setback in order to gain a job opportunity so that he may one day gain valuable work experience to leverage into career growth later, fatalistic shortsightedness often prevails to dictate actions. The incentive to remain on the beneficiary rolls is too strong for many to resist, and benefiting from redistribution sadly becomes a multi-generational way of life for many families as higher levels of benefits act as a distinctive to work.[233] Milton Friedman proposed an interesting solution to this problem: the negative income tax, explained in chapter 5. Ideas such as these are needed to break the current welfare trap whereby people remain unemployed to continue collecting benefits, single mothers continue having babies to collect benefits, and those that are physically able pretend to be too impaired for work.

Politics

Once redistribution is decided upon by government actors and the property and income of private individuals seized, decisions must be made on how to allocate the newly acquired resources. As the welfare state grows and redistribution becomes a greater priority, more will be taken for the purposes of redistribution, and the payouts will grow larger. As the payouts grow, competing groups will fight harder to get a larger piece of the redistribution pie.[234] Unionists representing labor will lobby that a larger portion of the redistribution wealth should go to lower-income workers. Rent-seekers of certain economic sectors will want the wealth to come their way so they can remain profitable in the face of growing competition from abroad or from industry disruptions such as improved efficiency or the availability of a new substitute. This one is particularly interesting.

As business sectors struggle to keep pace in a changing economic landscape, economic theory tells us that the resources being used in this business are no longer being used productively, and they should be freed up for use elsewhere. The struggling business will argue the opposite. They will cite the jobs that will be lost if their company should go under, and they will appeal to nationalism and argue that "made in America" should be prioritized. They will further argue that consumers are somehow better off paying more for a smaller basket of goods, provided those goods come from the failing businesses. The struggling businesses will appeal directly to the government to receive taxpayer-funded subsidies so they can enjoy more profits. In many industries, it has become easier for inefficient companies to make more money lobbying the government for favors than it is for enhancing performance in the marketplace.[235]

The sugar industry in the United States is a perfect example

165

of this. The United States has restrictive tariffs in place against foreign imported sugar while it subsidizes the production of sugar domestically. The result is an artificially high price of sugar caused by government policies of wealth redistribution in order to satisfy the sugar industry lobbyists.[236] As the price of sugar reaches new highs, foodstuff companies look to sugar alternatives—such as high fructose corn syrup—as an ingredient to keep their products affordable and attractive to consumers. Without these subsidies, the sugar industry would be less profitable, and less sugar would be grown in the United States. Rather than focus on the jobs that would be lost, the focus should instead be on the opportunities that will arise by freeing up resources that were once tied down in the inefficient production of a product in which the United States lacks a global competitive advantage. Instead of redistributing wealth to sugar producers and allowing market forces to work, sugar could be imported at a much lower cost, and food and snack companies could return to using pure cane sugar in their products. The consumers would be much better off, and the resources once used in an inefficient process can be reallocated to something that is more efficient, raising standards of living for all Americans.[237] Corn producers also receive subsidies in the same manner as sugar producers, but the result is different. Unlike sugar, the United States possesses a climate and topography that is ideal for the crop, making the country the world's leading corn producer.[238] Whereas sugar can be grown abroad and imported for a much lower cost than growing it domestically, corn can be grown cheaply here, meaning that it is a crop in which the United States has a competitive advantage.

Although the United States already has a competitive advantage in the production of corn, the 1970s saw massive subsidies granted for corn producers, leading to widespread overproduction of the crop.[239] With so much corn being produced in excess of our ability to consume it, much is exported. Due to the competitive advantage the United States possesses in the production of corn but lacks in the production of sugar combined with the subsidies for each, the price of corn has fallen whereas the price of sugar has risen, and this is due to the fact that if market forces were allowed to function properly, sugar would be imported while corn would continue to be produced domestically. As a result of the subsidies and tariffs, corn syrup has taken the place of sugar as a leading ingredient in soft drinks and other products. In a case of sad irony, the United States produces so much corn due to the subsidies that if such a quantity was brought to market, the price would plummet to the point where many farmers would experience a financial loss. Looking out for the corn industry, the government even pays some farmers NOT to bring their corn to market, and instead either to destroy the product or—the more common scenario—to not grow it at all.[240] On the one hand, the government subsidizes corn production leading to more acres of land being used for an over-planting of the crop, and on the other hand, the government pays farmers not to grow it in order to guarantee a minimum profit margin on the corn actually grown.

Many Americans fail to understand the relationship between wealth redistribution in the form of subsidies and the products they buy on a regular basis. Continuing the example of the sugar and corn industries, rather than demanding the government to cease the subsidies, they will instead heap blame on the producers of soft drinks and candy, accusing them of using less healthy sugar substitutes in an effort to pick every penny out from the consumers' pockets while disregarding the negative health aspects of the sugar substitutes. Corporations will be accused of being immoral and heartless, and they will be blamed for America's rising obesity epidemic when in actuality it is the wealth redistribution from taxpayers to sugar and corn producers that is really to blame, and there are still further effects of this kind of wealth distribution that cause a misallocation of capital goods.

Once government officials give in to the pressure to redistribute wealth and grant subsidies, usually because they in turn are receiving endorsements, they will redistribute resources towards failing sectors of the economy to prop up businesses. For a while, the recipients will enjoy heightened profits. As resources are redistributed to them however, the cost of materials and capital goods used in those businesses will rise as their price is bid up via the subsidy dollars. Soon these special interest businesses will not be reaping the larger profits they once enjoyed when the subsidy was first granted, but instead will see their profits level out. Even with their excess profits evaporating due to the increased value of the capital goods going into the production of whatever these businesses are making, they will still be receiving the subsidies. Now, they will fight even harder to retain them, for losing them will spell imminent financial disaster.[241] They will once again cite all the jobs that will be lost should their businesses be allowed to fail, but nothing is ever said of the jobs that do not exist but otherwise would if only the resources that would have been used in their creation were not redistributed to inefficient market sectors. When the government subsidizes profits, the value of goods used in these businesses rises. If the value of these capital goods is higher in an inefficient sector with government subsidies than they are in an actual productive and efficient sector without subsidies, the resources will be horrendously misallocated. Nothing will be said of the three jobs that could have been created in the efficient sector because they are unseen and unrealized. What is seen is the one job that is saved.[242]

Like maggots on a rotting carcass, legions of government bureaucrats will assemble around the redistribution economy to handle the transfers and entertain the lobbyists' efforts. As these government employees entrench themselves in the network of redistribution, they have the incentive to do whatever they can to expand the status of their target markets, for their jobs and livelihoods depend on redistribution continuing as a policy. They also can expect their wages to rise as their respective governmental offices grow in power. If they handle more redistribution, they will argue that the responsibility they bear warrants more compensation. If it were not so tragic, one would call it blissfully comedic: thousands of government bureaucrats, young and old, strut down the streets of Washington D.C. every day wearing their clearance badges around their necks. Their jobs are to compete with each other to see the most resources allocated to their departments for redistribution purposes, and each of them will tell you that the entire economy would collapse if they were not there to hold it all together. It is waste on top of waste.

Case: Social Security

The Social Security program is currently the US government's largest redistribution initiative.[243] Many Americans have a general lack of understanding of Social Security and its functions. Some falsely believe that the program is a fund that accepts contributions from workers and then pays them in their old age in a similar manner as an annuity. It is important to note that Social Security does not hold—or even responsibly invest—the funds it receives from workers. Instead, current contributions are passed directly to recipients as current benefits which make the program little more than an ill-conceived, government-sponsored Ponzi scheme.[244] Worse still, congressional lawmakers have borrowing capabilities with the fund's cash reserves. Tempted by a political incentive to provide goodies now and leave the bill to future politicians, elected officials have seen to it that the cash reserves of Social Security are used to invest in—or more accurately, purchase—government debt in order to grant the government access to the funds, essentially creating yet another taxpayer liability.[245] Changing demographics are also adding pressure. As the nation's population grows older, the baby boomers are retiring and drawing from the system in increasing numbers. When Social Security started in the Great Depression era, its recipient to contributor ratio was comfortably sustainable, but changing demographics have consistently lowered the contributor to recipient ratio. At the beginning of the program, there were over 35 million covered workers and only 220,000 beneficiaries, a ratio of 159 to 1. The ratio has significantly trimmed down to a measly 2.8 to 1 and is still dropping.[246] Current estimates predict that the fund will not be able to meet its obligations within the next few decades.

Perhaps the greatest tragedy of this pending social experiment failure is the way it siphons vast amounts of wealth off an individual throughout his working life and then gives him relatively little by comparison when he reaches the withdrawal age in his 60's. Once he comes of age and begins his withdrawals, he is given a few hundred dollars per month for the remainder of his life. Many seniors rely on this income to avoid complete impoverishment, and that is often cited as a justification for Social Security, but I pose the question to the reader: if the government had not levied an additional tax against him from the age at which he held his very first job until the day he retired, would he not be substantially better off financially? If one were able to opt-out of Social Security and hypothetically invest the money that would have otherwise gone to Social Security taxes into mutual funds or exchange-traded funds on a monthly basis throughout his working life, his level of wealth at retirement age would be several times greater. As of 2019, 6.2% of an employee's salary during his working life is robbed of him by the horrendous Federal Insurance Contributions Act Tax (FICA).[247] Imagine if over 6% of the entirety of your life's income could have been invested into a mutual fund with high-yield dividends and compounding interest instead of a low-return, worn-out safety net. Proponents of Social Security will argue that some people are not fiscally responsible enough to save, and Social Security ensures that these people at least have some level of income to rely on. To this, a free thinker would respond that people should have the liberty to lead their lives as they see fit, and they should also have to bear the consequences if those decisions were not wise and lead to poor results. Creating a society where people are taken care of if they choose not to prepare for retirement only encourages people to not make those preparations.[248]

Lastly—and most importantly—contributors to the Social Security scheme have no say in the matter. They never voluntarily entered into an agreement to take care of retirees in the form of monthly payments on the promise that they will one day be taken care of themselves. Attempts to resist paying Social Security taxes will bring government enforcers to one's doorstep. There is no choice. If given freedom of choice, most people—especially the young who have their whole working lives ahead of them—would likely opt out of paying into Social Security, forgo whatever benefits they would have been due at old age, and then the entire system would instantly collapse. There is a reason that Social Security is mandatory, and that reason is that the program is so terrible that only through force of arms and submission of the people can it be conducted. And even so, the program is still projected to fail. As the fund is bled dry and the Ponzi scheme collapses, the government will either raise taxes or cut benefits, both of which will cause protests and grumbling. The government is also relying heavily on certain demographic factors and subterfuge—such as raising the eligibility age—to keep the program afloat for as long as it can, all while selling the idea that Social Security remains necessary to take care of our elderly. Ironically, this argument runs counter to government monetary policy which is to inflate the dollar to encourage exports and domestic spending.[249] Long has the Federal Reserve made it its policy to inflate the dollar, and this hurts pensioners, Social

Security recipients, and fixed-income retirees the most—in other words, the elderly.

Since Social Security is not a savings account or annuity, but instead a direct Ponzi scheme-type arrangement, the resulting redistribution takes place in real-time. Current workers are taxed, and those taxes go directly to eligible recipients. Since the funds are not held or invested—aside from being occasionally looted by politicians via debt purchasing—but instead paid out to recipients, Social Security can only continue so long as future workers can be counted on to continue paying into the system. As the ratio of recipients to contributors approaches 1:1 and beyond, threats to the viability of the arrangement emerge which must be addressed to ensure the continuity of the program.

The major changes to Social Security that can be made to keep it functional are quite unpopular to discuss but will become necessary as the program becomes more distressed. The first solution would be to raise taxes. Raising taxes will generate a quick boost to the contributions, but as taxes increase, the incentive to work decreases. Workers on the margin may decide to be less productive to offset the higher taxes, and economic efficiency will decrease. An increase in taxes will hurt low-income earners more than high-income earners as well. Although the system is currently set up for high-income earners to pay more in taxes as a proportion of their income, they are more able to part with money before their standard of living suffers. Raised taxes on low-income workers will force them into difficult trade-off situations before their high-income peers.

The second course of action would be to slash benefits. Cutting benefits would save Social Security from some of its liabilities and relieve the pressure it faces, but this would once more hurt low-income people disproportionately. Poor individuals have a heavier reliance on Social Security than do wealthy people, and wealthy individuals would hardly notice the reduced benefits, as they are likely also drawing from retirement accounts, passive income vessels, hard assets like land and rental properties, etc. Slashing Social Security benefits would cause the low-income dependents into difficult situations, while the wealthy would merely be inconvenienced.

Alternatively, the government can raise the Social Security eligibility age. This would buy time for the program as well as generate extra revenue; people who would otherwise already be drawing from the system would instead be contributing to it for a few more years as they close out the difference between the old and new eligibility ages. Once more, low-income earners are hurt the most by this policy, just as they are unfairly affected by the policy in its current state. Social Security is much of a game of chance. One can work his entire life and pay into the system, finally reaching the age of eligibility and to make his first withdrawal. If he were to live another three hundred years after reaching eligibility age and draw Social Security payments each month, the program would come under heavy strain by this individual, as his contributions over the years would not outweigh his withdrawals. Instead, if he were to die immediately upon reaching the withdrawal age, Social Security would be the big winner, as one spent his entire life paying into it but took nothing out.

In our world today, high-income individuals tend to live longer than low-income individuals. Higher earners can more readily afford better dietary options whereas low-income earners must rely more on processed food that fits their budget. In old age, high-income earners can more easily afford healthcare and can pay for it for more extended periods of time, whereas poorer individuals cannot. Since wealthier people are expected to live longer than poor people, yet both have the same eligibility age to begin withdrawing Social Security payments, it can be expected that the wealthy individual will draw more out of the program than his less wealthy counterpart.[250] Even though the wealthy have paid more into Social Security on the net than low-income people, the fact that they are expected to live longer—thus make more monthly withdrawals—coupled with the fact that Social Security tax harms low-income earners more than it does the wealthy makes Social Security overall a redistribution program whereby wealth flows from the poor to the rich, all while giving the government another source of taxpayer funds to borrow against and enrich themselves with the necessary administration of such a large program.

Social Security should be abolished, or at least privatized and made voluntary. Current dependents should be eased out of the system and those that have not yet begun paying into it should be given the option not to. Social Security cannot be sustained into the distant future and will eventually require a massive and recurring taxpayer bailout. Reform and repeal are crucial, though highly unlikely to be discussed with any degree of seriousness until the day of reckoning due to how unpopular the politician will be who attempts to make any proposals. Politicians will continue borrowing from the cash reserves to fund their current public expenditures, leaving the problem for a future day, and it is our children who will eventually pay the price.

9 Healthcare

"When we give government the power to make medical decisions for us, we in essence accept that the state owns our bodies."
- Ron Paul, 2002.[251]

Healthcare is a broad term that encompasses a substantial portion of economic output in the United States, and it has been growing as a percentage of GDP. There are many conceptions of healthcare floating about, but they all boil down to the fact that like other aspects of the economy, healthcare is nothing more than a collection of goods and services provided to consumers—and produced and distributed by suppliers—just like other goods and services, only now pertaining to health and medicine.

We do not have a free market in healthcare in the United States, nor do we have a fully nationalized system either. We have a mixed market with both private suppliers handling some aspects and the government handling others. This chapter will take a more extensive look at why we have a mixed system, the rationales behind why government plays such a large part in the provision of healthcare, and offer a brief analysis of the detrimental effects of government involvement along with hypothetical alternatives to fully privatize healthcare and create a more customer-focused and efficient market.

Government involvement in healthcare dates back to early civilizations. The ancient Romans for instance would employ architects to build aqueducts and sanitation systems such as public latrines in order to enhance a city's overall hygiene level, thus preventing the spread of contagion which could cause civil unrest.[252] In more recent times, the government has taken a more personal role. Many today argue that the government should not only oversee general health initiatives for the population at large, but should also have direct control over every health aspect of a person's life. Like most government initiatives to infiltrate market processes, the original proposition remained limited in scope but has morphed into something new and enormous. One original key idea for government involvement in healthcare is the thought that the government can protect the consumer by bridging any gaps in information asymmetry. Through government initiative, people can potentially be better equipped to identify qualified doctors, and they can determine which drugs are safe to use, essentially creating a paternalistic framework whereby the government safeguards the health and wellbeing of its citizens. Later, the notion that the government should protect people evolved into the idea that it should provide for them as well, especially regarding the poor. Their inability to afford healthcare has aroused anger in those that see it as unfair, while healthcare is being increasingly designated as a "human right," much like rights to life and property. Critics attack the current system and free-market proposals, arguing that healthcare is treated as a commodity that only the affluent may enjoy.[253] In response to this political pressure, the government has taken a more active role in providing healthcare to the poor and elderly over the last several decades, while still the people largely demand even more action.

Before going forward, it is important to pause and consider the idea of healthcare as a right. Healthcare is a privilege, and most certainly not to be considered as any type of natural or civil right. Healthcare is a service provided by people who work jobs for the benefit of themselves and their families; it is their product which they offer for sale, as there is a strong demand for it. To imply that one has a right to healthcare is to imply that one has a right to the

176

product of someone's labor, regardless of what that may be. French economist Thomas Piketty disagrees. He writes:

> For education and health, there is real equality of access for everyone regardless of income (or parents' income), at least in principle. Modern redistribution is built around a logic of rights and a principle of equal access to a certain number of goods deemed to be fundamental. At a relatively abstract level, it is possible to find justifications for this rights-based approach in various national political and philosophical traditions. The US Declaration of Independence (1776) asserts that everyone has an equal right to the pursuit of happiness. In a sense, our modern belief in fundamental rights to education and health can be linked to this assertion, even though it took quite a while to get there.[254]

This comedic misinterpretation of the Declaration of Independence by an alleged industry-leading expert explains the difficulty in convincing ordinary people why healthcare is not a right. The founding fathers believed that everyone should have the right to pursue their goals and ambitions provided they do not inhibit others' pursuit of theirs. They believed that all have the right to pursue happiness, but none are required to supply it to others as an entitlement. Seldom is a compelling argument offered to justify why healthcare, in particular, should be a right, but not other products of people's labor. Why should not pest control also be a "human right?" Does not everyone have the right to live in a termite-free home? Should not car repair be a right as well since everyone needs their cars to function properly in order to drive around? Thomas Piketty believes education and health care are fundamental goods, and by that virtue should be supplied by the state as a right to all. But who is to define what "fundamental" means, and where does this authority come from? Does the authority come from Buddha, the flying spaghetti monster, or some other deity? Why is Piketty's opinion to determine what fundamental rights are superior to anyone else's, and what if two people disagree and what a right should be? When privately produced goods and services that are not rights are arbitrarily deemed to be entitlements, only through force can they be brought to market as such. Declaring as rights things that are in fact not rights is one of the many ways in which people's true rights are violated.

The argument that healthcare should be a right is mostly emotionally charged, as images are conjured up of sick people dying when they could have otherwise had life-saving treatment if only they had more cash. The argument in favor of healthcare as a right implies that no one should have to die from being too poor to afford medical treatment. Two considerations are to be made: the first being that if I know my health will be looked after by the state—hence taxpayers and not myself—I will have the incentive to be more reckless with my health. Since I will not be directly paying for healthcare, I will be far more likely to use it when I would not have otherwise had I been the one paying for it. It is no coincidence that those already on government-provided medical programs take much more frequent trips to hospitals, while those that actually have to pay for their care take less.[255] If everyone is offered "free" care as a right, demand will rise dramatically as everyone rushes off to the hospitals for the most minor of health issues. Second, nationalizing healthcare removes market forces that serve crucial functions in allocating scarce resources. Without a profit/loss system, the ability to compete for doctors and medical professionals based on pay, and without a direct supplier-consumer relationship, the quality and availability of healthcare will decline.

The United Kingdom is a perfect example of this. Excessive wait times, exuberant costs passed onto the taxpayer, and a severe shortage of doctors plague the country's medical industry.[256] Most doctors in the UK are foreigners, as the nationalized system fails to adequately attract a sufficient number of British doctors.[257] With all of the problems that arise by government intrusion into the healthcare marketplace, why is it that some people continue advocating for even more government control, aside from the intellectually-bankrupt arguments that are often strictly emotional? The answer lies in the original reason for government involvement, as people believe that an expansion of the original mandate can bring benefits on a much larger scale.

In some regards, healthcare and education have similarities. If I am single with no kids in the school system, I do not directly benefit from the public provision of education. I do benefit from living among an educated populace. Likewise, if I do not get sick often and rarely use the healthcare system, I still benefit largely from living among healthy people. If people generally are not sick, there is a smaller chance that I will get sick. If people's pre-existing conditions are treated, they will be productive members of society, making available to me additional trading partners, enhancing my own welfare and standard of living. These indirect positive benefits ascribed to me from my society having a healthy populace justify to some degree my bearing some of the costs, even if I do not directly consume healthcare, but these costs must be covered by my voluntary cooperation, and not through the force of arms of government coercion.

By far, the two most expansive and most expensive traces of government involvement in the American healthcare system are Medicare and Medicaid, the former primarily designed to provide healthcare to the elderly, and the latter being designed to provide healthcare to the poor. Medicare is funded through earmarked funds taken from the paychecks of working Americans, much like a special tax and not too different from Social Security.[258] Current payers into the system are funding current withdrawals, a situation only sustainable so long as that which is taken out is less than that which is put in. With the rapidly aging population in the United States as the Baby Boomers ease their way into retirement, questions are now arising concerning Medicare's financial future. As healthcare costs have risen over the past decades, so too has the tax rate used to fund the Medicare program, especially in the last decade as the government takes larger strides into transforming the healthcare industry from a mixed economy to a command economy.[259] As the costs of the program continue rising due to changing demographics and rising healthcare costs in general, drastic changes will need to be made in order for the program to remain solvent. Either taxes will have to continue rising, benefits will have to be cut, eligibility requirements will have to be made more restrictive, or some combination of these will be needed in order for the program to avoid going bankrupt.

Medicaid is a healthcare program available to low-income individuals who cannot afford or do not have access to private insurance. Generally speaking, the program is designated to aid the needy and downtrodden; however, the system is very susceptible to abuse and fraud on an individual level, as people can easily feign disability or hardship to enroll. Like Medicare, Medicaid has seen rising costs over the years. The program is primarily provided through individual state governments but is also largely funded through the federal government.[260] Since state governments also contribute to its funding, it is a joint-funded program, but a larger portion of the federal funds is allocated to the poorest states, having the effect of taxpayers in some parts of the country paying the healthcare costs of people in other parts. This is also true at the state level, as Medicaid redistributes wealth from higher-income counties to lower-income counties.[261] While the states have some degree of leniency and control over determining certain eligibility requirements and which health conditions will be covered, the program is still mandated by the federal government, often drawing complaints from the states as the program is increasingly becoming an unsustainable burden on state finances. The situation has become a breeding ground for fraudulent practices. While states oversee their own individual Medicaid programs, the federal government only reimburses a part of the expenses, thereby creating an incentive for states to exaggerate their expenditures to receive larger paybacks.[262]

Universal Coverage

Despite the already extensive governmental oversight in the healthcare system, there are still calls for more involvement. Many desire the government to assume complete control over the production and provision of healthcare, and in effect adopt a single-payer system. The moral argument for why universal healthcare coverage should not be implemented has been briefly expanded upon, but there are pragmatic arguments against the concept as well that should be considered. Many desire universal coverage on the grounds that it will be "free." Clearly, there is no such thing as a free lunch. Universal healthcare would be paid for indirectly through significantly higher taxes, or government issuance of additional debt, making healthcare a state-provided service like education and police protection.

The image of the poor and downtrodden suffering from easily-curable diseases due to a lack of wealth and access to care tugs on our emotional heartstrings. The pursuit of universal healthcare is an attempt to ensure that the currently uninsured have access to care, but one should take a deeper look into the characteristics of those individuals that this applies to. First of all, a disproportionate number of uninsured are relatively young and healthy. Before the passing of the Affordable Care Act, upwards of

30% of the nation's uninsured were between the ages of 19 and 29, even though this group represented approximately 17% of the population.[263] A few of these individuals were uninsured by choice, as the cost of becoming insured did not outweigh their individual health risks.[264] The Affordable Care Act removed all semblance of choice and mandated that all citizens of the United States must carry a health insurance policy or take a financial penalty for lacking one. This stayed in effect for several years at the federal level and had its legality questioned and challenged in courts. Although the fee no longer stands at the federal level, many states have decided to take over and implement their own fees for not having health insurance.[265] For those that truly cannot afford health insurance, imposing a fine on them for lacking an ability to pay will not help alleviate their plight; on the contrary, it will just make their situation more difficult, as they will have even fewer resources with which to purchase health insurance after a financial penalty has been extracted from them.

The underlying idea behind universal healthcare is that people's medical needs should be taken care of by the state. People allegedly deserve to go about their daily lives unconcerned with health risks—be they general issues or unique to them as individuals—and not worrying about unexpected medical expenses because they live under a system that offers healthcare to everyone free of charge as an innate right. What they do not understand is that this system is one that compels everyone by force to pay into the collective pool which will lead to inferior health services rendered in reduced supply. The belief in universal health coverage in contemporary politics is a growing threat to our way of life. Its implantation will lead to higher costs, reduced care, few practicing medical professions, and real consequences for patients. The growing belief that the state has a responsibility to provide medical care to citizens, much the same as it is a father's responsibility to look after the welfare of his children, blinds people to the realities and negative side effects of the policy. Clamoring for universal coverage may be a relatively new demand by a growing number of people opposed to free markets, but people have been advocating for government involvement in the health industry in other ways for a long time.

Pharmaceutical Drugs

In, *Free to Choose*, economist Milton Friedman elaborates on the purpose, founding, and functions of the Food and Drug Administration. Any drug on the market today must pass FDA approval and inspection prior to its being sold to consumers. The idea here is that the consumers need government protection from nefarious pharmaceutical companies that would distribute cheap and potentially unsafe drugs to us with horrible side effects if they were allowed to. This rationale ignores the notion that companies who kill their customers cannot expect consistent repeat business. Nonetheless, we now see the benefits of having safe medicine emerging from government oversight in healthcare: people can consume drugs prescribed by their doctors knowing that the drugs have already passed inspection and that side effects will not be experienced that are not already disclosed. So what is the problem here? With such a high degree of government oversight in drug administration, there are massive—and even horrific—unseen costs that go unaccounted for in the larger healthcare debate. Patients everywhere are suffering and dying because they do not have access to potentially life-saving drugs that the FDA has either not approved of yet or has already banned. Having a drug pass through the FDA is a lengthy process. The FDA will test and test again under countless trials to ensure that all potential side effects of a given drug become known. While this is going on, people in need of the drug are having to go without.[266] Consider the following scenario: hundreds of people have a terminal disease that may or may not be cured by a new drug that is slowly moving through the approval process. While these people wait for years for the drug to become available to them, more and more succumb to the fatal effects of the disease. Because their deaths occurred naturally and were spread out over time, they become mere statistics. The drug is never put under public scrutiny since it was never consumed.

Now consider the other scenario where the drug is rushed to market without undergoing all the possible trials to discover all the side effects. If the drug were to cure several hundred people but cause immediate death to some others, there would be a public outcry. The media would demonize the pharmaceutical company responsible for releasing an unsafe product in order to capitalize on people's fatal diseases. The media and others would not focus on the lives saved by the drug that would have otherwise been lost had the drug been withheld, but would instead focus solely on the lives lost to the drug's immediate side effects –lives that would have been eventually lost to the disease.[267] What can be done about this? The simple answer is: let the market decide.

Whenever a prototype drug is under development, it should be made readily available to consumers with varying degrees of marketability. Some drugs will be marked as fully tested, making them safe for all consumers and appealing to those that are more risk-averse. Others can be marked as "under development," or "trials ongoing," making their effectiveness and side effects somewhat unknown, but still allowing the drug to be available to consumers who either do not have the time to wait for successful clinical trials or are so uncomfortable in their suffering that they are willing to accept a higher level of risk. Still, other drugs could be marked as purely experimental, with their side effects and effectiveness highly unknown. These would appeal to individuals who simply do not care about the risk or who are so short on time and so adversely affected by an illness that they are ready to throw a Hail Mary.[268] In any of the above cases, products are available to consumers, and consumers are free to choose based on their needs and desires. The reduced government oversight would diminish healthcare costs, and medical malpractice suits would go down as well, further applying downward pressure on the cost of medical care.

One of the major contributors to high healthcare costs is Americans' eagerness to file lawsuits in the name of medical malpractice. This lawsuit trigger-happy mentality forces physicians to pay extremely high premiums for medical practice insurance, and these costs trickle down to the patients. If prescribed drugs were available to consumers in more broad categories ranking from risky and experimental to safe and tested, with consumers able to choose based on their own preferences, they will have less with which to fault the medical professionals when side effects are experienced. In today's world, prescribing an FDA approved drug to a patient and declaring with confidence that there will be no side effects, only to have the patient become the one statistical anomaly that develops unforeseen side effects, will inevitably result in expensive litigation. Removing government oversight from drugs is just one way to reduce healthcare costs. Removing it from the health insurance business is another.

Health Insurance

Insurance is an interesting concept in financial engineering. Essentially, insurance is a way to reduce risk by pooling that risk with others and then paying a premium for the arrangement. The farmer who relies on his crops for his livelihood can reduce his risk by purchasing insurance against crop failure, which would pay him a predetermined sum in the event such failure occurs. Homeowners do the same thing when they purchase flood and fire insurance. The sudden loss of a house would be financially devastating to most families, so it is worth a monthly premium payment for most individuals to pool that risk with other homeowners and insure the houses. Some of the earliest examples of insurance involve ancient merchant vessels in the classical era. If you as a merchant of the ancient times own a single ship, or if you do not own a ship but own the cargo being carried on the ship, and then were to lose your property to pirates en route, you would experience a total loss. However, if you had a 10% ownership stake in 10 different ships, total ownership would remain the same, but the risk would be spread among many vessels so that the sudden loss of one would not cause bankruptcy. Likewise, if you as a merchant split your cargo among several different ships, the risk would be spread and in this way, a person can insure himself.[269]

Insurance made its way to healthcare, and for good reason. Should a person suffer an unexpected injury and is no longer able to work, he would be cut off from his livelihood. Paying monthly insurance premiums ensures that he will receive a payout in the event the insured event happens, allowing him not to have to endure financial hardship he would otherwise experience if he was not insured. Similarly, one can purchase insurance against illness or developing certain diseases. Having such insurance covers a person's expenses when he or she visits the hospital or becomes sick. Due to evolutionary trends in the health industry, the cost of insurance has been rising—as has the cost of healthcare—to the point where many Americans are opting for the highest deductible plans they can obtain, or they are dropping out of the system altogether.[270] Even with insurance, a visit to the hospital can set a person back financially with such debt that many are instead choosing to avoid hospitals altogether. As the costs of ambulance rides increase, people are relying on alternatives such as Uber, or driving themselves if they can manage, which pose safety hazards for all.[271] People have medical insurance premiums deducted from their regular paychecks, but still avoid the hospitals, thereby omitting benefits they pay for. The question then becomes: why are health insurance costs rising?

Insurance is most efficient when it acts as a limited financial arrangement between those willing to be paid in order to bear risk, and those willing to pay to have risk removed. In the current insurance landscape, we have introduced new parties and entities to the transaction. Health insurance is provided to us, not by speculators who have an incentive to ensure that only as much risk is insured that is desired, but instead by third-party health insurance companies whose layers of bureaucratic procedures and government-imposed regulations interfere with the insurance process and act as unnecessary intermediaries. Rather than take on the necessary function of health risk speculators for voluntary clients, the government has regulated the industry to the point where mandates are so extensive that the entire character of the insurance business has been transformed.[272]

For starters, the US government has mandated that all citizens are now required by law to carry insurance. This violates the rights of those who would be willing to pass on insurance, and it creates a two-fold problem with regards to health insurance costs. The first being that insurance companies no longer have a need to convince people who would otherwise forgo insurance that they need it. These people are now captive consumers, required by law to buy the product. The second issue is that by requiring everyone to consume some minimum amount of a product, with that amount being determined by the government, there is an increased demand for the product which drives up its price.

Next, we move on to the agency issues. Paying insurance companies, either directly or through wage deductions, and then having those insurance companies pay our medical expenses changes the way we consume healthcare from how we would if we just paid for our expenses directly. When we go to the hospital under the current system, we pay out-of-pocket for some minimum amount (the deductible), and then the insurance company covers the rest, subject to negotiation with the health service provider. Up until our deductible is met, we try to economize our healthcare. If we are not to meet the deductible on a given medical requirement, we desire only the healthcare we truly need. Say for example you are visiting your physician for a regular checkup and are paying out-of-pocket. After your checkup is complete, the doctor may ask: "Since you're here, would you like to be tested for prevention of disease XYZ?" You would then be faced with a cost-benefit analysis.

To determine whether or not the benefits of preventative healthcare is worth the cost, one should consider the odds of contracting the disease in question. If those odds turned out to be 0.0001% of contracting the disease without the preventative healthcare, but the costs amounted to several thousand dollars in order to be tested, you would likely determine that the cost is not worth it, and would decline the doctor's offer to consume additional healthcare. If however you met your deductible during the regular checkup, and anything extra is now covered by insurance, the additional cost to you is zero regardless of how minuscule the benefits are. Since the personal cost has now been reduced to zero, you have little reason to decline the additional healthcare. From the physician's side of things, he is able to bill your insurance for all services performed, so he has a great incentive to provide you with far more healthcare than you actually need. With his incentive to oversupply you with care, and your lack of incentive to refuse anything offered after the deductible has been met, the overall amount of healthcare consumed will increase across the board, and costs are passed on to insurance companies who are not directly involved in the patient-doctor relationship.[273]

As healthcare costs are increased by heightened demand, insurance companies raise their premiums and reduce their benefits, passing the costs onto the consumers. So when next time you are at the doctor's office and he suggests additional services followed by the mantra that the services are "free" to you since insurance will cover it, remember that there is no such thing as a free lunch, and you will eventually bear the costs in some way or another. The healthcare professionals will make money, the insurance companies will remain profitable, and you will be left in the wind with higher insurance premiums due to increased healthcare demand.

Government

There are four parties to consider with regard to how healthcare is consumed in the US: you as the consumer, the physicians and medical professionals as the suppliers, the insurance companies as the intermediaries, and the government as the referee. Recall how the insurance companies and the physicians have a profitable arrangement whereby the physicians oversupply and overcharge, and the insurance companies charge consumers higher premiums in order to pay the hospitals for that excess supply. You as the consumer have the incentive to change the system whereby you can have access to better care at lower prices, while they have the incentive to keep things as they are, creating a conflict of interest. Due to the highly regulated nature of the healthcare industry, The government—not the free market—is the vessel through which change in the healthcare industry takes place. On the one hand, politicians recognize your pain and desire your vote, so they preach reform and talk of how they will make healthcare more affordable—usually through populist rhetoric that if enacted would actually make costs soar—but nevertheless sounds appealing to the average voter so long as no one does too much research into the issue. On the other hand, politicians also need financing for their campaigns, and they accept that the resources provided to them by the healthcare industry lobbyists are necessary. Furthermore, the healthcare industry will fight much harder to resist change, while people's ability to request change is far more limited. As a result, the healthcare industry and insurance companies carry the day, and they use the government as an instrument to maintain the current system at the consumer's expense.[274]

The solutions to the healthcare problem in the US are rather straightforward: remove the force of government and replace it with free-market mechanics. By allowing market forces to work, costs will be lowered, and people will get more of what they need at prices they can more easily afford. By having states remove their stipulations that everyone must have health insurance or face a financial penalty if they lack insurance, people who genuinely do not want insurance coverage or do not consume enough healthcare to justify purchasing a policy will opt-out, lowering the aggregate demand for healthcare and subsequently lowering its cost for those that stay in. Additionally, the government can abandon other anti-consumer stances, allowing consumers to shop across state lines for their health insurance, ensuring that they have more access to the policies they want. Good policies offered by superior companies will be more highly sought after while the inferior insurance companies will lose business. If consumers are not captive, resources can go to their best uses, and the best services will force out the bad, improving the marketplace.[275]

The above are just some preliminary and even modest suggestions for healthcare insurance reform, but more radical reform is also needed, and it stems from the fundamental root of insurance in general. Insurance is an agreement between two primary parties: the speculator willing to bear the risk and the insured who is willing to pay others to take the risk for him. Insurance is designated to provide payments to the insured in the event their unforeseen or insured events come to pass. Most health expenses do not have these characteristics. In fact, most health expenses are both predictable and common among everyone.

Pregnancies and deliveries, routine check-ups throughout one's life, and elderly care are predictable medical expenses, yet they are insured. Having insurance against regular and predictable occurrences defies the very nature of insurance and introduces those third parties with their high administrative costs and incentives to use the government to profit at the consumer's expense.

We must separate and distinguish the two main forms of medical expenses from each other: that which is common and predictable, and that which is unforeseen and meets the criteria of risk-bearing events. Regarding the former, routine healthcare expenses must be treated like all other goods and services consumed, not subject to insurance, and paid for directly by the consumer. Should this come to pass, consumers will have more incentive to consume healthcare wisely, avoiding unnecessary consumption, and lowering costs. Physicians will not be able to over-prescribe medication as easily since insurance is no longer picking up the tab, and they will have more incentive to supply the best care to their customers—the patients—as they do not wish to lose business to competing hospitals that do a better job of satisfying patient needs. Under this system healthcare costs would be lower, freeing up resources to be used for the actual insurable events, such as catastrophe insurance to cover accidents, physical dismemberment, sudden and unforeseen illness, and other healthcare expenses which cannot be predicted. These events will be treated the same as insurance against property, where the insured is willing to pay to have the risk removed, but still has the freedom to abstain if he feels the costs are not worth the benefits. Certain employers and other organizations may have their own, private stipulations requiring that their affiliates have insurance, much the same as many mortgage underwriters require property insurance before underwriting a mortgage loan, but it is not the place of the government to insert itself in the healthcare industry with its costly and wasteful Medicare/Medicaid programs along with its increasing encroachments on individual choice, mandating that everyone must carry an insurance policy regardless of his risk tolerance and preferences. Those involvements interfere with free-market mechanics that would align incentives in such a way that both consumers and suppliers of healthcare operate in ways that benefit all involved parties to the greatest extent possible and in as most efficient manner as possible, not to mention the moral argument against government involvement in healthcare dealing with freedom of choice, the practical argument stating that government ensures less healthcare is available and at higher costs and lower quality, or even the civic argument in which one could make the case that government in healthcare is well in excess of its constitutional mandate. The solutions for fixing healthcare in the US are many, but they can all be summarized as follows: remove government from the equation and let the free market work.

10 Education

"In short, some of the least qualified students, taught by the least qualified professors in the lowest quality courses supply most American public school teachers...That educators who have repeatedly failed to do what they are hired to do, and trained to do, should take on sweeping roles as amateur psychologists, sociologists, and social philosophers seems almost inexplicable — except that they are doing it with other people's money and experimenting on other people's children."
- Thomas Sowell, 1992.[276]

In the early days of the United States, education was largely privatized. As time passed, the state took on an increasingly more involved role in subsidizing and providing education to the point where today, education is one of the larger areas of public expenditure on the state and local level.[277] As the state became more involved in education, the US witnessed a rise in overall education levels among the general population.[278] With schools springing up out of the ground at the taxpayers' expense paired with compulsory laws requiring children to be enrolled in school, it is no wonder that there are far more high school diploma holders today than there were in decades prior. More may not necessarily mean better, however, as the provision of education is becoming increasingly burdensome on local and state governments. Costs per student have dramatically risen over the last few decades, as have administrative and overhead costs.[279] Lobbyists and lawmakers engage in schmoozing and dealing in order to ensure that certain subjects are taught, certain books are used, and certain zoning laws are passed. Indeed, as the government becomes more involved in education, costs will rise and bureaucracy will grow.[280] Evidence suggests that just because the state spends more now on education than it ever has in the past, results may not improve. Education levels and the success of students are not as correlated with the amount of financial resources committed to them as the politicians and lobbyists would have you believe. In short, more public spending on education does not result in a more highly educated population.

The increase in public spending on education can be explained in many different ways. Schools are integrating new technologies now more than they ever have in the past, and more financial resources are required to ensure that schools have the latest science lab equipment or computers in the library.[281] Schools have been decreasing their class sizes, implying that more teachers are necessary to teach the same amount of students—or in other words, more input is required for the same output, causing a rise in cost.[282] Teachers' unions and established interest groups are becoming more assertive in their demands, forcing costs up, and finally, schools have been engaging more in additional spending on pursuits unrelated to academics, such as elaborate sports programs and the hiring of non-teaching staff than they had in decades passed; and given how generally unprepared the average American high school graduate is for the "real world," one cannot help but question whether or not that fourth athletic workout room or the hiring of an ineffective guidance counselor is a good use of public funds.[283]

As public spending on education increases without a corresponding increase in results, the public becomes skeptical at political proposals to divest further financial resources into the hole. They surmise that the last batch of money did not improve things—nor did the one prior—so why should this new proposed spending spree be any different? American schools are falling behind, and government attempts to forcefully yank it forward tend to make matters worse. Horrific governmental policies like "No Child Left Behind," and newer teaching curriculum such as the "Common Core" math system ensure that the quality of education is reduced to its lowest common denominator. With public schools appearing to engage each other in a race to the bottom, more parents consider private education to ensure their children are not being set up to fail. Some argue that privatized education creates unnecessarily high levels of inequality, as it is unfair for students who do not have the opportunity to attend private institutions.[284] Below are just some of the more common arguments for public education versus privatized education.

Public Education

Unlike national defense or an interstate highway system, education cannot be considered a public good by definition. Education is a good that can easily exclude individuals from its consumption, and it cannot be jointly consumed either.[285] Unlike two individual citizens who are living in the United States at a given time that both simultaneously enjoy the benefits of national defense or can both drive their cars on the interstate at the same time, no two individuals can receive the same education. The education that I received is exclusive to me, and its impressions on my life cannot be shared by another. You can, however, take the exact same courses at the exact same time with the exact same teachers, eventually receiving the same diploma as me, but we still received mutually exclusive education. A simple way of putting it would be to extrapolate how no two individuals can wear the same hat at the same time.

With education not meeting the criteria to be considered a public good, it is nonetheless offered to citizens as a government service. Outside of the public sector, the private marketplace also offers education and has seen growing enrollment numbers over the last few years while having experienced an extended period of decline in the years prior.[286] There is a pendulum effect between private and public education. During the era of the nation's founding up until the mid-1800s, almost all education was offered privately until the government tasked itself with building schools and offering education through taxation.[287] An almost exclusively privatized system gave way to public schools until a vast majority of all graduating high school seniors were doing so underneath the government's mantle, despite evidence indicating that private schools offer better educational opportunities for America's youth. Private schools consistently outperform public schools on average, and parents are choosing to send their kids there rather than public schools if the choice is realistic for their household.[288] Given how education is not to be considered a public good, nor is it superior in quality to its free-market alternative, one must ask why the government should be involved in the education business at all.

Proponents of public education argue that education creates benefits to uninvolved third parties, and thus they should be made to pay. When people are educated, everyone is made better off. Standards of living across the board will rise as a populace becomes more educated, as a more highly educated society will be expected to be more efficient and productive. Even if a person does not have children enrolled in schools and is not directly involved in the consumption of public education, he is still made better off by other people sending their children to school.[289] For example, when I frequent my pizza parlor and am greeted by a smiling teenager working his first summer job, I place my order, pay, and leave. When I pay for my pizza, I expect to receive the appropriate amount of change back. That teenager's ability to calculate how much change I am to receive—or be able to perform addition and subtraction with the register—is derived from his education, an education in which I did not partake; and yet when I receive the appropriate amount of change back, I have benefited from his consumption of education. I do not have to do the calculations for him or wait while he fetches his manager to perform them. He figures up the change, settles with me, and then I am free to go about my business. Proponents of tax-funded education argue that I should pay into the system of education since I receive benefits from others being educated, and it is a fair argument to make. Arguments against public education are best emphasized from a performance standpoint, highlighting how resources are wasted in the public sector, whereas even fewer resources invested in education could achieve better results if left in the private sector.

Individual Incentives

From an individual's perspective, the incentive to become educated is very strong, particularly in the early stages of education. Incentives then change as children grow older and develop unique talents and skills, and the incentives become tailored to individual ambitions and desired career paths. The incentive to complete secondary education is strong for all, as everyone stands to reap societal benefits from completing the K-12 education track.[290] Regarding post-secondary and advanced education, the incentive structure changes. Only an aspiring neurosurgeon has the incentive to complete all levels of medical study to become a practitioner in that field, but he shares with everyone else the need to know how to read and write. There is an inverse relationship between education levels and the overall well-being of society, as the degree at which society is made better off by a well-educated populace decreases as education levels increase. From a personal perspective, it is important for me and my life that everyone I encounter knows how to read, write, and perform basic arithmetic—that way we can at least communicate and conduct business. It is not so important for me that everyone I encounter needs to understand how to perform brain surgery as effectively as the neurosurgeon. The teller at my bank or the plumber I contract with will likely not add value to the services they render to me by knowing advanced concepts in theoretical quantum physics, but they will add value to their services if they can read, write, and understand how to perform common calculations. The same is true for everyone; in fact, society would actually begin to suffer if everyone pursued education to the greatest extent possible. Instead of being productively employed providing goods and services to their fellow man, people would be wasting their valuable time and energy obtaining education levels that are not at all relevant to their lives. If enough people did this, there would be a significant decrease in the amount of goods and services brought to market, and overall standards of living would decrease. One could already make the argument that society is quickly reaching that point, as the number of college graduates has risen substantially over the years prompting responses suggesting that the average worker is overeducated for whatever position he holds.[291]

Everyone has the incentive to obtain elementary levels of education so he may function in society. Beyond the necessities, education is individual-specific. If a man's best opportunity for employment lies in the medical field, he has the incentive to complete medical school. Should this man also be better able to serve me as a medical professional than he could as something else, I too have the incentive to see him complete medical school. Without public subsidies, paid for by me and the rest of society, our struggling medical student may not be able to afford school, and he may prematurely withdraw before completing his education due to financial hardship. His withdrawal will force him to seek employment in another field, one in which he does not have a competitive advantage. Perhaps he will become an electrician, a plumber, a musician, a teacher, or any number of alternatives. Whatever other career path he may pursue as an alternate, his contribution to the marketplace will not be his greatest possible potential contribution, as his skills are best suited to the medical field. Society as a whole is made worse off by his withdrawal. From this perspective, one can see why public funds are held for educational purposes, as they help ensure people have the opportunity to pursue those careers in which they can be most productive, but this comes at a severe cost. Public funds and assurances of subsidies have made the cost of education swell over the years, with the cost per pupil having almost doubled in the last two decades.[292] A completely private system would have schools compete with each other for the customers (students), and would have the incentive to keep their costs down. Tax dollars backstopping the public school budgets and ensuring that students always have the ability to pay for their schooling have removed all incentive for schools to keep costs down, as they do not operate with profit and loss constraints.

Fairness

One of the most cited arguments in favor of government-provided education is that of fairness, or equality of opportunity. Should education be completely privatized, so the argument goes, only privileged children of wealthy parents would receive better educational opportunities, as their parents could afford to send them to superior schools while the less affluent children would never have the chance to excel.[293] Though true that public schools in wealthy neighborhoods and suburbs tend to be all-around superior to public schools within the inner cities, proponents of public education may argue that the difference would be even greater if the education system was fully privatized.

Regardless of educational opportunities, wealthy children will always have advantages over those who are less well off. Even without factoring in the material advantages of having more wealth and being able to enjoy more consumer consumption, children of high-income households are far more likely to develop good habits and a strong work ethic. They will see their parents' aptitude and learn by example, coming to understand that hard work and more dedication to education will pave the way to better jobs and higher incomes down the road, and their parents will be there to guide them and instill these values.[294] They will not grow up with the impression that they are victims of an oppressive system, but instead with the impression that they can be high-achievers if they dedicate themselves. With these advantages already in place, many would argue that these children should not receive additional advantages in the form of better educational opportunities that are closed off to others, justifying the role of government as a referee so to speak, leveling out the playing field. The reality, however, is that although students are more equal in a public school system than in a private one, they are more equal in so far as that everyone receives a lower quality education overall.[295]

For reasons to be explained in more detail later, the quality of public education has declined to the point where people are beginning to ask—and in places of extreme failure such as Chicago and Detroit, demand—how it can be better provided while still remaining a government-provided service. In other words, they continue to want education financed through compulsory taxes and administered by government bureaucrats, but they want the performance and efficiency of the free market. Several proposals have been made over the past few decades in an attempt to find a blend between free-market efficiency and governmental provision, some of which have been tried and experimented with to see how the education system can be improved.

School Vouchers

A voucher is essentially a paid ticket that entitles its bearer to the underwritten good or service. In education, vouchers are a way the government can continue financing education, but it allows for more freedom of choice for the parents as to how their tax dollars are spent, seeing as though their tax dollars paid for the voucher. Under a voucher system, parents of school-aged children would receive a voucher that covers the cost of education for their children, which they would then redeem at a school of their choosing. This system allows parents access to public financing, but also allows competition between the schools, providing them with incentives to improve their educational opportunities and quality. As students are drawn to the better schools, more vouchers are redeemed at that institution, and the school makes more money. Schools that fail to attract students will be forced to make amends and cut costs or would be forced by the market to have to close their doors entirely. This system will help provide schools the crucial incentive to be both more efficient and more effective, an incentive which many currently lack.[296]

A voucher system would have many deficiencies. For starters, the higher-performing schools may arbitrarily decide to raise their tuition rates in excess of what the voucher guarantees. If a voucher-holding family cannot afford to pay the difference between the voucher's value and the cost of the school, their children will be excluded from an educational opportunity. One reason schools may raise their prices relates to student body volume. If top-performing schools attract too many students, schools would recognize the demand and raise prices to the point where the number of students able to attend the school is reduced to the number of students the school is able to sustain. This would effectively eliminate the overcrowding issue. Schools are limited as to how many students they can fit in their classrooms and halls, so some form of rationing must take place, either through higher prices or more strict admissions standards. In either case, the end result would be a more exclusive web of high-tier schools subsidized publicly that exclude certain children whose parents also hold the vouchers, but cannot afford the difference or meet the tougher admission standards. Even with this potential risk of lower-income students being edged out of the system to prevent overcrowding, school vouchers still poll strongly among lower-income families indicating that these families are willing to try something new in order to escape the current system.[297]

The supporters of school vouchers may not be aware of how the vouchers make easier the abusive and fraudulent practices in which school officials engage, and also general wasteful shenanigans. With vouchers, schools compete for students in order to have the students redeem their vouchers at that particular school, but the schools may not always be acting in the students' best academic interests. Remember that the students themselves hold no vouchers—it is the parents and legal guardians that dispense of the vouchers on behalf of the children in pursuit of education. Rather than looking after students' interests, schools will have the incentive to court the parents in order to attract a larger volume of voucher redemptions, and sometimes that which makes the parents happy is not in the students' best interests. Vouchers will also pull some students out of the private school system and foist them onto the taxpayer, whereby they may re-enroll in their private schools again, only this time under the voucher program—increasing educational costs to the public. Furthermore, students leaving a public school to redeem a voucher at a private one reduces the revenue of the public school without equally reducing its operating costs. Fixed costs such as maintenance remain even if a few of the students leave and take their vouchers with them, although it is worth mentioning that most of a school's costs are variable.[298] The private sector already does an exceedingly good job educating thousands of American youth, but with vouchers being distributed to all parents of school-aged children, public funds would have to be dispersed to individuals who would otherwise not have received them or may not need them.

School vouchers certainly have flaws, but they have a great number of merits as well. They arouse passionate debate between advocates for public education and advocates for a greater degree of choice for parents. Although vouchers can act as a redistribution tool moving financial resources from the taxpayers' pockets into the hands of private educational institutions, those private schools are more effectively and more efficiently able to educate, thus resulting in net savings to taxpayers when school vouchers are implemented.[299]

Public School Choice

Another experimental method through which the current school system can be improved would be to remove zoning restrictions. Currently, public schools each have geographic zones that determine which kids may attend which school. Often these zones will be incoherent, with children being zoned for schools several miles away and having long commutes while living just down the street from another school. Private schools are not restricted by zones but have other admissions criteria, so it is not uncommon for private schools to have children enrolled whose parents are willing to drive the extra mile. But for public schools, oftentimes it can be difficult for parents when their zoned schools are far away, and it can be difficult for the children as well given how early they must embark on a school bus and how late is the hour when they finally return home. If zoning restrictions are suddenly removed, allowing any parent to send their children to any school of their choice, schools will then have to compete with each other to attract students just as they would under a voucher system.

Proximity to parents will be one advantage for attracting students, but should the closest school be undesirable, parents would not be restricted by zoning ordinances to send their children there. An equilibrium will arise within the school system. As more parents send their children to better schools, these schools will become crowded, making them less desirable—which will factor into parental choice. An inferior school that is closer to home may not be as desirable as the better school further away, but if the better school is bursting at the seams with students, and parents begin to feel as though the crowd affects their children's educational experience in a negative way, they will reconsider the schools closer to home.[300] This equilibrium within a competitive school system will ensure that overcrowding is naturally mitigated without removing the incentives for schools to continually strive for excellence in order to attract students.

In olden times, there did not exist much competition among schools for students. There were few public schools, and students had little choice but to attend whichever was closest to them. Homeschooling was much more common, but as public school attendance grew, education moved out of the home and into the public system. Today, homeschooling has seen a significant comeback as a preferred method of obtaining education for children, with most homeschooling occurring due to parental dissatisfaction with the public school system or due to religious convictions and preferences.[301] Many parents also believe that they are better equipped to educate their own children than the schools, making homeschooling a choice of welfare. Laws pertaining to homeschooling differ across state lines, and it comes as no surprise that states with more relaxed laws have higher percentages of parents that choose to homeschool relative to those states that are more restrictive.[302] Because so small of a percentage of children are homeschooled, and because homeschooling is conducted at the parents' expense and not the public's, most 3rd party observers care little for how it is handled so long as a child's education is not outright neglected. Homeschooling and private schools hurt the parents by having them pay twice for their child's education, once through taxes to fund public schools, and again through tuition for private schools or opportunity costs for homeschooling.

University Level

An interesting contrast exists between elementary and high school education in the United States compared to higher education. Globally speaking, the United States performs poorly in education compared to the rest of the world in both elementary and high school, but the reverse is true of secondary education. The United States is home to one of the world's best university systems, drawing students from all over the world each year to pursue college and advanced degrees—and although foreign enrollment has dipped somewhat in the past few years, the United States still remains one of the world's top destinations for foreign students seeking to complete their college degrees abroad.[303] So what makes the American university system superior to the elementary and high schools relative to the systems of other countries? With the exception of students that graduate high school but choose not to attend college, the universities in the United States have the same students that passed through the elementary and high school systems, so there is clearly more to be explained in order to understand why colleges outperform those of other countries while the high schools do not.

An obvious factor is that of zoning laws and district regulations. The university system has more market forces being applied to it than the high school system. With universities, students have their choice of school and are not limited by zones. The freedom of mobility among students forces colleges to compete with one another for student enrollment, while elementary and high schools operating under zoning laws do not have this incentive.

Another, but less apparent factor explaining the difference between the universities and high schools is the makeup of teaching faculty. Competition between schools to attract teachers ensures that rates of pay remain competitive and merit-based, as better-performing professors that conduct more research are able to command higher salaries at the best universities. Further, fields of study that command more marketable applications such as science and engineering yield higher professor salaries than do the social sciences with fewer market applications, creating incentives for educators of a higher caliber to dedicate their careers to those fields, and this also works to address the oversupply of faculty in one field and the shortage of faculty in another.[304] These incentives align to ensure that professorial talent—like all scarce resources should be—is allocated to its highest-valued use.

Although post-secondary education institutions are not without a strong element of bloated bureaucracy and waste, high schools suffer from even more bureaucratic afflictions than the universities, ensuring that these incentives are significantly stronger at the university level. First, new-hire high school teachers are usually paid about the same regardless of discipline, and discrepancies in salary will largely be confined to different geographic locations when compared to each other.[305] Second, promotions and raises are based on seniority, not merit. Third, unless the teacher in question is just a good-hearted soul, she has no incentive to do a good job, either for herself or her students, as pay and promotions are guaranteed and not based on merit, while the zoning method of allocating students to schools ensures that her school need not worry about losing students to schools with better teachers. The students she teaches are a captive audience, career advancements are based on seniority rather than merit creating a "run-out-the-clock" situation, and pay and promotions are granted regardless of specialization fields.[306] These perverse incentives create educational fiascoes where the quality of education decreases, all at the students' expense of personal growth and development.

11 National Defense

"Of all the enemies of public liberty, war is perhaps the most to be dreaded, because it comprises and develops the germ of every other. War is the parent of armies. From these proceed debts and taxes. And armies, debts, and taxes are the known instruments for bringing the many under the domination of the few...No nation could preserve its freedom in the midst of continual warfare."
- James Madison, 1795.[307]

A nation's defense constitutes the most well-defined public good. Citizens are pooled together, taxed, and then given a service; that service being the armed protection of their lives and property by military force. All citizens receive the same amount of protection regardless of how much or how little they contribute to its funding, as the bullets fired by a soldier on a distant battlefield create as much protection for the nation's homeless as they do for the nation's wealthiest citizens, although a nation's wealthiest citizens can be said to have more to lose in the event the nation is overtaken by hostile powers, therefore his higher tax contribution to funding the military is proportionate to what he has at stake.[308]

Nations can have vastly different military objectives, and even the same nation can have vastly different objectives across different time periods. Some nations may be surrounded by hostile powers that covet its natural resources, others may be dealing with religious fanatics attempting to purge their land of nonbelievers, while others may be seeking to expand their own dominions at their neighbors' expense. The resources of each nation-state are limited, as is the taxable capacity of its citizens to finance military adventures. As citizens are taxed, the public must decide what to do with the money. Should it allocate more towards schools and roads, service its outstanding debt, or increase the military budget? How might a nation decide how it intends to use its tax dollars regarding national defense compared to the alternatives? No dollar can be spent twice, so resources allocated to defense come at the cost of some other project being starved of resources that it also could have used.[309]

A nation's military budget largely depends on the type of foreign policy it pursues. If a given nation aspires to be aggressive and impose its will on other nations and peoples, it can increase defense spending to help project itself onto the world stage. This is largely practiced today by nations with higher defense spending such as the United States, Russia, China, and others.[310] By spending more on the military and increasing one's military strength, a nation can militarily "persuade" other nations to see things in a new light. Such influence comes at a grave cost at times, as the imposition of a nation's will onto other peoples and cultures will often stir resentment, actually increasing the dangers to that nation's citizens in the form of insurrections, terrorist attacks, and targeted tourist kidnappings. When a nation imposes its will on others through military force, it will harm its own citizens by antagonizing foreign hostile individuals who are unwilling to yield. Ideally, a mere demonstration of force would be enough to deter other nations and potential terrorists from striking, and as a government increases its defense spending, it can project more force up until the point where defense spending prohibits productive economic activity. In the words of Theodore Roosevelt, "Speak softly, but carry a big stick."[311]

What amount of defense spending is necessary for a given country—or the United States in particular—to safeguard its people while securing its national interests abroad? Just how big should our stick be and how loud should our voice echo? The answer lies within what should by now be a familiar framework: the cost-benefit analysis.

As the cost of military spending increases, the additional benefits of defense go down for every new dollar spent.[312] There comes a point when an extra dollar spent on defense will not generate a dollar's worth of defense benefits. It is at this point when defense spending should cease. Finding such a point is especially difficult in the case of national defense. Unlike with roads, education, or health care, it is more difficult to quantify the benefits of defense spending. As one writes this book on a dining room table in central Alabama, he is relatively safe from a terrorist attack or invasion from foreign powers, but just how safe is he? How might his safety be affected if national defense spending were cut in half or doubled? Given that there is no such quantifiable unit to measure safety, and that even if there were, such changes in the number of units by lowering or boosting spending would be highly speculative in nature, we cannot entirely say for certain what the effects would be, but we can at least make some reasonable approximations.

Alongside the costs and benefits of national defense, fiduciary spending must also be considered in terms of efficiency to ensure that our taxed dollars spent on the military return the highest material benefit in terms of defense. Military defense contracts should be scrutinized for wasteful spending, weapons manufacturing should be analyzed to see if it is being conducted as efficiently as possible, and are the people a nation employs as soldiers most suited to that use? Everything is determined at the margin.[313]

As mentioned, the appropriate amount of wealth spent on a nation's defense will vary depending on what that nation's objectives are. Nations that seek only to protect themselves from foreign invaders will likely spend less on national defense than will nations that seek to leave a dominating imperial footprint on the globe—perhaps not in absolute terms—but likely in relative ones, unless the nation concerned only with border defense finds itself in the target crosshairs of the imperial nation, in which case the former will have to increase defense spending in order to more adequately protect itself.

A nation's interests regarding its military policy can be divided into tiers of importance, with all nations having some of the more basic ones, while only select aggressive nations share the less common military objectives. All nations, regardless if they are passive or aggressive, seek to protect themselves and their territory against foreign invasion. Tax revenue spent on the military will first satisfy this goal. Once the nation is secured, passive and peaceful nations will likely cease their defense spending and funnel their collected taxes into more civic projects, while aggressive and warlike nations will continue their military spending. After spending enough to ensure domestic borders are protected, a nation will engage in military spending that protects its political and economic interests abroad. From there, a nation will spend to protect its allies from foreign invasion, much like the United States and its relationship with NATO countries. Then the nation will spend and exert military influence to secure the interests of its allies. Perhaps after that, a nation will spend on national defense in the name of humanity, such as delivering oppressed peoples from the hands of their local despots.[314]

As each tier of objectives is met, military spending is allocated to new objectives that decrease in importance, but the cost of satisfying each new objective increases, as it is significantly more expensive to field an army large enough to police the world than it is to merely secure one's borders. Every new military expense outside of the most significant goal of domestic security will benefit the nation less and less until costs no longer make military spending worthwhile.[315] Many might argue that the United

States has long since passed this point, as CIA-funded rebels are currently opposed to Pentagon-backed "freedom fighters" all across the Middle East and other regions in what amounts to a massive cash burn and faulty foreign policy whereby the one hand is acting in friction with the other, with the overall objectives being unclear or undefined across groups.[316] Another consideration weighing against the nation's current foreign policy is the fact that today's paid allies are likely tomorrow's enemies, as the United States is currently fighting groups funded decades ago during the Cold War, particularly in Afghanistan and other locations that actively fought against the Soviet Union.[317]

Countries like the United States go to great lengths to increase influence on the world stage. As these nations spend more on the military, either by funding their own, those of their allies, or covert groups acting on their behalf, they can project more of their power onto the world. When a nation grows in military strength, other nations' military strength will decline relative to the nation in question. In order to further their own objectives and safeguard their own interests against what might be perceived as a growing adversary, these nations may increase their own military spending in an effort to catch up to the leader in pursuit of military primacy.

Suppose there are two nations that are equal in military strength, and one decides to embark on a military spending spree in order to increase its power at the expense of its neighbor. Assuming its neighbor does not increase its own military spending, even a modest amount of military spending can allow the first nation to become stronger relative to the passive country. The first nation may now bully and overpower the second nation from its new position of strength. There is potential for the first nation, after having spent more on the military, to acquire benefits due to its projection of force that outweigh the costs of increased military spending, and these benefits will be extracted by subordinating the second nation who must now yield its interests to those of the nation with more force and a stronger military.

To avoid having its national interests overshadowed by a potentially hostile neighbor, the second nation may decide to abandon its passive approach and engage in military spending of its own. As the passive nation becomes active and spends to catch up to the first nation, the marginal benefits of military spending decrease for the first nation to the point where they reach previous levels of parity prior to either side increasing their military power. Both nations have consumed a greater portion of their wealth to bolster their military, yet neither acquired an advantage relative to the other. Nations that participate in this kind of behavior jockey back-and-forth on the world stage, each competing against each other to see who has deeper pockets. Whichever side can spend the most on its military can enjoy the advantages of leading the pack at the expense of the others, yet tremendous amounts of wealth are consumed in the process, and the economic benefits of achieving military primacy over one's neighbors are simply not there and do not justify the expense.[318] Whereas we could have had a bridge, we have a tank. Whereas we could have had a hospital, we have a battleship. Politicians must focus on the true defense needs of a nation, and cease spending on military hardware when the benefits no longer outweigh the costs. Currently, the United States has a larger military budget than the next ten nations combined—most of whom are allies—with a budget almost three times larger than China's and roughly ten times more than Russia.[319] Given how far ahead United States defense spending is compared to what may be considered its principal geopolitical foes, one could make the case that the US has a relative advantage at their expense. We are safe, our allies are safe, and our interests abroad are secured, and yet the United States continues to spend so much of its wealth on endless wars and military adventures.

Military Spending in Democracy

As with all economic questions regarding spending, one should ask: "What do we get in return?" Does a dollar spent yield a dollar or more worth of benefits? Military spending is no exception. Defense spending should equal the limit where the additional benefits of defense are equal to the costs of acquiring them. Any further spending past this point will result in a net loss of welfare, as more wealth is destroyed in pursuit of diminishing benefits. In the realm of politics, the motives behind defense spending may not be so straightforward.

Resources that are allocated to defense create a curious phenomenon. Any amount of wealth spent on bolstering the military is wealth that cannot be used elsewhere, such as building schools and roads. It may however be seen as an investment, from a certain point of view. Though wealth spent on the military prohibits that same wealth from being consumed, it may provide for even greater consumption of wealth in the future, should the military objectives be appropriate to that end. If a country is to be annihilated in armed conflict and its people carried off in slavery, they can be said to have a very low standard of living awaiting them in the near future, provided they survived. If, however, that nation had amplified its defense spending prior to being overtaken by another hostile power, it may have survived the war intact—or even appeared strong enough to force its enemies to back down before firing a shot—and that nation would have secured its future. Their standard of living would be much higher if they could win or prevent war through a show of force than it would be if they were defeated and enslaved. As such, their military spending acts as an investment in their own future abilities to continue engaging in economic activity and everyday life. The transition of European armies from feudal levies and mercenary hires in the Middle Ages to standing professional armies of the early modern period occurred under this premise. Many Germanic principalities came to understand during the Thirty Years' War and its subsequent devastation that in order not to suffer annihilation, they would have to "invest" in standing armies rather than rely on limited mercenaries and levies in order to secure their future existence.[320]

It is also necessary to investigate the rationale behind military spending from the point of view of those who make the decisions. Current defense spending can allow for surviving or deterring armed conflict in the future, thus ensuring future consumption and economic activity continue for the people, but the resources must be spent in the present. This weighs on the incentives politicians face. Politicians' main incentives are to get reelected, and the most assured way of winning elections is to make one's voter base happy; to make them happy, throw some spending their way. Money spent on military defense is money not spent on other types of consumption or goodies, such as public works and services that would benefit voters immediately. Given that military spending provides future benefits at the expense of present consumption, politicians serving short terms in office would have less incentive to engage in defense spending, as the politicians coming into office after them are the ones who would reap the political benefits. A king or emperor does not face such incentives. His reign is guaranteed for life, and he has a much longer time horizon than does an elected representative. Since he has no need to court the peoples' favor in order to stay in office, he does not need to engage in frivolous spending to win their votes, thus he will be more likely to engage in military spending which provides benefits deep into the future.[321]

While despots and dictators may have more incentive to engage in military spending than do democratically elected politicians, the United States offers itself as a contrarian example. In the House of Representatives and the Senate, it is not uncommon to see politicians win multiple elections and remain in office for decades at a time. No term limits enable them to stay in power provided they keep winning elections, and given that so many hail from solid blue or solid red geographic regions, many of them can comfortably assume that they can remain in office as long as they wish, provided they keep the young upstarts out of their way and ensure that they remain in their parties' good graces.[322] When American politicians anticipate spending many decades in office rather than just one or two terms, the time horizon incentives shift. Now they are faced with incentives to ensure that present spending will bring both present *and* future benefits. Even though they were democratically elected and should have all the incentive to only focus on the short term, their bias against military spending is muted somewhat, and they are more likely to approve defense spending bills...especially when they can also keep kicking the can down the road and delaying the inevitable day when the bill comes due.

The marriage between defense spending and politicians' incentives are mired in corruption and waste. Factories producing military hardware and munitions are often located in the congressional districts of the Congressmen who are on the committees overseeing the military and related expenditures. Initiatives to downsize the military by closing unnecessary bases will meet stiff resistance from these individuals who will argue that the military activities in their particular districts are of the utmost importance to our national security. As it stands, military spending in their districts represents a redistribution of money from the rest of the country directly to their voter base, allowing them to boast of all the new jobs they provided for their constituents—paid for by someone else with money that has better uses. To top it off, these politicians who are self-proclaimed military experts know exactly what this nation needs to boost its security...it needs more of whatever is being produced or supplied from the military factories located in their districts and an expansion of the military presence in those districts in order to draw more federal funds.[323]

Business of Defense

Imagine walking into a car dealership on a given day. You are quickly greeted by a smiling salesman eager to do business with you. He shakes your hand as he asks, "How can I help you today?" You smile back and describe the type of car you are currently in the market to buy, and he then proceeds to show you several different models that fit your description. After some consideration, you eventually select a car that you fancy and make your purchase. Such a scenario is quite common in the United States. Now, imagine that instead of a car dealership, you stroll into the lobby of a Lockheed Martin facility. Rather than being greeted by a chummy sales representative, you are met by a confused receptionist who wonders which important visitor you are and why you are not marked on the calendar. You approach the desk and say, "Hello, I'm in the market to buy an F-22 Raptor fighter jet. How much will this cost, and do you offer financing?" You are then escorted back outside by security.

How do companies like Lockheed Martin remain in business when they do not sell their products to willing buyers? The answer is that they are set up almost exclusively to supply defense-related goods to the military, and the revenue from their contracts with the United States government keeps them profitable.[324] Military goods are unique. The armed forces purchase many goods and services for which they are the only customer. A great deal of what they demand would not have suppliers if not for the demand they themselves create. Furthermore, military demand often requires new developments in technology which becomes the responsibility of the suppliers. Companies like Lockheed Martin are often contractually obligated to heavily invest in research and development of the new military technology, and given that there can only be one customer for the would-be finished product, the investment is surrounded by many uncertainties.[325]

The level of uncertainty with a given military goods purchase can determine how the government chooses to pay for it via your tax dollars. If little or no research and development is needed, and the time frame for which the goods must be supplied is clearly defined, government and defense suppliers usually agree to a flat rate contract whereby the government pays a predetermined amount and receives a predetermined amount of goods in return. When details on goods are not as clear, when costs are not always certain, and there may be a heavy amount of research and development involved on behalf of the supplier, a fixed rate may not always be feasible.[326]

When the production of national defense goods involves uncertainty, the government often allows suppliers to shift this uncertainty onto the government's tab, making it responsible for delays and increased costs. The government often will agree to maintain a fixed rate fee for the procurement of defense goods, but then will also agree to cover the costs of supplying them, whatever those costs may be. Under this common arrangement, suppliers have less incentive to control expenses and produce goods efficiently. With their market secure and the taxpayers covering their costs, inefficiencies and even opportunities for fraudulent behavior creep in. Even worse still, defense suppliers will sometimes convince the government to pay back a percentage of the costs as a profit to the supplier. These agreements will no doubt foster negligent overspending and waste.[327]

A more appropriate type of business deal includes incentives for the suppliers to cut costs, not maximize them, though this may not be an efficient path either. The government can provide an incentive to the supplier to cut costs by offering to pay a percentage of the savings back to the supplier, but this may encourage the supplier to design and offer inferior products at lower costs in order to maximize the kickback. There is no single ideal business arrangement whereby the government can receive the highest quality defense goods at the lowest possible costs. The nature of the public sector, agency problems, misaligned incentives, bureaucratic waste and producers, moral hazard, and a score of other obstacles will ensure that each possible scenario of supplying defense goods to the government will feature high volumes of waste, or will provide the taxpayer with shortcuts and inferior products.

Opportunity Cost of Defense

For every amount of wealth allocated to national defense, that wealth can no longer be allocated towards any of its near-infinite alternative uses. The steel used to build a tank cannot also be used to construct a new bridge. The same concept holds true regarding soldiers. When a person enlists or is drafted into the military, that person cannot simultaneously enter the private sector and provide goods and services to the marketplace. He is removed from the workforce (a wealth-creating role), and placed in an army uniform (a wealth-consuming role). Given that a person cannot both be at home producing wealth as a worker while being abroad on a distant battlefield consuming wealth as a soldier, how should a nation field its army?

A nation can produce an army in one of two ways: voluntarily or through coercion. When it opts for the voluntary route, it offers competitive wages to soldiers to attract them away from other occupations they may be suited for. When using coercion, a nation conscripts its soldiers by force. Circumstances determine which method will be adopted by the government.

Should a government find itself strapped for cash and willing to violate the natural rights of its citizens by forcing them to engage in involuntary service, conscription is the most appropriate method to supply an army with bodies. When employing a volunteer-only army, the government must attract soldiers by offering wages that draw the individuals away from other professions they might engage in, which makes the government a competitor in the domestic labor market. This could quickly become costly, as most people may not be willing to do the type of work involved in soldiery at the same pay they could get doing something else. With conscription, the government plays its trump card in the labor market that allows it to remove itself as a competitor. No longer must the government attract willing volunteers at competitive rates, as it can simply take labor by coercive means. It theoretically could take the labor it desired without offering any wage at all, as conscripted citizens have no choice but to either serve or flee. With conscription in place, the cost of staffing an army is shifted away from government and onto those unfortunate individuals that were conscripted, as well of course as the people not conscripted who will see their standards of living go down, as otherwise productive people were just forcibly removed from the economy. Those forcibly drafted into the military are now required to work for lower wages than they could otherwise earn in other occupations, as the very existence of the draft is proof that the wage offered by the government to serve in the military is too low to attract people voluntarily.[328]

Another important aspect of the draft is its destructive effect on the economy. Labor is a resource, and standards of living are highest when labor is most effectively employed in its most effective uses. For many people, serving in the military is not the best opportunity available to them, as they can earn a living substantially greater if they were to engage in productive activity providing goods and services at home. In a competitive market without government interference, labor will allocate itself to its highest-valued use through the price system, as higher wages will attract labor to its most needed occupation. Under a draft where people whose best opportunities to employ their labor lie elsewhere, they may see themselves forcibly yanked from their productive professions and put into an army uniform. People who could best serve their fellow man as a doctor, car mechanic, lawyer, businessman, or any other profession are now thrown into an occupation that may not be suitable to their talents.[329]

Labor will be horrendously wasted under conscription, and inefficiencies in the labor market will translate to lower productive activity and lower standards of living, never mind the violation of a person's rights to do what he wants with his own self. Many argue that the presence of the draft is a violation of the 13th Amendment to the Constitution—the amendment which abolished slavery at the end of the Civil War. In order to ensure the draft stayed protected and legal, a Supreme Court ruling in 1916 declared that there will be some instances in which the 13th Amendment does not apply and that a person's liberty will be surrendered to an extent in which his "involuntary service" is needed as it relates to certain situations in which enforcement of duties "owed" to the government by an individual is required.[330] In other words, you are protected by the Constitution from having to perform involuntary service, unless the requester of that involuntary service is the federal government, in which case you can bid your rights to self farewell.

The biggest problem associated with maintaining an army of all volunteers (from the government's perspective) is its cost, especially if the army is to be large and expansive. At a given wage rate, anyone willing to be a soldier and perform those duties at that pay rate would willingly sign up, but in order to attract additional soldiers, the government would have to increase the rate of pay in order to accommodate those that are unwilling to enlist at the lower rate. Once every individual willing to join the military at this new heightened rate signs up, the government would once again have to raise wages in order to attract additional people. The cost will rise as the army grows, as higher tiers of labor are bid away from their private-sector alternatives. With a draft, the government would have to pay the same rate for every soldier regardless of what that person could earn in the private sector, and the government could set this rate arbitrarily low to cut down on costs, as it would not need to compete for labor as it would relying on willing volunteers. This effectively pushes a large portion of the costs of having a large military onto the soldiers themselves who are forced to earn low wage rates against their true earning potential.[331] If the government's military objectives are limited, a small army staffed with willing volunteers is the most efficient way to supply defense at the lowest cost. But when the government requires a massive army to achieve any number of military objectives, it can institute a draft and force the cost of the army onto the conscripted soldiers who must now "work" for less than they could earn elsewhere.[332]

Although the United States still has a draft, it has not conscripted anyone since the Vietnam War. The United States has relied strictly on volunteers for its more recent military adventures, and yet, the military force of the United States is felt on every corner of the globe. Given that the United States has one of the world's largest armies, but relies on volunteers and not conscripts, it is no wonder that the expense of maintaining the army and paying its wages outpace other nations by a wide margin.[333] Indeed, the military objectives of the United States extend so far beyond securing the homeland from the threat of foreign invasion, it makes little sense to continue relying on volunteers from the government's perspective.[334] At any point, the government could decide to force the costs of its outrageously large military on its own soldiers by forcibly conscripting them and cutting their pay. This would allow it to continue its policy of policing the world without the hefty price tag. The costs would be borne primarily by those in uniform. A more reasonable suggestion would be for the

222

United States to rethink its military objectives and return to a more fundamental and constitutional vision of national defense, whereby the military is only deployed to the extent it is needed to protect American citizens, and nothing else.

National defense is a sticky topic from an economic stance. The free market relies on the consent of its participants and voluntary cooperation to provide goods and services at the lowest cost. Military objectives require threatening force, coercion, and in the event settlements cannot be reached, violence. For different nations, might makes right, and a strong military will be able to extract more advantage in the event of conflict. With a zero-sum mindset, where one nation's enhanced strength comes at the expense of another's, most nations—including poor and developing ones—elect to have a strong military to either ward off potential attackers or subjugate enemies.[335]

Governments often take a more nationalistic approach to satisfy the needs of the military over the needs of the people, as the needs of the military are easily justified when making the claim that having a military enables the needs of the people to begin with. Fear peddlers are quick to claim that having no military will inevitably result in everyone being conquered and enslaved. A herd mentality often develops among the people to support their military, as supporting it and its objectives—regardless of what those objectives may be—is the patriotic thing to do.[336] Usually, the more outspoken and visual the support—such as bumper stickers and conspicuous, military-themed shirts—the more a person can expect societal approval...at least within the southern United States which have higher enlistments per capita than other regions.[337] Criticism of the military, its objectives, and often the government itself as it pertains to pursuing foreign policy can often result in wild backlash and social stigmatization. Ironically this occurs most frequently in the American South where conservatives are often the most vocal about supporting the military, while often the most critical of any socialism initiative at the federal level outside of protectionism and tariffs.[338] Given that national defense is a public good, meaning that taxes are levied and the good is supplied by the government, the United States military is an example of collectivization. With a current budget that consumes nearly a third of the country's GDP, the United States military is actually one of the largest socialist institutions in the history of human civilization.

Conclusion

"Underlying most arguments against the free market is a lack of belief in freedom itself." - Milton Friedman, 1962.[339]

Is government really necessary, or is it just something that humans continue to subject themselves to because the idea of a world without one is too scary to imagine or too fanatical? From the earliest humans that formed tribal societies to the modern nation-states, people have lived and died having their lives governed by people other than themselves. The nature of governance has varied widely across human history and the human experience with government. Ranging from the mostly free societies of advanced capitalist countries of today to the totalitarian regimes of failed central planning states of yesteryear, from the ancient tribes of primitive organization to the religious states in which service to the king is pleasing to the Almighty, people have always had a justification for their governments. They equate government to civilization, and they assume that removing one from the equation will necessarily cause a removal of the other. To deny the necessity of government or even advocating that it should be more limited in scope often prompts jeers and mockery, such as people deriding a government critic with the phrase: "Move to Somalia if you don't believe in government!"

Images of failed states where geographic regions are divided between competing warlords come to most people's minds when they are asked to imagine a society without government. Many believe that we need the government to provide services, keep the peace, and uphold civilization. I ask the reader the following: is what we have actually civilized? Even in the United States—the established bastion of personal freedom and economic opportunity—what is civilized and what is not deserves a thorough investigation.

An entrepreneur seeking to open a business must complete hundreds of pages of regulatory paperwork and comply with costly regulations that more often than not fail to protect the consumer while increasing the cost of doing business. Consumers are limited in their choices on how to live their lives, as the government dictates which products do and do not make it to store shelves, often in what quantities depending on tariffs and import quotas of the time, and it even manipulates the items' costs. All of these affect your standard of living and interfere with your freedom to determine how to best live your life.[340]

Imagine yourself enjoying a nice social gathering with some friends, perhaps catching up with each other after many years apart. You excuse yourself to the restroom and return to find several pizza boxes on the table. One of your friends looks to you, and the following dialogue takes place:

> "We ordered pizza while you were away. You need to chip in $5 to contribute towards its cost," your friend says confidently.

> You respond, "But I don't even like pizza."

> "It does not matter," replies your friend. "By being at this party, you have implied consent that you would pay for anything the majority of us decides to do. If you do not pay, we will seize the money regardless and forcibly lock you in the closet for not complying."

The United States government approaches its citizenry in a similar manner. What may seem like a silly anecdote is essentially the model of government we live under. Is this really civilized? When a person exerts his efforts and labor to produce something and trade it away, or when he exerts his labor for someone else and receives a paycheck in return, he is entitled to the fruits of that labor. His income is his property, and he alone has the right to determine how it is to be used or disposed of. When any portion of his income is seized via taxation, his rights have been violated regardless of anything he in turn receives from the government. If a burglar breaks into your house and steals your property, is the theft made right by him sweeping off your porch and trimming your hedges before he leaves? After all, you benefited from his services, even if you did not consent to them. The same can be said of today's government-provided goods and services.

For people who do not consent to the taking of their property for the provision of goods and services in which they did not voluntarily enter into an agreement with another consenting party to acquire, the arrangement was only made possible through force and the threat of violence. In the United States, a significant portion of a person's confiscated property paid to the government via taxation or through other means does not even return to the payer in the form of government services. A great deal of wealth is squandered on wasteful government programs, schemes of redistribution, payouts to political pundits and cronies, or converted to weapons used in wars that are not in the country's national interests. What can be done to correct this ongoing error?

In order for us to achieve a better life for ourselves, it is essential that we replace faith in government with faith in the free market. No arrangement has brought more people out of poverty in a faster time period than the free market has managed. No other system more successfully allows people to live free of tyranny and decide for themselves how to best achieve their different goals and dreams.[341] It is a great tragedy that in the US, a crisis—be it social or economic—is caused by the government, blamed on free markets, and addressed with more government, inevitably leading to a greater crisis down the road. Until people understand that the free enterprise system is truly the answer to solve many of the country's underlying problems, we will continue witnessing extended periods of growth in government authority and involvement in markets. This can only result in further distortions of the economic system that makes our livelihoods possible.

The free market works. Government-provided goods and services are more costly to provide and are of inferior quality to those of the private sector. In many cases, the government has outright banned the private sector from competing—such as with the postal service—in order to ensure that government monopolies stay in effect. It is important to understand that monopolies only exist in perpetuity when protected by the government. In a free market system, a monopoly can only form if a company is providing a good or service to the market so efficiently that consumers continue patronizing the business. Entrepreneurs will always be on the lookout for profit-creating opportunities, and if they find a way to provide consumers with what they want at a superior quality or lower price than the established competitor, they will compete and capture business. Monopolies take hold when the government bans competition or subsidizes the firm to the point where others cannot compete.[342] Free markets allow for competition while the government takes competition away, and competition enables economic progress. Suppose the horse and buggy industry successfully lobbied the government to prevent the ascension of the automobile. Suppose the government prevented the light bulb in favor of protecting the jobs of candle makers. Through government involvement in the market system, progress is thwarted.

Given that the government retards if not outright halts

economic progress while delivering inferior goods and services at exuberant costs to consumers who not all of them consented to pay, it is simply amazing that so much is left in the hands of the government to begin with. While private schools exist, the majority of individuals receive their education via the government. While private security exists, the government provides policing and military that protects the vast majority of us. Roads are filled with potholes, public pensions are underfunded, the postal service is teetering on bankruptcy, as are other government-provided services like Medicare and Medicaid. Government has the power to tax, and this prevents it from behaving judiciously. Whereas a businessman must constantly seek to please his customers or lose their business, the government can simply force people to use its services and raise their taxes if the service cannot be provided at current cost levels. On his campaign in 1964, then Presidential candidate Ronald Reagan delivered a televised speech in which he said the following:

> Public servants say, always with the best of intentions, 'What greater service we could render if only we had a little more money and a little more power.' But the truth is that outside of its legitimate function, (the) government does nothing as well or as economically as the private sector.[343]

The current mixed system is broken, inefficient, and violates people's rights across a wide spectrum...and yet popular support continues to cry out for more. All that is needed is one more layer of regulation to prevent the next financial crisis, one more program of redistribution to make everyone equal, one more breach of government into the healthcare system to ensure healthcare for all...please do not be fooled. There is no other person who better understands your life than you do, and there is no other person who can tell you how to live it better. Assuming people are evil, how can it be wise to select a small number of them, give them authority over others, and give them the power to exert that authority? Assuming people are inherently good, how can it be reasonable to believe that a small number of them clustered together can have more collective insight into the wants and needs of consumers than the millions of dispersed individuals who through no government action or central planning have all spontaneously come together in the market to create the most prosperous economy the world has ever seen?

The natural state of man is poverty, and poverty has been the story of man's existence on Earth throughout most of his stay. Only in the last century and a half have standards of living risen enough to pull millions of people out of the life of subsistence and into the life of plenty. It is no coincidence that this anomaly is occurring at the same time in history that markets have been allowed to function more freely than they have in previous periods, but this is becoming increasingly threatened with government interference in market mechanics. Let us not lose this progress. Let this brief chapter of human prosperity not be a temporary achievement in the continuing story of humanity. Let us restore faith in the markets—and in ourselves—to safeguard that prosperity for the future.

Endnotes

Introduction

1. Munday, Stephen. *Markets and Market Failure*. Oxford: Heinemann (2000), 62.

2. Zemeckis, Robert. *Cast Away* (2000; Los Angeles, CA: 20th Century Fox, 2017), DVD.

3. Lawrence, Francis. *I Am Legend* (2007; Burbank, CA: Warner Bros., 2008), DVD.

Chapter 1 Collective Action

4. Hayek, F.A. *The Road to Serfdom.* Caldwell, Bruce (ed.). Chicago: The University of Chicago Press (2007), 163.

5. Von Mises, Ludwig. *Human Action: A Treatise of Economics,* Indianapolis: Liberty Fund (2007), 42.

6. Ridley, Matt. *The Rational Optimist: How Prosperity Evolves,* New York: Harper Collins (2010), 56.

7. Hobbes, Thomas. *Leviathan,* London: Penguin Books (1985), 186.

8. Rousseau, Jean-Jacques. *On the Social Contract.* Trans. Donald Cress. Indianapolis: Hackett (1987), 24.

9. Locke, John. *Second Treatise of Government.* ed. C.B. Macpherson. Indianapolis: Hackett (1980), 109.

10. Olson, Mancur. *The Logic of Collective Action: Public Goods and the Theory of Groups.* Cambridge: Harvard University Press (1965), 53-60.

11. Frohlich, Norman, & Oppenheimer, Joe. "I get by with a little help from my friends." World Politics, vol. 23, no. 1. Cambridge: Cambridge University Press (1970), 104-120.

12. Buchanan, James. *The Collected Works of James M. Buchanan Vol. 6. Cost and Choice: An Inquiry in Economic Theory.* Indianapolis: Liberty Fund (1999), preface.

13. Von Mises, Ludwig. *Human Action: A Treatise of Economics,* Indianapolis: Liberty Fund (2007), 99.

14. Sen, Amartya. "Markets and Freedoms: Achievements and Limitations of the Market Mechanism in Promoting Individual Freedoms." *Oxford Economic Papers, V*ol. 45, no. 4. Oxford: Oxford University Press (1993), 521.

15. Mill, John Stuart. *On Liberty,* London: John W. Parker & Son (1860), 7-13.

16. Buchanan, James & Tullock, Gordon. *The Collected Works of James M. Buchanan Vol. 3. The Calculus of Consent: Logical Foundations of Constitutional Democracy.* Indianapolis: Liberty Fund (1999), 76-86.

17. Ibid.

18. Black, Duncan. "On the Rationale of Group Decision-Making." *Journal of Political Economy,* Vol. 56, no. 1. Chicago: University of Chicago Press (1948), 23-34.

19. Francis Fukuyama. *The Origins of Political Order: From Prehuman Times to the French Revolution,* New York: Farrar, Straus, & Giroux (2011), 53-55.

20. Bernstein, William. *A Splendid Exchange: How Trade Shaped the Modern World,* New York: Atlantic Monthly Press (2008) 22-26.

21. Buchanan, James. "An Economic Theory of Clubs." *Economica,* Vol. 32, no. 152. London: Wiley (1965), 1-14.

22. Fouirnaies, Alexander & Hall, Andrew. "How Do Electoral Incentives Affect Legislator Behavior?" (2018)

23. Johnsen, Christopher; Weingast, Barry; Shepsle, Kenneth. "The Political Economy of Benefits and Costs: A Neoclassical Approach to Distributive Politics." *Journal of Political Economy,* Vol. 89, no. 4. Chicago: University of Chicago Press (1981), 642-664.

24. Downs, Anthony. *An Economic Theory of Democracy,* New York: Harper & Brothers (1957), 244-271.

25. Friedmon, Milton & Rose. *Free to Choose: A Personal Statement,* New York: Harcourt Brace Jovanovich (1980), 291.

26. Gwartney, James. "Private Property and Freedom in the West." *The Intercollegiate Review,* Spring/Summer. Delaware: Intercollegiate Studies Institute (1985), 39-40.

27. Sowell, Thomas. *Basic Economics: A Common Sense Guide to the Economy, 4th ed.* New York: Basic Books (2011), 41-47, 237-251.

28. Wenar, Leif. *The Stanford Encyclopedia of Philosophy.* Zalta, Edward (ed). Stanford: Metaphysics Research Lab (2017).

29. Rousseau, Jean-Jacques. *On the Social Contract.* Trans. Donald Cress. Indianapolis: Hackett (1987), 64.

30. Jefferson, Thomas. *The Thomas Jefferson Papers: Thomas Jefferson to James Madison. Vol XV 27 March 1789 to 30 November 1789,* Princeton: Princeton University Press (1958), 392-398.

31. Friedmon, Milton & Rose. *Free to Choose: A Personal Statement,* New York: Harcourt Brace Jovanovich (1980), 131-149.

32. Williams, Walter. *Race and Economics: How much can be Blamed on Discrimination?* Stanford: Hoover Institution Press (2011) 106-109, 135-141.

33. Read, Leonard. "I Pencil: My Family Tree as Told by Leonard Read." Irvington: FEE (1958).

34. Hayek, Friedrich. *The Fatal Conceit: The Errors of Socialism.* (ed.) W.W. Bartley III. London: Routledge (1988), 76-77.

Chapter 2 Rights and Regulations

35. Madison, James. *The Federalist Papers No. 48*. New York: Bantam Classics (2003), 300-301.

36. Buchanan, James. *The Collected Works of James M. Buchanan Vol. 6. Cost and Choice: An Inquiry in Economic Theory.* Indianapolis: Liberty Fund (1999), 43-44.

37. Rachels, Chase. *A Spontaneous Order: The Capitalist Case for a Sateless Society.* Createspace Independent Publishing (2015), 69.

38. Acemoglu, Daron; Johnson, Simon; Robinson, James. "Institutions as a Fundamental Cause of Long-run Growth." *Handbook of Economic Growth.* 1 (2005), 297.

39. Powell, Benjamin. "Private Property Rights, Economic Freedom, and Well Being." *Economic Education Bulletin* 43, No. 11, American Institute for Economic Research (2002), 1-3.

40. Rose, Joseph. "Remembering Portland's Disastrous Yellow Bike Project." The Oregonian Oregon Live, (2016).

41. Office of the Under Secretary of Defense. *Defense Budget Overview: Fiscal Year 2018, Revised* Feb. 13, 2018.

42. LaFarve, Wayne. *Criminal Law* 5th ed. St. Paul: Thomson Reuters (2010), 834.

43. Emshwiller, John; Fields, Gary. "Federal Asset Seizures Rise, Netting Innocent with Guilty." *The Wall Street Journal* (Aug 22, 2011).

44. Keenan, Kevin; Walker, Sam. "An Impediment to Police Accountability? An Analysis of Statutory Law Enforcement Officers' Bill of Rights." *Public Interest Law Journal* 14:185 (2005), 186-194.

45. Neily, Clark & Schweikert, Jay. "As the Supreme Court Considers Several Qualified Immunity Cases, A New Ally Joins The Fight." Cato Institute (01/17/2020).
https://www.cato.org/blog/supreme-court-considers-several-qualified-immunity-cases-new-ally-joins-fight

46.   Cohen, Mark. "Measuring the Costs and Benefits of Crime and Justice." *Criminal Justice.* Washington D.C.: National Institute of Justice (2000), 265-278.

47.   Alchian, Armen. "Some Economics of Property Rights." *Il Politico* 30 No. 4 (1965), 816-829.

48.   Cockshott, Paul; Cottrell, Allin. *Towards a New Socialism.* Nottingham: Russell Press (1993), 7-27.

49.   Marx, Karl. *Das Kapital vol III.* New York: Penguin Press (1981), 647.

50.   Page, John. "The East Asian Miracle: Four Lessons for Development Policy." NBER *Macroeconomics Annual* 9 (1994), 219-69.

51.   Acemoglu, Daron; Robinson, James. *Why Nations Fail: The Origins of Power, Prosperity, and Poverty.* New York: Crown Business (2012), 72-73.

52.   Shleifer, Andrei. "Understanding Regulation." *European Financial Management* Vol. 11 No. 4 (2005), 439-445.

53.   *Free To Choose.* "Who Protects the Consumer?" Ep. 7. Directed by David Filkin. Public Broadcasting Service (1980).

54.   Ibid.

55.   Brook, Yaron & Watkins, Don. *Free Market Revolution: How Ayn Rand's Ideas Can End Big Government.* New York: Palgrave Macmillan (2012), 162-176.

56.   Ibid.

57.   Ibid.

58.   Gwartney, James; Lee, Dwight; Stroup, Richard. *Common Sense Economics: What Everyone Should Know About Wealth and Prosperity.* New York: St. Martin's Press (2005), 89.

59.   Stigler, George. "A Theory of Oligopoly." *The Journal of Political Economy* Vol. 72 No. 1 (1964), 44-50.

60.   Williams, Walter. *Race and Economics: How much can be blamed on discrimination?* Stanford: Hoover Institution Press (2011), 61.

61.   Tullock, Gordon. "The Transitional Gains Trap." *The Bell Journal of Economics* Vol. 6 No. 2 (1975), 671-678.

62.   Becker, Gary. "Public Policies, Pressure Groups, and Deadweight Costs." *Journal of Public Economics* Vol. 28 No. 3 (1985), 329-347.

63.   Ibid.

64.   *The Big Short.* Directed by Adam McKay. Hollywood, CA: Paramount Pictures (2015)

65.   Draca, Mirko; Fons-Rosen, Christian; Vidal, Jordi. "Revolving Door Lobbyists." *American Economic Review* Vol. 102 No. 7 (2012), 3731-3748.

Chapter 3 The Road and The Radio
66.   Higgs, Robert. "The Siren Song of the State." *The Free Market* Vol. 25 No. 09. (2007).
67.   Carpenter, Amanda. "Clinton: 'Something Has to Be Taken Away from Some People," *TownHall*, June 04, 2007.
68.   Holcome, Randall. *The Economic Foundations of Government.* New York: New York University Press (1994), 184-185.
69.   Samuelson, Paul. "The Pure Theory of Public Expenditure. *Review of Economics and Statistics.* Vol. 36 No. 4 (1954), 387-389.
70.   Weisbrod, Burton. "Collective Consumption Services of Individual-Consumption Goods." *The Quarterly Journal of Economics.* Vol. 78 No. 3 (1964), 473.
71.   Demsetz, Harold. "The Exchange and Enforcement of Property Rights." *Journal of Law and Economics.* Vol. 7 (1964), 20.
72.   Stroup, Richard. "Free-Riders and Collective Action Revisited." *The Independent Review.* Vol. 4 No. 4 (2000), 487.
73.   Cowen, Tyler. "Public Goods." The Concise Encyclopedia of Economics. The Library of Economics and Liberty.
74.   Gwartney, James; Lee, Dwight; Stroup, Richard. *Common Sense Economics: What Everyone Should Know About Wealth and Prosperity.* New York: St. Martin's Press (2005), 17.
75.   Lott, John. *Freedomnomics: Why the Free Market Works and other Half-Baked Theories Don't.* Washington D.C.: Regnery Publishing, Inc. (2007), 89-90.
76.   Congdon, William; Kling, Jeffrey; Mullainathan, Sendhil. *Policy and Choice: Public Finance through the Lens of Behavioral Economics.* Washington D.C.: Brookings Institution Press (2011), 134.
77.   Rothbard, Murray. *For a New Liberty: The Libertarian Manifesto.* Auburn: The Ludwig Von Mises Institute (2006), 247.
78.   Toscano, Paul. "The Ten Biggest U.S. Government Contractors." *CNBC* (04/08/2011).
79.   "FY 2020 Budget Estimates." U.S. Air Force: March, 2019.
80.   Johansen, Lief. "Some Notes on the Lindahl Theory of Determination of Public Expenditures." *International Economic Review.* Vol. 4 No. 3 (1963), 346-358.

81. Brown, Jeffrey. "Reconsidering the Gas Tax: Paying for What You Get." *Access* Vol. 19 (2001), 1910-1915.

82. Cowen, Tyler. "Public Goods." *The Concise Encyclopedia of Economics.* The Library of Economics and Liberty.

83. Barrett, Scott. *Why Cooperate: The Incentive to Supply Global Public Goods.* Oxford: Oxford University Press (2007), 13.

84. Olson, Mancur. *The Logic of Collective Action: Public Goods and the Theory of Groups.* Cambridge: Harvard University Press (1965), 48.

85. Rachels, Chase. *A Spontaneous Order: The Capitalist Case for a Sateless Society.* Createspace Independent Publishing (2015), 173-184.

86. Ibid.

87. Lott, John. *Freedomnomics: Why the Free Market Works and other Half-Baked Theories Don't.* Washington D.C.: Regnery Publishing, Inc. (2007), 79-82.

Chapter 4 The Theoretical Framework of Government Intervention

88. Rand, Ayn. "The Nature of Government." Foundation for Economic Freedom (03/01/1964). https://fee.org/articles/the-nature-of-government-by-ayn-rand/

89. Pillion, Dennis. "Wastewater Spill Wipes out 175,000 Fish North of Birmingham." *AL.com* (Jun 14, 2019).

90. Caplan, Bryan. "Externalities." *The Concise Encyclopedia of Economics.* The Library of Economics and Liberty.

91. Ibid.

92. Dahlman, Carl. "The Problem of Externality" in *The Theory of Market Failure,* ed. Tyler Cowen. Fairfax: George Mason University Press (1988), 209-210.

93. Coarse, Robert. "The Problem of the Social Cost." *The Journal of Law and Economics.* Vol 3 (1960), 1-44.

94. Sowell, Thomas. *Basic Economics: A Common Sense Guide to the Economy 4th ed.* New York: Basic Books (2011), 433-434.

95. Chapman, Gretchen; Galvani, Alison; Ibuka, Yoko; Li, Meng; Vietri, Jeffrey. "Free-riding Behavior in Vaccine Decisions: An Experimental Study." PloS One (2014), 1.

96. Caplan, Bryan. "Externalities." *The Concise Encyclopedia of Economics.* The Library of Economics and Liberty.

97. Friedman, Milton. *Capitalism and Freedom 40th ed.* Chicago: The University of Chicago Press (2002), 26-27.

98. Holcome, Randall. *The Economic Foundations of Government.* New York: New York University Press (1994), 201.

99.   Bator, Francis. "The Anatomy of Market Failure" in *The Theory of Market Failure,* ed. Tyler Cowen. Fairfax: George Mason University Press (1988), 35.

100.   Friedman, Milton. *Capitalism and Freedom 40th ed.* Chicago: The University of Chicago Press (2002), 25-26.

101.   Sandmo, Agnar. "Pigouvian Taxes" in *The New Palgrave Dictionary of Economics, 2nd edition,* ed. Steven Durlaf & Lawrence Bloom. London: Palgrave Macmillan (2008), 4,947-4,957.

102.   Kousky, Carolyn; Kunreuther, Howard; Lingle, Brett; Shabman, Leonard. "The Emerging Private Residential Flood Insurance Market in the United States." *Wharton Risk Management and Decision Processes Center* (2018), 5.

103.   Howard II, James. *Socioeconomic Effects of the National Flood Insurance Program.* Switzerland: Springer (2016), 13.

104.   Thompson, Peter. "Public Goods." *Wiley Online Library,* 2008.

105.   Stigler, George. "The Theory of Economic Regulation." *The Bell Journal of Economics and Management Science.* Vol. 2 No. 3 (1971) 3-21.

106.   Tietenberg, Tom. "The Tradable-Permits Approach to Protecting the Commons: Lessons for Climate Change." *Oxford Review of Economic Policy* Vol. 19 No. 3 (2003), 400-419.

Chapter 5 Income Tax

107.   Bastiat, Federic. *Economic Sophisms.* Translated by Arthur Goddard. New York: Foundation for Economic Education (1996), 95.

108.   Rachels, Chase. *A Spontaneous Order: The Capitalist Case for a Sateless Society.* Createspace Independent Publishing (2015), 214-215.

109.   Rogge, Benjamin. *A Maverick's Defense of Freedom.* Indianapolis: Liberty Fund (2010), 238.

110.   Mauro, Madison; Wei, Emma; York, Eria. "Tax Freedom Day 2019 is April 16th." *The Tax Foundation* (April 10, 2019).

111.   Rachels, Chase. *A Spontaneous Order: The Capitalist Case for a Sateless Society.* Createspace Independent Publishing (2015), 214-215.

112.   Mankiw, Gregory; Weinzierl, Matthew; Yagan, Danny. "Optimal Taxation in Theory and Practice." *Journal of Economic Perspectives* No 03. Vol 04. (2009), 147-174.

113.   Bloomquist, Kim. "Tax Evasion, Income Inequality and Opportunity Costs of Compliance." *Proceedings. Annual Conference on Taxation and Minutes of the Annual Meeting of the National Tax Association* Vol 96. (2003), 91-104.

114. Forbes, Steve; Ames, Elizabeth. *How Capitalism Will Save Us*. New York: Crown Business (2009), 296-297.

115. Bryant, Joseph. "What's So Bad About It? Birmingham Water Works Board Members Detail Opposition to State Legislation." *AL.com* (Apr. 21, 2015).

116. Hazlitt, Henry. *The Failure of New Economics*. Princeton: D. Van Nostrand Company (1956), 184-185.

117. Ferguson, Andrew. "Bubble on the Potomac: The New Affluence Flooding the Nation's Capital Sets It Apart from the Country It Governs." *Time Magazine* (05/28/2012).

118. Beck, Emma. "Cutting That Bagel Will Cost You: Weird State Tax Laws." *USA Today* (03/31/2013).

119. Olson, John. "What are Payroll Taxes and Who Pays Them?" *The Tax Foundation* (07/25/2016).

120. Kagan, Julia. "Income Tax." *Investopedia* (08/28/2019).

121. Norton, Rob. "Corporate Taxation." The Concise Encyclopedia of Economics. The Library of Economics and Liberty.

122. Ibid.

123. McCardle, Megean. "Why We Should Eliminate the Corporate Income Tax." *The Atlantic* (10/28/2010).

124. Cooper, John. *Woodrow Wilson: A Biography*. New York: Vintage (2009), 216-218.

125. Higgs, Robert. *Crisis and Leviathan: Critical Episodes in the Growth of American Government*. Oxford: Oxford University Press (1987) 150-152.

126. Ibid. 30-32

127. "Historical Highest Marginal Income Tax Rates." Tax Policy Center (02/04/2020) https://www.taxpolicycenter.org/statistics/historical-highest-marginal-income-tax-rates

128. "The Budget and Economic Outlook: 2017-2027." Testimony by Keith Hall. Congressional Budget Office (02/02/2017).

129. Gellman, Barton. *Angler: The Cheney Vice Presidency*. New York: The Penguin Press (2008), 257-259.

130. Fullerton, Don. "The Laffer Curve" in *The New Palgrave Dictionary of Economics, 2nd edition,* ed. Steven Durlaf & Lawrence Bloom. London: Palgrave Macmillan (2008), 839.

131. Brooks, Arthur; Feulner, Edwin. "Why Tax Increases Don't Work." *USA Today* (12/05/2012).

132. Samuel, Henry. "Actor Gérard Depardieu to 'sell everything' in France." *The Telegraph* (09/04/2015).

133. Bartlett, Bruce. *The Benefit and the Burden: Tax Reform-Why We Need It and What It Will Take*. New York: Simon & Schuster (2012), 61-62.

134. Hall, Robert; Rabushka, Alvin.. *The Flat Tax (2nd ed.)*. Stanford: Hoover Institution Press (2007), 8-20.

135. Gilman, Martin. *No Precedent, No Plan: Inside Russia's 1998 Default*. Cambridge: The MIT Press (2010), 243-244.

136. Gale, William G. "Flat tax." *The Encyclopedia of Taxation and Tax Policy, Urban Institute Press,* Washington, D.C. (1999): 155-158.

137. Hall, Robert; Rabushka, Alvin.. *The Flat Tax (2nd ed.)*. Stanford: Hoover Institution Press (2007), 24-28.

138. Friedman, Milton. *Capitalism and Freedom 40th ed.* Chicago: The University of Chicago Press (2002), 191-194.

139. Black, Lewis. "Why Corporations Choose Delaware." Delaware Department of State Division, 2007.

140. Pomerleau, Kyle. "The United States Corporate Income Tax Rate is Now More in Line with Those Levied by Other Major Nations." *Tax Foundation* (02/12/2018).

141. Davison, Laura. "Soak-The-Rich Tax Plans Take Hold in the Entire Democratic Field." *Bloomberg* (02/22/2020).

142. Fullerton, Don; Metcalf, Gilbert. "Tax Incidence." *Handbook of Public Economics,* vol. 04, ed. Alan Auerbach & Martin Feldstein. Amsterdam: Elsevier Science, (2002), 1787-1872.

143. Mukherjee, Abhiroop; Singh, Manpreet; & Zaldokas, Alminas. "Do Corporate Taxes Hinder Innovation?" *Research Briefs in Economic Policy* no. 79. (2017).

144. Jark, Daniel. "Corporate High-Yield Bonds Vs. Equities: What's the Difference?" *Investopedia* (07/09/2019).

145. Rosenthal, Steven; Austin, Lydia. "The Dwindling Taxable Share of U.S. Corporate Stock." *Tax Notes* (2016), 923-934.

146. Dubay, Curits. "Taxation of Debt and Equity: Setting the Record Straight." *The Heritage Foundation* (09/30/2015).

147. Barry, Christopher; Mann, Steven; Mihov, Vassil; Rodriguez, Mauricio. "Corporate Debt Issuance and the Historical Level of Interest Rates." *Financial Management* Vol. 37 No 3 (2008), 413-430.

148. Egan, Matt. "Problem with Rising Rates: Corporate America has Binged on Debt." *CNN* (02/26/2018)

149. La Rocca, M.; La Rocca, T.; and Gerace, D. "A Survey of the Relation Between Capital Structure and Corporate Strategy." *Australasian Accounting, Business and Finance Journal* Vol. 2 No 2 (2008) 1-18.
150. Ibid.

Chapter 6 Consumption Tax
151. Smith, Adam. *An Inquiry into the Nature and Causes of the Wealth of Nations.* Canaan, Edwin (ed). New York: The Modern Library (1994), 929.
152. Ehrbar, Al. "Consumption Tax." The Concise Encyclopedia of Economics. The Library of Economics and Liberty.
153. Fullerton, Don; Metcalf, Gilbert. "Tax Incidence." *Handbook of Public Economics,* vol. 04, ed. Alan Auerbach & Martin Feldstein. Amsterdam: Elsevier Science, (2002), 1787-1872.
154. Gwartney, James; Lee, Dwight; Stroup, Richard. *Common Sense Economics: What Everyone Should Know About Wealth and Prosperity.* New York: St. Martin's Press (2005), 86-87.
155. Smith, Kyle. "Philadelphia's Soda War." *National Review* (01/14/2019).
156. Gifford Jr., Adam. "Whiskey, Margarine, and Newspapers: A Tale of Three Taxes," in William F. Shughart II, ed., *Taxing Choice: The Predatory Politics of Fiscal Discrimination.* New Brunswick, NJ: Transaction Publishers, Rutgers—The State University of New Jersey (1998), 57–77.
157. Edwards, Chris. "Special-Interest Spending and Corporate Welfare." *Cato Handbook for Policy Makers,* 8th ed. (2017), 543-549.
158. Sowell, Thomas. *Basic Economics: A Common Sense Guide to the Economy, 4th ed.* New York: Basic Books (2011), 41-47, 237-251.
159. Wan, William. "America's New Tobacco Crisis: The Rich Stopped Smoking, The Poor Didn't." *Washington Post* (06/13/2017). https://www.washingtonpost.com/national/americas-new-tobacco-crisis-the-rich-stopped-smoking-the-poor-didnt/2017/06/13/a63b42ba-4c8c-11e7-9669-250d0b15f83b_story.html

Chapter 7 Tax on Wealth
160. Gunther, Gerald, & Marshall, John. *John Marshall's Defense of McCulloch v. Maryland.* Stanford University Press (1969).

161. Gordon, Richard; Rudnick, Rebecca. "Taxation of Wealth" in *Tax Law Design and Drafting* Vol 1, ed. Victor Thuronyi. International Monetary Fund (1996).

162. Tanner, Michael. "Five Myths about Economic Inequality in America." *Policy Analysis* No. 797. Cato Institute., (09/07/2016).

163. Tanner, Michael. "The Real '1 Percent.'" Cato Institute, (11/08/2011).

164. William, Allen. "Mercantilism." In John Eatwell, Murray Milgate, and Peter Newman, eds., *The New Palgrave: A Dictionary of Economics.* Vol. 3. London: Macmillan (1987), 445–448.

165. Perry, Mark. "The Fixed-Pie Fallacy". *American Enterprise Institute.* (12/23/2006).

166. Ream, Roger. "What Causes Wealth?" *Foundation of Economic Education.* (08/01/1981).

167. Williams, Walter. "Capitalism and the Common Man: Are Wealthy Capitalists Really Obliged to 'Give Back'." *Foundation for Economic Education.* (01/01/2000).

168. Prychitko, David. "Marxism." *The Library of Economics and Liberty.*

169. Reed, Lawrence. "Great Myths of the Great Depression." *Foundation for Economic Education,* (2010), 12.

170. Wolla, Scott. "Why Are Some Countries Rich and Others Poor?" Economic Research. *Federal Reserve Bank of St. Louis,* (09/2017).

171. Mathias, Peter. *The First Industrial Nation: An Economic History of Britain 1700-1914.* New York: Charles Scribner's Sons (1969), 126.

172. Bastiat, Frédéric . *Economic Sophisms.* Translated by Arthur Goddard. New York: Foundation for Economic Education (1996), 83.

173. Hazlitt, Henry. The Failure of New Economics. Princeton: D. Van Nostrand Company (1956), 184-185

174. Alchian, Armen. *Economic Forces at Work.* Indianapolis, IN: Liberty Press (1977), 331.

175. Kagan, Julia. "What is Capital Gains Tax." Investopedia.com

176. Dempsey, Mike. "Capital Gains Tax: Implications for the Firm's Cost of Capital, Share Valuation, and Investment Decision-Making." *Accounting and Business Research* Vol. 28 No 2. (1998), 91-96.

177. Wurgler, Jeffrey. "Financial Markets and the Allocation of Capital." *Journal of Financial Economics* Vol. 58 No. 1-2. (2000), 187-214.

178. Kovenock, Daniel & Rothschild, Michael. "Notes on the Effect of Capital Gain Taxation on Non-Austrian Assets." *Economic Policy in Theory and Practice* (1987), 309.

179. Cox, Don & Johnston, Ken. "The Influence of Tax-Loss Selling by Individual Investors in Explaining the January Effect." *Quarterly Journal of Business and Economics* Vol. 35 No. 02 (1996), 14-20.

180. *Tax Incentives for Increasing Savings and Investments.* Hearings Before the Committee on Finance. United States Senate One Hundred Fist Congress, Second Session. Washington: US Government Printing Office (1990), 226.

181. Kagan, Julia. "Transfer Tax." Investopedia.com

182. Internal Revenue Service. "Instructions for Form 709" (2019). https://www.irs.gov/instructions/i709#idm140554799622736

183. Rothbard, Murray. *America's Great Depression 5th ed.* Auburn: Mises Institute (2000), 287.

184. Kagan, Julia. "Estate Tax Definition." Investopedia.com. https://www.investopedia.com/terms/e/estatetax.asp

185. Smyth, Albert. *The Writings of Benjamin Franklin, Vol X (1789-1790).* New York: Macmillan (1907), 69.

186. Zaritsky, H. and T. Ripy (1984), "Federal Estate, Gift, and Generation Skipping Taxes: A Legislative History and Description of Current Law." Report No. 84-156A.

187. Cho, Chloe & Huang, Chye-Ching. "Ten Facts You Should Know About The Federal Estate Tax." Center on Budget and Policy Priorities. (10/30/2017).

188. Tanner, Michael. "The Real '1 Percent.'" Cato Institute. (11/08/2011).

189. Lundeen, Andrew. "The Estate Tax Provides Less Than One Percent of Federal Revenue." The Tax Foundation. (04/07/2015).

190. Picketty, Thomas. *Capital in the Twenty-First Century.* London: The Belknap Press (2014), 240-242.

191. Ames, Elizabeth & Forbes, Steve. *How Capitalism Will Save Us.* New York: Crown Business (2009), 159-161.

192. Arnott, Robert, William Bernstein, and Lillian Wu. "The Myth of Dynastic Wealth: The Rich Get Poorer." *Cato J.* 35 (2015): 447.

193. Walczak, Jared. "State Inheritance and Estate Taxes: Rates, Economic Implications, and the Return of Interstate Competition." The Tax Foundation Special Report No. 235. Jul. 2017.

194. Gale, William; Hines Jr., James; Slemrod, Joel (Eds). *Rethinking Estate and Gift Taxation.* Washington D.C.: Brookings Institute Press (2001), 299.

195. Waldfogel, Joel. "The deadweight loss of Christmas." *The American Economic Review* 83, no. 5 (1993): 1328-1336.

196. Kagan, Julia. "Trust Definition." Investopedia.com
https://www.investopedia.com/terms/t/trust.asp
197. Kennon, Joshua. "What is a Trust Fund?" The Balance.
(01/13/2020).
198. Kenton, Will. "Step-Up in Basis." Investopedia.com
https://www.investopedia.com/terms/s/stepupinbasis.asp
199. Kagan, Julia. "Property Tax Definition." Investopedia.com
https://www.investopedia.com/terms/p/propertytax.asp
200. Harris, Benjamin & Moore, Brian. "Residential Property Taxes in
the United States." Urban-Brookings Tax Policy Center (2013), 1-13.
201. Shaw, Andy. "No-Bid Contracts Invite Government Corruption."
Better Government Association (11/15/2015).
202. Michel, Adam. "The New York Times is Wrong. The Rich Pay
More Taxes Than You Do." The Heritage Foundation (10/15/2019).
203. Gaines, James. "Homeownership Costs and Housing Affordability
Sensitivity." Texas A&M University: Real Estate Center (2006), 2.
204. Kuethe, Todd & Sherrick, Bruce. "The Taxation of Agricultural
Land in the United States." University of Illinois: Policy Matters
(10/15/2014).
205. Archibald, John. "Here's Why Alabama's Taxes are Unfair."
Al.com (01/14/2020)
https://www.al.com/news/2020/01/why-alabamas-taxes-are-unfair.html
206. Ibid.
207. Francis, Norton. "State Tax Incentives for Economic
Development." Urban Institute (02/29/2016).

Chapter 8 Redistribution
208. Williams, Walter. *All It Takes is Guts: A Minority View.*
Washington, D.C.: Regnery Publishers (1987).
209. Hall, Thomas. *Aftermath: The Unintended Consequences of Public
Policies.* Washington, D.C.: Cato Institute (2014), 24-26.
210. Pilon, Roger. *The Purpose and Limits of Government.* Washington,
D.C.: Cato Institute (1999), 18.
211. Hyman, David. *Public Finance: A Contemporary Application of
Theory to Policy 9th ed.* Mason: Thomson South-Western (2008), 261.
212. Rockwell Jr., Llewellyn. "The Menace of Egalitarianism." Auburn:
The Mises Institute (10/08/2015).
213. Hubbard, Glenn & Kane, Tim. *Balance: The Economics of Great
Powers from Ancient Rome to Modern America.* New York: Simon &
Schuster (2013), 193.

214. Higgs, Robert. "Nineteen Neglected Consequences of Income Redistribution." Independent Institute. (12/05/1994).

215. Jolink, Albert, and Jan Van Daal. "Gossen's laws." *History of political economy* 30, no. 1 (1998): 43.

216. Lerner, Abba P. *Economics of control: Principles of welfare economics.* Macmillan and Company Limited, New York, 1944. 23-40.

217. Higgs, Robert. "Nineteen Neglected Consequences of Income Redistribution." Independent Institute. (12/05/1994).

218. Lerner, Abba P. *Economics of control: Principles of welfare economics.* Macmillan and Company Limited, New York, 1944. 30.

219. Le Grand, Julian. *The Strategy of Equality: Redistribution and the Social Services.* Abingdon: Routledge (1982), 7-17.

220. Feser, Edward. "Taxation, Forced Labor, and Theft." The Independent Review (2000), 220.

221. Chodorov, Frank. *Out of Step: The Autobiography of an Individualist.* New York: The Devin-Adair Company (1962), 216-239.

222. Clar, Jeff; Levy, Leon; Tullock, Gordon. "The Poverty of Politics: How Income Redistribution Hurts the Poor." *Atlantic Economic Journal* Vol. 34. (2006), 47-62.

223. Scully, Gerald. "Measuring the Burden of High Taxes." NCPA Policy Report No. 215. National Center for Policy Analysis (1998), 1-18.

224. Blinder, Alan. "Distribution Effects and the Aggregate Consumption Function." *Journal of Political Economy* Vol. 83 No. 03. (1975), 447-475.

225. Friedmon, Milton & Rose. *Free to Choose: A Personal Statement,* New York: Harcourt Brace Jovanovich (1980), 108.

226. Athreya, Kartik; Owners, Andrew; Romero, Jessie; & Schwartzman, Felipe. "Does Redistribution Increase Output?" Federal Reserve Bank of Richmond. Policy Brief EB17-01 (2017).

227. Andreoni, James. "Privately Provided Public Goods in a Large Economy: The Limits of Altruism." *Journal of Public Economics* Vol. 35. No 01. (1988), 57-73.

228. Andreoni, James. "Giving With Impure Altruism: Applications to Charity and Ricardian Equivalence." *Journal of Political Economy* Vol. 97 No. 06. (1989), 1447-1458.

229. Frye, Brian L. "Solving Charity Failures." *Or. L. Rev.* 93 (2014), 166.

230. Tabor, Steven. "Assisting the Poor with Cash: Design and Implementation of Social Transfer Programs." World Bank Institute. Social Safety Net Primer Series (2002), 4-12.

231. Kodras, Janet E. "Labor Market and Policy Constraints on the Work Disincentive Effect of Welfare." *Annals of the Association of American Geographers* 76, No. 2 (1986), 228-246.

232. Free To Choose. "From Cradle to Grave." Ep. 4. Directed by David Filkin. Public Broadcasting Service (1980).

233. Blank, Rebecca & Haskins, Ron (eds.). *The New World of Welfare.* Washington, D.C.: Brookings Institution Press (2001), 81-85.

234. Kaiser, Robert. "How Lobbying Became Washington's Biggest Business-Big Money Creates a New Capital City, Washington and Politics are Transformed." The Washington Post (08/28/2008).

235. Sameroff, Anthony. "Why Big Business Prefers Lobbying Government to Competing in the Marketplace." Mises Institute (08/29/2019).

236. Sowell, Thomas. *Basic Economics: A Common Sense Guide to the Economy 4th ed.* New York: Basic Books (2011), 61-63.

237. Ibid.

238. Truitt, Gary. "Why Do We Grow All This Corn." Hoosier AG Today (09/29/2013).

239. Thompson, Tamara (ed.). *Childhood Obesity.* Farmington Hills: Greenhaven Press (2016), 57-58.

240. Osborn, Tim & Young, Edwin. "The Conservation Reserve Program: An Economic Assessment." No. 1473-2017-3842. 1990.

241. Flam, Harry, Torsten Persson, and Lars EO Svensson. "Optimal subsidies to declining industries: efficiency and equity considerations." *Journal of Public Economics* 22, no. 3 (1983): 327-345.

242. Friedmon, Milton & Rose. *Free to Choose: A Personal Statement,* New York: Harcourt Brace Jovanovich (1980), 292-294.

243. "The State of Social Security." The Heritage Foundation (2018).

244. Tanner, Michael. "Social Security, Ponzi Schemese, and the Need for Reform." *Cato Institute Policy Analysis* 689 (2011).

245. Forbes, Steve; Ames, Elizabeth. *How Capitalism Will Save Us.* New York: Crown Business (2009), 99.

246. Social Security Administration. "Social Security History." SSA.gov.

247. Krantz, Matt. "How To Opt Out Of Paying Social Security Tax." Investors.com (06/12/2010).

248. Munnell, Alicia H. "The Impact of Social Security on Personal Savings." *National Tax Journal* (1974): 553-567.

249. Tarver, Evan. "How Moves In The Fed Funds Rate Affects The US Dollar." Investopedia.com

250. Coronado, Julia Lynn, Don Fullerton, and Thomas Glass. "The Progressivity of Social Security." No. w7520. National Bureau of Economic Research, 2000.

Chapter 9 Healthcare

251. Paul, Ron. "Government Vaccinations." LewRockwell (12/10/2002). https://www.lewrockwell.com/2002/12/ron-paul/government-vaccinations/

252. Gargarin, M. and Fantham, E. (eds.). *The Oxford Encyclopedia of Ancient Greece and Rome, Volume 1*. Oxford: Oxford University Press (2010), 145.

253. Pereira, Anita. "Live and Let Live: Healthcare is a Fundamental Human Right." *Conn. Pub. Int. LJ* 3 (2003): 481.

254. Picketty, Thomas. *Capital in the Twenty-First Century.* London: The Belknap Press (2014), 479.

255. DiLorenzo, Thomas. "Socialized Healthcare vs. the Laws of Economics." The Mises Institute (07/28/2009).

256. Sowell, Thomas. *Basic Economics: A Common Sense Guide to the Economy 4ᵗʰ ed.* New York: Basic Books (2011), 571.

257. Bodkin, Henry. "Gap Between Number of Foreign Doctors and UK Trained Doctors Doubles in a Year, New Figures from GMC Show." The Telegraph (10/24/2019).

258. Neuman, Tricia. "A Primer on Medicare: Key Facts About the Medicare Program and the People it Covers." KFF (03/20/2015).

259. "What is the Additional Medicare Tax and Who Pays It?" The Internal Revenue Service (03/02/2016). https://www.irs.gov/newsroom/what-is-the-additional-medicare-tax-and-who-pays-it

260. Majaski, Christina. "Medicaid vs. Medicare: What's the Difference?" Investopedia (03/28/2020). https://www.investopedia.com/articles/personal-finance/081114/medicaid-vs-medicare.asp

261. Mirabile, Matthew P., Richard D. Levinson, and John Jack. "The Income Redistribution Effects of Medicaid: Application in New York State." *Socio-Economic Planning Sciences* 9, No. 5 (1975), 209-219.

262. Forbes, Steve; Ames, Elizabeth. *How Capitalism Will Save Us*. New York: Crown Business (2009), 172.

263. Collins, Sara R., and Jennifer L. Nicholson. "Rite of Passage: Young Adults and the Affordable Care Act of 2010." The Commonwealth Fund (2010).

264. Berk, Marc & Fang, Zhengyi. "Who are the Young Uninsured?" Health Affairs (02/07/2014).
https://www.healthaffairs.org/do/10.1377/hblog20140207.037072/full/

265. Norris, Louise. "Will You Owe a Penalty Under Obamacare?" Health Insurance (11/09/2019).
https://www.healthinsurance.org/obamacare/obamacare-penalty-calculato r/

266. Friedmon, Milton & Rose. *Free to Choose: A Personal Statement,* New York: Harcourt Brace Jovanovich (1980), 291.

267. Sowell, Thomas. *Applied Economics: Thinking Beyond Stage One.* New York: Basic Books (2004), 90-91.

268. Rachels, Chase. *A Spontaneous Order: The Capitalist Case for a Sateless Society.* Createspace Independent Publishing (2015), 145-146.

269. Weber, Max. *General Economic History.* New York: Cosimo Classics (2007), 205.

270. Beller, George A. "The Rising Cost of Health Care in the United States: Is It Making the United States Globally Noncompetitive?." *Journal of Nuclear Cardiology* 15, No. 4 (2008), 481.

271. Moskatel, Leon, and David Slusky. "Did UberX Reduce Ambulance Volume?." *Health Economics* 28, No. 7 (2019), 817-829.

272. Sowell, Thomas. *Applied Economics: Thinking Beyond Stage One.* New York: Basic Books (2004), 76-78.

273. Barros, Pedra & Martinez-Giralt, Xavier. *Health Economics: An Industrial Organization Perspective.* New York: Routledge (2012), 179-213.

274. Weissman, Steven. "Perspective: Skyrocketing Healthcare Costs are Caused By Political Corruption." University of Southern California Center for Health Journalism (06/21/2016).

275. Gratzer, David. *The Cure: How Capitalism Can Save American Health Care.* New York: Encounter Books (2006), 98.

Chapter 10 Education

276. Sowell, Thomas. *Inside American Education: the Decline, the Deception, the Dogmas.* New York: The Free Press (1993).

277. Macaig, Michael. "States That Spend the Most (and the Least) on Education." Governing (06/04/2019).

https://www.governing.com/topics/education/gov-state-education-spending-revenue-data.html

278. Hornbeck, Dustin. "Federal Role in Education has a Long History." The Conversation (04/26/2017). https://theconversation.com/federal-role-in-education-has-a-long-history-74807

279. "Expenditures per Pupil for Elementary and Secondary Public Schools (Dollars)." Science and Engineering Indicators (04/29/2020). https://ncses.nsf.gov/indicators/states/indicator/public-school-per-pupil-expenditures/map/2016

280. Andrews, Lewis. "Public School Cronyism is Fueling the Pension Crisis." The American Conservative (08/13/2019). https://www.theamericanconservative.com/articles/public-school-cronyism-is-fueling-the-pension-crisis/#:~:text=The%20effect%20of%20so%20many,their%20mutual%20advantage%2C%20showing%20only

281. Cuban, Larry. *Oversold and Underused: Computers in the Classroom*. Cambridge: Harvard university press (2009), 68-99.

282. "Teachers and Pupil/Teacher Ratios." National Center for Education Statistics (2014). https://nces.ed.gov/programs/coe/pdf/Indicator_CLR/coe_clr_2014_04.pdf

283. Ripley, Amanda. "The Case Against High School Sports." *The Atlantic* (2013). https://www.theatlantic.com/magazine/archive/2013/10/the-case-against-high-school-sports/309447/

284. Wingfield, Adia. "Abandoning Public Education Will Be Considered Unthinkable 50 Years from Now: Private and Charter Schools, and Public Schools in Expensive Communities, Fuel Inequality." Vox (04/03/2019). https://www.vox.com/2019/3/27/18226303/public-private-school-choice

285. DeAngelis, Corey. "Schooling is Not a Public Good." Foundation for Economic Education (01/26/2017). https://fee.org/articles/schooling-is-not-a-public-good/?gclid=EAIaIQobChMI7NHn-bTx6QIVlZOzCh1iGgAFEAAYASAAEgI40fD_BwE

286. "Private School Enrollment." National Center for Education Statistics (2020). https://nces.ed.gov/programs/coe/indicator_cgc.asp

287. Murphy, Robert. "The Origins of the Public School." The Foundation for Economic Education (07/01/1998). https://fee.org/articles/the-origins-of-the-public-school/

288. Bedrick, Jason. "Yes, Private Schools Beat Public Schools." Cato Institute (03/28/2014). https://www.cato.org/publications/commentary/yes-private-schools-beat-public-schools

289. Hall, Joshua C. "Positive Externalities and Government Involvement in Education." *Journal of Private Enterprise* 21, No. 2 (2006).

290. Mitra, Dana. "The Social and Economic Benefits of Public Education." *Pennsylvania State University* (2011).

291. Joubert, Clement. "The Effects of Overeducation." World Economic Forum (11/17/2014). https://www.weforum.org/agenda/2014/11/the-effects-of-overeducation/

292. Duffin, Erin. "U.S. Public Schools: Average Expenditure per Pupil 1980-2017." Statistica (03/13/2020). https://www.statista.com/statistics/185135/average-expenditures-per-pupil-in-public-schools/#:~:text=U.S.%20public%20schools%20%2D%20average%20expenditure%20per%20pupil%201980%2D2017&text=An%20average%20of%2013%2C094%20U.S.,the%20academic%20year%20of%202017.

293. Murnane, Richard & Reardon, Sean. "The Role of Private Schooling in Contributing to the Increase in Inequality of Educational Outcomes Between Children from Low- and High-Income Families." Russell Sage Foundation (2014). https://www.russellsage.org/awarded-project/role-private-schooling-contributing-increase-inequality-educational-outcomes-between

294. McCullough, Tom. "How Wealthy Parents can Raise Responsible, Grounded Kids." Barrons (02/20/2019). https://www.barrons.com/articles/how-wealthy-parents-can-raise-responsible-grounded-kids-51550665849

295. Friedmon, Milton & Rose. *Free to Choose: A Personal Statement,* New York: Harcourt Brace Jovanovich (1980), 150-188.

296. Ibid.

297. McDonald, Kerry. "The Strongest Support for School Vouchers Comes from Lower-Income Families." Foundation for Economic Education (10/14/2019). https://fee.org/articles/the-strongest-support-for-school-vouchers-comes-from-lower-income-families/

298. Leuken, Martin. "How to Accurately Calculate the Fiscal Impact of School Voucher Programs." EdChoice (09/27/2016).

https://www.edchoice.org/engage/how-to-accurately-calculate-the-fiscal-impact-of-school-voucher-programs/
299. Ibid.
300. Allende, Claudia; Gallego, Francisco, & Neilson, Christopher. "Approximating the Equilibrium Effects of Informed School Choice." Princeton University Mimeo, 2019.
301. McDonald, Kerry. "Homeschooling and Educational Freedom: Why School Choice is Good for Homeschoolers." Cato Institute (09/04/2019).
https://www.cato.org/publications/briefing-paper/homeschooling-educational-freedom-why-school-choice-good-homeschoolers
302. Bhatt, Rachana. "Home is Where the School Is: The Impact of Homeschool Legislation on School Choice." *Journal of school choice* 8, No. 2 (2014), 192-212.
303. Younger, Jon. "Attracting Top International Students Helps All of Us: Here's Why It Matters." Forbes (12/14/2018).
https://www.forbes.com/sites/jonyounger/2018/12/14/attracting-top-international-students-helps-all-of-us-heres-why-it-matters/#5812abe72f7a
304. Langton, Nancy & Pfeffer, Jeffrey. "Paying the Professor: Sources of Salary Variation in Academic Labor Markets." *American Sociological Review* (1994), 236-256.
305. Hansen, Michael & Quintero, Diana. "Scrutinizing Equal Pay for Equal Work Among Teachers." Brookings (09/07/2017).
https://www.brookings.edu/research/scrutinizing-equal-pay-for-equal-work-among-teachers/
306. Chud, Howard. *Something Is Terribly Wrong: The Sad Truth About Education in America.* Indianapolis: Dog Ear Publishing (2009), 15.

Chapter 11 National Defense
307. Madison, James. "Political Observations," April 20, 1795, in Philip R. Fendall (ed.) *Letters and Other Writings of James Madison* Vol. 04. Philadelphia: J.B. Lippincott & Co. (1865), 491.
308. Gertcher, Frank & Weida, William. *The Political Economy of National Defense.* Boulder: Westview Press (1987) 46-49.
309. Gertcher, Frank & Weida, William. *The Political Economy of National Defense.* Boulder: Westview Press (1987) 4-7.
310. Tian, Nan; Fleurant, Aude; Kuimova, Alexandra; Wezeman, Pieter D.; Wezeman, Siemon T. "Trends in World Military Expenditure, 2019" Stockholm International Peace Research Institute (04/27/2020).

311. Platt, Suzy (ed). *Respectfully Quoted: A Dictionary of Quotations.* New York: Barnes & Noble (1993), 123.

312. Jolink, Albert, and Jan Van Daal. "Gossen's laws." *History of political economy* 30, no. 1 (1998): 43.

313. Gertcher, Frank & Weida, William. *The Political Economy of National Defense.* Boulder: Westview Press (1987) 46-47.

314. "The Military Spending Debate." Charles Koch Institute.

315. Kennedy, Paul. *The Rise and Fall of the Great Powers: Economic Change and Military Conflict from 1500 to 2000.* New York: Random House (1987), xvi.

316. Davis, Daniel. "US Failed to Set Attainable Military Objectives in Syria." Military Times (10/25/2019). https://www.militarytimes.com/opinion/commentary/2019/10/25/us-failed-to-set-attainable-military-objectives-in-syria/

317. Feifer, Gregory. *The Great Gamble: The Soviet War in Afghanistan.* New York: Harper Collins Publishers (2009), 97-99.

318. Drezner, Daniel W. "Military Primacy Doesn't Pay (Nearly As Much As You Think)." *International Security* 38, No. 1 (2013), 52-79.

319. Tian, Nan; Fleurant, Aude; Kuimova, Alexandra; Wezeman, Pieter D.; Wezeman, Siemon T. "Trends in World Military Expenditure, 2019" Stockholm International Peace Research Institute (04/27/2020).

320. Mears, John A. "The Emergence of the Standing Professional Army in Seventeenth-Century Europe." *Social Science Quarterly* (1969), 106-115.

321. Brauner, Jennifer. "Military spending and democracy." *Defence and Peace Economics* 26, No. 4 (2015), 409-423.

322. Greenberg, Dan. "Term Limits: the Only Way to Clean Up Congress." *Heritage Foundation* (1994).

323. Friedman, Milton & Friedman, Rose. *The Tyranny of the Status Quo.* New York: Harcourt Brace Jovanovich Publishers (1984), 78.

324. Amir, Amir & Weiss, Stanley. "Lockheed Martin Corporation." Encyclopedia Britannica (02/27/2020). https://www.britannica.com/topic/Lockheed-Martin-Corporation

325. Gertcher, Frank & Weida, William. *The Political Economy of National Defense.* Boulder: Westview Press (1987) 8-10.

326. Ibid.

327. Friedman, Milton & Friedman, Rose. *The Tyranny of the Status Quo.* New York: Harcourt Brace Jovanovich Publishers (1984), 76-77.

328. Bingley, Paul, Petter Lundborg, and Stéphanie Vincent Lyk-Jensen. "Opportunity Cost and the Incidence of a Draft Lottery." (2014).

329. Becker, Gary & Becker, Guity. *The Economics of Life: From Baseball to Affirmative Action to Immigration, How Real-World Issues Affect Our Everyday Life.* New York: McGraw-Hill (1997), 198.
330. Butler v. Perry, 240 U.S. 328, 333 (1916)
331. Bingley, Paul, Petter Lundborg, and Stéphanie Vincent Lyk-Jensen. "The Opportunity Costs of Mandatory Military Service: Evidence from a Draft Lottery." *Journal of Labor Economics* 38, No. 1 (2020), 39-66.
332. Warner, John T., and Beth J. Asch. "The economic theory of a military draft reconsidered." *Defence and Peace Economics* 7, no. 4 (1996): 297-312.
333. Warner, John & Asch, Beth. "The Record and Prospects of the All-Volunteer Military in the United States." *Journal of Economic Perspectives*, 15 No. 2 (2001), 169-192.
334. Becker, Gary & Becker, Guity. *The Economics of Life: From Baseball to Affirmative Action to Immigration, How Real-World Issues Affect Our Everyday Life.* New York: McGraw-Hill (1997), 198.
335. Dunne, Paul, & Perlo-Freeman, Sam. "The Demand for Military Spending in Developing Countries." *International Review of Applied Economics* 17, No. 1 (2003), 23-48.
336. Bacevich, Andrew. *The New American Militarism: How Americans are Seduced by War.* Oxford: Oxford University Press (2005), 2-7.
337. DeVore, Chuck. "States That Defend Us—Where Do Our Military Volunteers Call Home?" Forbes (02/19/2020). https://www.forbes.com/sites/chuckdevore/2020/02/19/states-that-defend-uswhere-do-our-military-volunteers-call-home/#79d5aebd534c
338. Manak, Inu. "Are Republicans Still the Party of Free Trade?" Cato Institute (05/16/2019). https://www.cato.org/blog/are-republicans-still-party-free-trade

Conclusion

339. Friedman, Milton. *Capitalism and Freedom 40th ed.* Chicago: The University of Chicago Press (2002), 15.
340. Brook, Yaron & Watkins, Don. *Free Market Revolution: How Ayn Rand's Ideas Can End Big Government.* New York: Palgrave Macmillan (2012), 162-176.
341. "The Role of Government in a Free Society." In Milton Friedman Speaks (videotape publication). New York: Harcourt Brace Jovanovich, 1980. Lecture delivered at the Hoover Institution, Stanford University (02/09/1978).

342. Brook, Yaron & Watkins, Don. *Free Market Revolution: How Ayn Rand's Ideas Can End Big Government.* New York: Palgrave Macmillan (2012), 155.
343. Reagan, Ronald. "A Time for Choosing." (1964).

Bibliography

Acemoglu, Daron, and James A. Robinson. *Why Nations Fail: The Origins of Power, Prosperity, and Poverty*. Currency, 2012.

Akerlof, George A., and Robert J. Shiller. *Animal Spirits: How Human Psychology Drives the Economy, and Why It Matters for Global Capitalism*. Princeton university press, 2010.

Alchian, Armen Albert, and Ronald H. Coase. *Economic Forces at Work*. Indianapolis: Liberty press, 1977.

Allison, John A. *The Financial Crisis and the Free Market Cure: Why Pure Capitalism is the World Economy's Only Hope*. McGraw Hill Professional, 2012.

Appleby, Joyce. *The Relentless Revolution: A History of Capitalism*. WW Norton & Company, 2011.

Bacevich, Andrew J. *The New American Militarism: How Americans are Seduced by War*. Oxford University Press, 2013.

Barrett, Scott. *Why Cooperate?: The Incentive to Supply Global Public Goods*. Oxford University Press on Demand, 2007.

Bartlett, Bruce. *The Benefit and the Burden: Tax Reform-Why We Need It and What It Will Take*. Simon and Schuster, 2012.

Baskin, Jonathan, Jonathan Barron Baskin, and Paul J. Miranti Jr. *A History of Corporate Finance*. Cambridge University Press, 1999.

Bastiat, Frédéric. *Economic Sophisms*. Oliver and Boyd, 1873.

Baumol, William J. *The Free-Market Innovation Machine: Analyzing the Growth Miracle of Capitalism*. Princeton university press, 2002.

Becker, Gary, and Beler GN. *The Economics of Life: From Baseball to Affirmative Action to Immigration, How Real World Issues Affect Our Everyday Life*. No. 306.3/B395. McGraw-hill, 1997.

Ben-Ami, Daniel. *Ferraris For All: In Defense of Economic Progress*. Policy Press, 2012.

Bernstein, Peter L., and Peter L. Bernstein. *Against the Gods: The Remarkable Story of Risk*. New York: Wiley, 1996.

Bernstein, William J. *A Splendid Exchange: How Trade Shaped the World*. Grove/Atlantic, Inc., 2009.

————. *The Birth of Plenty: How the Prosperity of the Modern World was Created*. International Marine, 2004.

Bethell, Tom. *The Noblest Triumph: Property and Prosperity Through the Ages*. Macmillan, 1999.

Bhagwati, Jagdish. *In Defense of Globalization*. Oxford University Press, 2004.

Blank, Rebecca M., and Ron Haskins, eds. *The New World of Welfare*. Brookings Institution Press, 2004

Blinder, Alan S. *After the Music Stopped: The Financial Crisis, the Response, and the Work Ahead*. No. 79. Penguin Classics, 2013.

Bloom, Howard. *The Genius of the Beast: A Radical Re-vision of Capitalism*. Prometheus Books, 2010.

Brook, Yaron, and Don Watkins. *Free Market Revolution: How Ayn Rand's Ideas Can End Big Government*. St. Martin's Press, 2012.

Buchanan, James M. *The Collected Works of James M. Buchanan*. Liberty Fund, 1999.

―――. *What Should Economists Do?*. Liberty Fund Inc., 1979.

Chancellor, Edward. *Devil Take the Hindmost: A History of Financial speculation*. Farrar, Straus, Giroux, 1999.

Chernow, Ron. *Alexander Hamilton*. Head of Zeus Ltd, 2016.

Clark, Gregory. *A Farewell to Alms: A Brief Economic History of the World*. Vol. 25. Princeton University Press, 2008.

Cockshott, W. Paul, and Allin Cottrell. *Towards a New Socialism*. Spokesman Pr, 1993.

Cohen, Daniel. *Globalization and Its Enemies*. MIT press, 2007.

Colton, Timothy J., and Robert H. Legvold, eds. *After the Soviet Union: From Empire to Nations*. WW Norton, 1993.

Congdon, William J., Jeffrey R. Kling, and Sendhil Mullainathan. *Policy and Choice: Public Finance Through the Lens of Behavioral Economics*. Brookings Institution Press, 2011.

Cooper Jr, John Milton. *Woodrow Wilson*. Vintage, 2009.

Cowan, Robin, and Mario J. Rizzo, eds. *Profits and Morality*. University of Chicago Press, 1995.

Cowen, Tyler. *Creative Destruction: How Globalization is Changing the World's Cultures*. Princeton University Press, 2009.

―――, ed. *The Theory of Market Failure: A Critical Examination*. George Mason University Press, 1988.

Cuban, Larry. *Oversold and Underused*. Harvard university press, 2009.

D'Aveni, Richard. *Strategic Capitalism: The New Economic Strategy for Winning the Capitalist Cold War*. McGraw Hill Professional, 2012.

Diamond, Jared. *Collapse: How Societies Choose to Fail or Succeed*. Penguin, 2011.

———. *The World Until Yesterday: What Can We Learn from Traditional Societies?*. Penguin, 2013.

Durlauf, Steven N., and Lawrence Blume, eds. *The New Palgrave Dictionary of Economics*. Vol. 2. London, UK: Palgrave Macmillan, 2008.

Ehrenberg, Ronald G., and Robert S. Smith. *Modern Labor Economics: Theory and Public Policy*. Routledge, 2016.

Elkins, Stanley, and Eric McKitrick. *The Age of Federalism: The Early American Republic, 1788-1800*. Oxford University Press, 1995.

Feifer, Gregory. *The Great Gamble: The Soviet War in Afghanistan*. New York: Harper, 2009.

Ferguson, Niall. *Civilization: the West and the Rest*. Penguin, 2012.

———. *The Ascent of Money: A Financial History of the World*. Penguin, 2008.

———. *The Cash Nexus: Money and Politics in Modern History, 1700-2000*. Penguin UK, 2013.

Ferling, John. *Jefferson and Hamilton: The Rivalry that Forged a Nation*. Bloomsbury Publishing USA, 2013.

Franklin, Benjamin. *The Writings of Benjamin Franklin: 1767-1772*. Vol. 5. Macmillan, 1906.

Friedman, David. *Hidden Order: The Economics of Everyday Life*. HarperBusiness, 1997.

———. *The Machinery of Freedom: Guide to a Radical Capitalism*. Open Court Publishing Company, 1989.

Friedman, Milton. *Capitalism and Freedom*. University of Chicago press, 2009.

———. *Money Mischief: Episodes in Monetary History*. HMH, 1994.

Friedman, Milton, and Rose Friedman. *Free to Choose: A Personal Statement*. Houghton Mifflin Harcourt, 1990.

———. *Tyranny of the Status Quo*. Penguin, 1985.

Friedman, Thomas L. *The Lexus and the Olive Tree: Understanding Globalization*. Farrar, Straus and Giroux, 2000.

Forbes, Steve, and Elizabeth Ames. *How Capitalism Will Save Us: Why Free People and Free Markets are the Best Answer in Today's Economy*. Currency, 2011.

Foster, Richard, and Sarah Kaplan. *Creative Destruction: Why Companies that are Built to Last Underperform the Market—And How to Successfully Transform Them*. Currency, 2011.

Fukuyama, Francis. *The Origins of Political Order: From Prehuman Times to the French Revolution*. Farrar, Straus and Giroux, 2011.

Gagarin, Michael. *The Oxford Encyclopedia of Ancient Greece and Rome*. Vol. 1. Oxford University Press on Demand, 2010.

Gellman, Barton. *Angler: The Cheney Vice Presidency*. Penguin, 2008.

Gersemann, Olaf. *Cowboy Capitalism: European Myths about the American Reality*. Cato Institute, 2004.

Gilder, George. *Wealth and Poverty: A New Edition for the Twenty-first Century*. Regnery Publishing, 2012.

Gilman, Martin G. *No Precedent, No Plan: Inside Russia's 1998 Default*. MIT Press, 2010.

Goldin, Claudia, and Gary D. Libecap, eds. *The Regulated Economy: A Historical Approach to Political Economy*. University of Chicago Press, 2008.

Gratzer, David. *The Cure: How Capitalism Can Save American Health Care*. Encounter Books, 2009.

Griswold, Daniel. *Mad About Trade: Why Main Street America Should Embrace Globalization*. Cato Institute, 2009.

Gwartney, James D. *Common Sense Economics: What Everyone Should Know About Wealth and Prosperity*. Macmillan, 2016.

Hall, Robert E., and Alvin Rabushka. *The Flat Tax*. Hoover Press, 2013.

Hall, Thomas E. *Aftermath: The Unintended Consequences of Public Policies*. Cato Institute, 2014.

Hamilton, Alexander, James Madison, and John Jay. *The Federalist Papers*. Oxford University Press, 2008.

Hayek, Friedrich August. *The Fatal Conceit: The Errors of Socialism*. Vol. 1. Routledge, 2013.

Hayek, Friedrich August. *The Road to Serfdom: Text and Documents: The Definitive Edition*. Routledge, 2014.

Hazlitt, Henry. *The Failure of the "New Economics"*. Ludwig von Mises Institute, 1959.

Higgs, Robert. *Crisis and Leviathan*. New York: Oxford University Press, 1987.

Hobbes, Thomas. *Leviathan*. JM Dent, 1914.

Holcombe, Randall G. *The Economic Foundations of Government*. London: Macmillan, 1994.

Hyman, David. *Public Finance: A Contemporary Application of Theory to Policy 9th ed.* Thomson South-Western, 2008.

Hubbard, Glenn, and Tim Kane. *Balance: The Economics of Great Powers from Ancient Rome to Modern America*. Simon and Schuster, 2013.

Hume, David. *A Treatise of Human Nature*. Courier Corporation, 2003.

James, Harold. *The Creation and Destruction of Value: The Globalization Cycle*. Harvard University Press, 2009.

Johnson, Simon, and James Kwak. *White House Burning: Our National Debt and Why It Matters to You*. Vintage, 2013.

Kennedy, Paul. *The Rise and Fall of the Great Powers: Economic Change and Military Conflict from 1500 to 2000*. Vintage, 2010.

Kotkin, Stephen. *Armageddon Averted: The Soviet Collapse, 1970-2000*. Oxford University Press, 2008.

LaFave, Wayne R. *Principles of Criminal Law*. Thomson/West, 2003.

Lal, Deepak. *Reviving the Invisible Hand: The Case for Classical Liberalism in the Twenty-first Century*. Princeton University Press, 2006.

Le Grand, Julian. *The Strategy of Equality: Redistribution and the Social Services*. Vol. 13. Routledge, 2018.

Lerner, Abba P. *Economics of Control: Principles of Welfare Economics*. Macmillan and Company Limited, New York, 1944.

Lewis, Michael. *The Big Short: Inside the Doomsday Machine*. Penguin UK, 2011.

Lipset, Seymour Martin, and Jason M. Lakin. *The Democratic Century*. Vol. 9. University of Oklahoma Press, 2004.

Locke, John. *Second Treatise of Government: An Essay Concerning the True Original, Extent and End of Civil Government*. John Wiley & Sons, 2014.

Lott, John R. *Freedomnomics: Why the Free Market Works and Other Half-baked Theories Don't*. Simon and Schuster, 2007.

Lynch, Timothy, ed. *After Prohibition: An Adult Approach to Drug Policies in the 21st century*. Cato Institute, 2000.

Madison, James. *Letters and Other Writings of James Madison*. Vol. 2. Lippincott, 1867.

Martinez-Giralt, Xavier, and Pedro Barros. *Health Economics: An Industrial Organization Perspective*. Routledge, 2013.

Marx, Karl. *Das Kapital*. Anaconda Verlag, 2013.

Mathias, Peter. *The First Industrial Nation: The Economic History of Britain 1700–1914*. Routledge, 2013.

Mandelbaum, Michael. *The Ideas that Conquered the World: Peace, Democracy, and Free Markets in the Twenty-first Century*. Hachette UK, 2004.

Meier, Kenneth J. *The Political Economy of Regulation: The Case of Insurance*. Suny Press, 1988.

Meller, Patricio. *The Unidad Popular and the Pinochet Dictatorship: A Political Economy Analysis*. Springer, 2000.

Mueller, John. *Capitalism, Democracy, and Ralph's Pretty Good Grocery*. Princeton University Press, 2001.

Von Mises, Ludwig. *Human Action*. Lulu Press, Inc, 2016.

———. *Socialism*. Ludwig von Mises Institute, 1981.

———. *The Theory of Money and Credit*. Skyhorse Publishing, Inc., 2013.

Munday, Stephen CR. *Markets and Market Failure*. Heinemann, 2000.

Olson, Mancur. *The Logic of Collective Action: Public Goods and the Theory of Groups, Second Printing with a New Preface and Appendix*. Vol. 124. Harvard University Press, 2009.

Ormerod, Paul. *Butterfly Economics*. Faber & Faber, 2011.

Paine, Thomas. *Paine: Political Writings*. Cambridge University Press, 2000.

Paulson Jr, Henry M. *On the Brink: Inside the Race to Stop the Collapse of the Global Financial System—With Original New Material on the Five Year Anniversary of the Financial Crisis*. Business Plus, 2013.

Phillips, Kevin. *Wealth and Democracy: A Political History of the American Rich*. Random House Digital, Inc., 2003.

Picketty, Thomas. *Capital in the Twenty-First Century.* The Belknap Press, 2014.

Pilon, Roger. *The Purpose and Limits of Government.* Cato Institute, 1999.

Pipes, Richard. *Property and Freedom*. Vintage, 2007.

Platt, Suzy, ed. *Respectfully Quoted: A Dictionary of Quotations*. Barnes & Noble Publishing, 1993.

Powell, Jim, Paul Johnson, and James Powell. *The Triumph of Liberty: A 2,000-year History, Told Through the Lives of Freedom's Greatest Champions*. Free Press, 2000.

Rachels, Chase, and Stephan Kinsella. *A Spontaneous Order: The Capitalist Case for a Stateless Society*. Christopher Chase Rachels, 2015.

Radelet, Steven. *The Great Surge: The Ascent of the Developing World*. Simon and Schuster, 2015.

Reid, Gavin C. *Classical Economic Growth: An Analysis in the Tradition of Adam Smith*. Blackwell, 1989.

Ridley, Matt. *The Origins of Virtue*. Penguin UK, 1997.

———. *The Rational Optimist: How Prosperity Evolves.* Harper Perennial, 2011.

Roberts, Keith. *The Origins of Business, Money, and Markets*. Columbia University Press, 2011.

Roemer, John E., and John E. Roemer. *Free to Lose: An Introduction to Marxist Economic Philosophy*. Harvard University Press, 2009.

Röpke, Wilhelm. *A Humane Economy: The Social Framework of the Free Market*. Open Road Media, 2014.

Rosenberg, Nathan, and Birdzell LE Jr. *How the West Grew Rich: The Economic Transformation of the Industrial World*. Basic books, 2008.

Rothbard, Murray Newton. *America's Great Depression*. Ludwig von Mises Institute, 1972.

———. *For a New Liberty: The Libertarian Manifesto*. Ludwig von Mises Institute, 1978.

Rousseau, Jean-Jacques. *Rousseau: The Social Contract and Other Later Political Writings*. Cambridge University Press, 2018.

Sachs, Jeffrey D. *The End of Poverty: Economic Possibilities for Our Time*. Penguin, 2006.

Sandel, Michael J. *What Money Can't Buy: The Moral Limits of Markets*. Macmillan, 2012.

Schumpeter, Joseph A. *Capitalism, Socialism and Democracy*. Routledge, 2013.

Seabright, Paul. *The Company of Strangers: A Natural History of Economic Life-Revised Edition*. Princeton University Press, 2010.

Shcharansky, Anatoly, Natan Sharansky, and Ron Dermer. *The Case for Democracy*. Public Affairs, 2004.

Sherman, Howard J. *Radical Political Economy*. Basic Book, 1972.

Shlaes, Amity. *The Forgotten Man: A New History of the Great Depression*. Random House, 2009.

———. *The Greedy Hand: How Taxes Drive Americans Crazy and What to do about It*. Random House, 2012.

Sirico, Robert. *Defending the Free Market: The Moral Case for a Free Economy*. Regnery Publishing, 2012.

Smith, Adam. *The Wealth of Nations: An Inquiry into the Nature and Causes of the Wealth of Nations*. Harriman House Limited, 2010.

Smith, Norman Kemp. *Immanuel Kant's Critique of Pure Reason*. Read Books Ltd, 2011.

Sorkin, Andrew Ross. *Too Big to Fail: The Inside Story of How Wall Street and Washington Fought to Save the Financial System—and Themselves*. Penguin, 2010.

Sorman, Guy. *Economics Does Not Lie*. Encounter Books, 2009.

De Soto, Hernando. *The Mystery of Capital: Why Capitalism Triumphs in the West and Fails Everywhere Else*. Civitas Books, 2000.

D'Souza, Dinesh. *The Virtue of Prosperity: Finding Values in an Age of Techno-affluence*. Simon and Schuster, 2002.

Sowell, Thomas. *Applied Economics: Thinking Beyond Stage One*. Hachette UK, 2008.

———. *Basic Economics: A Common Sense Guide to the Economy*. 5th. Basic Books, 2015.

———. *Inside American Education*. Simon and Schuster, 1992.

———. *On Classical Economics*. Yale University Press, 2006.

Stumpf, Samuel Enoch. *Socrates to Sartre: A History of Philosophy*. New York: McGraw-Hill, 1993.

Thompson, Tamara, ed. *Childhood Obesity*. Greenhaven Publishing LLC, 2016.

De Tocqueville, Alexis. *Democracy in America*. Vol. 10. Regnery Publishing, 2003.

Toomey, Patrick J. *The Road to Prosperity: How to Grow Our Economy and Revive the American Dream*. John Wiley & Sons, 2009.

Veryser, Harry C. *It Didn't Have to Be This Way: Why Boom and Bust Is Unnecessary—and How the Austrian School of Economics Breaks the Cycle*. Open Road Media, 2014.

Weber, Max. *General Economic History*. Transaction publishers, 1981.

———. *The Protestant Ethic and the "Spirit" of Capitalism and Other Writings*. Penguin, 2002.

Weida, William J., and Franklin L. Gertcher. *The Political Economy of National Defense*. Routledge, 2019.

Williams, Walter. *All It Takes is Guts: A Minority View*. Gateway Books, 1987.

———. *Race & Economics: How Much can be Blamed On Discrimination?* Hoover Press, 2013.

Wills, Garry. *A Necessary Evil: A History of American Distrust of Government*. Simon and Schuster, 2002.

Wintrobe, Ronald. *The Political Economy of Dictatorship*. Cambridge University Press, 2000.

Wolf, Martin. *Why Globalization Works*. No. 3. Yale University Press, 2004.

Woods, Thomas E. *Back on the Road to Serfdom: The Resurgence of Statism*. Open Road Media, 2014.

Zaltman, Gerald. *How Customers Think: Essential Insights Into the Mind of the Market*. Harvard Business Press, 2003.

www.ingramcontent.com/pod-product-compliance
Lightning Source LLC
Chambersburg PA
CBHW030612220526
45463CB00004B/1262